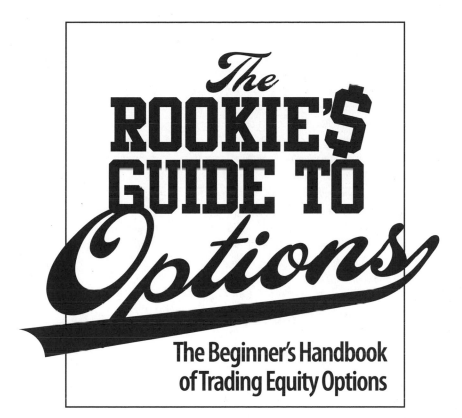

The ROOKIE'S GUIDE TO Options

The Beginner's Handbook of Trading Equity Options

BY MARK D. WOLFINGER

W&A
PUBLISHING

P.O. Box 849, Cedar Falls, Iowa 50613
www.w-apublishing.com

Published by W&A Publishing, Cedar Falls, Iowa

In the publication of this book, every effort has been made to offer the most current, correct and clearly expressed information possible. Nonetheless, inadvertent errors can occur, and rules and regulations governing personal finance and investing often change. The advice and strategies contained herein may not be suitable for your situation, and there is a risk of loss trading options, stocks, commodity futures, and foreign exchange products. Neither the publisher nor authors shall be liable for any loss of profit or any other commercial damages, including but not limited to special, incidental, consequential, or other damages, that is incurred as a consequence of the use and application, directly or indirectly, of any information presented in this book. If legal, tax advice or other expert assistance is required, the services of a professional should be sought.

Library of Congress Control Number: 2007941613
ISBN: 978-1-934354-04-9
ISBN-10: 1-934354-04-X

Printed in the United States of America

10 9 8 7 6 5 4 3 2 1

This book is dedicated, with love, to Penny, my life partner of 17 years.

Contents

Introduction

You are about to enter the world of options. My goal is for readers to gain a complete understanding of options and how to use them to your investment advantage. You should come away with a clear understanding of options—how they work and how you can make money by incorporating option strategies into your investment methods.

In the sports world, a rookie is someone in his or her first year of professional play. The term also refers to someone who is new to a profession. This book was written for newcomers to the world of options—not necessarily investment rookies, but option rookies. It contains substantial background information on options and detailed descriptions of six option strategies. These are not the only option strategies available, but they were chosen because they make it easy for you to enter the world of options—and I use only these strategies for my personal trading.

Most investors who enter this realm are familiar with investing in the stock market from the standpoint of owning individual stock or mutual funds. If that's your experience, it should be a smooth transition when you add options to your arsenal of investment tools. Equity options are related to stocks. The term used to describe that relationship is "derivative." The value of an option is derived from the value of an individual stock or group of stocks, such as an index.

Some investors come to the options world with little or no investing experience. If that describes you, it may require a bit more effort to get up to speed, but it should not be a problem. Although it's possible to go into involved mathematics when discussing options, in keeping with the goal of making this an enjoyable learning experience, this book uses nothing more complicated than simple arithmetic.

This book was written for all investors who are interested in expanding their investing knowledge. Options are versatile investment tools that can be used in a wide variety of strategies. This book will teach you to use options intelligently—and that means using them as they were originally designed: to reduce risk.

Who can benefit from reading this book?

Are you a very conservative investor who wants to protect the value of a stock market portfolio? You can use options to accomplish that. And you can obtain that insurance protection at little or no cost. Interested? Options are for you.

Are you a fairly conservative investor looking for a way to invest in the stock market with reduced risk of loss? Options are for you. You have fewer losing trades when you use options to reduce risk.

Are you someone who has never used options but is familiar with the workings of the stock market? Options are for you. Depending on your investment objectives and just how much risk you are willing to assume, there are suitable option strategies.

Are you an aggressive investor—someone who is much more interested in making money than in protecting current assets? Options are for you. There are strategies available that provide the opportunity to make substantial returns on your investment—with limited risk.

Are you a gambler? Or do you have extra cash burning a hole in your pocket? Well, you can use options also. My purpose in writing this book is to encourage the more conservative use of options, but if you prefer to take chances, that's your decision. But, at least let me show you how to use options so that you have a reasonable chance of being successful. There's no need to throw your money away.

Whatever your investment objectives, options can help you achieve your goals:

- capital preservation,
- slow and steady growth with reduced risk,
- aggressive growth with limited risk, or
- speculation.

I'm sure you already understand how options work (even if you don't realize it). The concept behind options is common in our daily lives—rain checks, bus transfers and insurance policies are all examples of common "options." Options can be used in very complicated strategies, but the good news is that there are enough simple, easy-to-understand strategies that allow you to meet your investment goals.

The methods taught in this book do not represent a get-rich-quick scheme. It will require some effort, but if you take time to understand the concepts presented in these pages, you will come away with the ability to make good investment decisions.

The detailed examples and step-by-step instructions that accompany each strategy make this book the best available primer on options. Rather than just tell you what you "should" do, this book takes you through the decision-making process. When it comes to trading options, you'll discover that you often have many alternatives from which to choose. Each example provides reasons why each of the available choices may be appropriate for you and your circumstances. As you experience the decision-making process, you'll begin to understand which variables are most important for your goals, making it much easier to make these decisions on your own.

There is more to trading than making money—it's also about being satisfied with your investment decisions. That means trading within your comfort zone. It's important to be confident that your investment choices are sound and you are satisfied with the reward potential for a given trade. But the risk required to earn the potential reward also must be acceptable. When risk is too high, then the investor is truly gambling. If the reward is too small, then you are better off with U.S. Treasury bills. There is no need to own investments that keep you awake with worry. Options allow you to reduce risk, and hopefully rest easy.

About this book

In writing this book, my objective is to provide easy-to-understand options instruction and explain how to use options to reduce risk with a higher percentage of profitable trades. You will learn all you need to know to trade options with confidence. We'll talk about the risks and rewards that come with using options as we examine what there is to gain (or lose) by adopting basic option strategies.

Because this book is intended to show the average investor how to use the options markets to make money, we must start at the beginning. That requires an explanation of what an option is and how an option works—both in our everyday lives and in the stock market.

Although this book is intended for option rookies, there is enough meat for the investor who already has option trading experience. Re-reading these pages as you gain experience will provide insights you may have missed the first time, making this book useful for many years to come.

Some Tips on Getting the Most Out of this Book:

Many chapters conclude with a brief quiz that is a helpful review for the material under discussion. You'll find the answers toward the end of the book. Also, please read the footnotes. They are not citations but provide information that is useful to your complete understanding of the topic.

Part I

Option Essentials

Chapter 1

Options Basics

Our discussion is limited to options involving stock market investments. Those include options on individual stocks, stock indexes and some exchange traded funds (ETFs). Many other options exist, such as options on commodities and currencies. Once you understand how stock options work, you'll also understand the principles concerning other types of options.

The stock options discussed here should not be confused with employee stock options. Those are given to the employees of some companies as part of their compensation packages. Employee stock options are similar to the stock options under discussion—but are more limited because they are not traded on an exchange and cannot be bought and sold.

What is an option?

An option is a contract between two parties: one person buys the option and another sells the option. The price at which the transaction occurs is referred to as the premium.

The premium is quoted on a per-share basis. Because the option contract represents 100 shares of stock, the premium the buyer pays to the seller is that per-share premium multiplied by 100. Thus, if you sell one option at $1.20, you receive $120.

There are two types of options:
A call option gives its owner the right to buy and a put option gives its owner the right to sell:

- a specified item (called the underlying asset),
- at a specified price (called the strike price),
- for a specified period of time (any time before the option's expiration date).

Thus, in return for paying a premium to purchase an option:

- The owner of a call option has the right (but not the obligation) to buy the underlying asset at the strike price any time before the expiration date.
- The owner of a put option has the right (but not the obligation) to sell the underlying asset at the strike price any time before the expiration date.

The underlying asset is almost always 100 shares of a specified stock or ETF. Certain options on indexes are similar but have a very important distinction. We'll cover those differences when we discuss trading index options in Part III.

That's all there is to an option. Options are not complicated investment tools, despite their intimidating reputation. It's true that options can be used in complex strategies, but it's far more fun to use options in one of the many easy-to-understand strategies that helps you make money at the same time that your investment risk is reduced.

How does an option work?
An option grants to its owner certain rights. An option imparts certain obligations on the seller.

Rights of an option owner
If the option owner chooses to do what the contract allows, and if that decision is made before the expiration date, then the option owner is said to exercise his or her rights. Once the option expires, all rights expire with it. Thus, it is crucial for option owners to make a final decision before expiration. But, don't be concerned; option expirations occur monthly, on a regularly scheduled basis, making it easy for everyone to know when options expire. We'll discuss expiration in greater detail later.

When an option is exercised, the option is cancelled and cannot be used again. The exerciser buys (if it's a call option) or sells (if it's a put option) 100 shares of the specified stock at the strike price.

Most of the time the option owner does not choose to exercise the option. As you will see later, it's usually a better idea for the individual investor who owns options to sell those options rather than exercise. But there are exceptions, so it is important to understand your rights when you own an option.

{ *NOTE: As stated above, the option owner has the right, but not the obligation to exercise. The term "but not the obligation" is very important. Many option novices fail to grasp the importance of this point. When you own an option, you are in control. You may choose to exercise your right to buy (call) or sell (put) the underlying asset at the strike price. But no one can force you to do so. The term "option" comes from the Greek word meaning choice. And it's strictly your choice—as long as you make that decision before the option expires. The astute reader may wonder, "if I don't exercise the option, what else can be done with it?" Good question. The answer is discussed later in this chapter.*

Obligations of an option seller
When you sell an option, you agree to accept certain obligations, specifically to honor the terms of the option contract. You are only so obligated if the option owner elects to exercise. Thus, you may be called upon to honor the contract, but it's

also possible that the option expires worthless. If the option does expire worthless,[1] your obligations are cancelled and the premium collected when you sold the option represents your profit.

- If you sell a call option (that you don't own) you may become obligated to sell the underlying asset at the strike price. Don't be confused. The call buyer has the right to buy the underlying asset. The call seller may become obligated to sell that asset.
- If you sell a put option (that you don't own) you may become obligated to buy the underlying asset at the strike price.
- If you sell an option that you own, the slate is wiped clean and you have no remaining position. You have neither the rights of an option owner, nor the obligations of an option seller.

There are two ways to cancel the option seller's obligations:

- When the option expires, the option seller is released from all obligations.
- If the option seller buys the identical option (this is called a closing transaction) before being assigned an exercise notice, then the position is cancelled, along with any obligations.

{ *NOTE: The owner of an option controls the situation and may decide to exercise the option any time before it expires. The option seller has no control and must wait for the option owner's decision. For clarification: When you sell an option, you may not request or demand that the option owner exercise the option. You have no say in the matter. The decision rests entirely with the option owner.*

When the option is exercised, a randomly selected seller of that option is assigned an exercise notice and is obligated to fulfill the conditions of the

contract. How the specific seller is chosen is discussed in greater detail in Chapter 5. Thus, the person who receives the assignment notice[2] must sell 100 shares of stock at the strike price (if it's a call option), or buy 100 shares at the strike price (if it's a put option). There is no escape. Once you have been assigned that exercise notice, the option is cancelled, the trade occurs and you must honor your commitment. In the real world, you don't have to do anything. Upon learning of the assignment notice, your broker takes care of the entire process. If you are assigned an exercise notice on a call option, the shares are removed from your account, and cash (100 x the strike price) is deposited. It's the same as if you sold 100 shares of stock overnight. If you are assigned on a put option, 100 shares are deposited into your account and the cash to pay for those shares is removed. It's the same as if you bought 100 shares overnight. This process occurs when the markets are closed and your broker informs you that the transaction has occurred.

One further point: When an option owner exercises an option, if you are assigned an exercise notice, you do not learn of the assignment immediately. Your broker notifies you of the assignment before the market opens for trading the following business day. If assignment occurs on expiration Friday, you learn of the assignment when your broker notifies you. That notification usually arrives Monday morning (before the opening), but your online broker should notify you by Sunday afternoon.

To give you a better understanding of the entire process that consists of buying, selling and exercising an option, let's look at some examples of how options are used in our everyday lives.

Call options in our daily lives

You may not be aware, but you probably use call options frequently. Have you ever shopped at a

---

1. *An option expires worthless when expiration day arrives and its owner declines to exercise.*
2. *Receiving an "assignment notice" is the same as being assigned an exercise notice.*

supermarket and tried to buy an advertised special, only to discover that the store had run out of the item? If so, did the customer service department offer to give you a rain check? That rain check is a call option, because it gives you the right (but not the obligation) to purchase the sale item (underlying asset) at the sale price (strike price) for a limited period of time (until the option expires, usually 30 days). You have no obligation to exercise your rights to buy the sale item, but you have the right to do so. Because you paid nothing for that rain check, the premium for your call option is zero.

If you take public transportation and buy a transfer, that transfer is a call option whose underlying asset is another ride. This time, the strike price is zero, because there is no further cost when you exercise your right to take that second ride. But, you must use the transfer before it expires. This option is not free, but the cost of the transfer (premium) is substantially less than the cost of paying a new fare.

When you take public transportation and believe you can accomplish your task in time (before the transfer expires) to use the transfer to travel to another destination (or return to your starting point), then it's probably a good investment to take the risk of paying the small premium to buy the transfer. After all, that transfer gives you the right to take that second ride at a substantial savings. If you are not ready to use the transfer before it expires, then you are not obligated to drop whatever you are doing to take that bus or train. It's your transfer (option) and you are in control. You may throw away the transfer (allow it to expire worthless) if you so choose.

These are only two examples of common call options that we experience in everyday life.

Put options in our daily lives

Put options are also commonly used, and it's a safe bet that you are already familiar with them.

If you own an expensive item, such as a car, a home, or perhaps some artwork or a fancy piece of jewelry and if you own an insurance policy on that item, then you own a put option. In exchange for paying an annual premium, your policy allows you to sell that item to your insurance company if it is lost, stolen or destroyed. The insurance company pays your claim by paying cash (strike price) as a settlement that provides you (or is supposed to provide you) with enough money to replace the item.

These insurance policies are more limited than the put options discussed in this book because you don't have the freedom to exercise your option at any time. Thus, you cannot force the insurance company to buy your item any time you choose to sell. But it does allow you to sell under certain conditions (lost, stolen or damaged beyond a certain point), as outlined in the insurance policy.

What can you do with an option?

Once you buy an option (in Chapter 3 we'll discuss why anyone would want to buy or sell an option), there are three different actions you can take.

Remember, if you are the seller of an option, your choices are limited. You can repurchase the option you sold and thereby cancel your obligations. If you don't repurchase, then you must wait, and there are two possible outcomes: either the option expires worthless or you are assigned an exercise notice. There is nothing else you can do.

But the option owner has choices. Let's examine those choices, by returning to the supermarket and continue discussing the rain check you received. Assume this rain check is good for three one-pound cans of your favorite brand of coffee. The regular price is $5 per pound, and the sale price is $4 per pound. The rain check expires in 30 days.

Choice 1: Exercise your option. One week later (or any time during the 30-day lifetime of the rain check) you return to the store and find that coffee is once again in stock and it's priced at $5 per pound.

- The market price ($5) of the underlying asset is above the call's strike price ($4).
- That means the option is "in-the-money" and has an "intrinsic value."
- The intrinsic value is the amount by which the option is in the money, or the difference between the market price and the strike price ($1 in this example).

You take three cans of coffee and place them in your shopping cart. When you reach the checkout line, you give your rain check to the cashier. When you do that, you are exercising your option and the cashier is being assigned an exercise notice that obligates the supermarket to deliver the coffee (the underlying asset) at the discounted price of $4 per pound (the strike price). You pay $12 for three pounds of coffee. That option no longer exists.

Choice 2: Sell your option. On your next shopping trip, you notice that coffee is selling at its regular price of $5 per pound. But, you were recently introduced to another brand and are no longer interested in exercising your option. While looking at the coffee display, you notice a young woman place two cans of your former brand in her shopping cart. You tell her that you have a discount coupon providing a $2 discount on the coffee purchase and that you would be happy to split the savings by selling that coupon (please don't refer to it as a call option, as the other person would never understand) for $1. (In the real world you would be a Good Samaritan and give away the rain check because you have no use for it. But this is a lesson on how options work and people don't give away their stock options.) At first your fellow shopper is resistant to the idea, but you convince her the coupon is genuine and she agrees to your proposal.[3] It's a good deal for both of you. She saves $1 and you make

$1. The supermarket loses the $2 it would have earned if the option expired worthless. You now have a short-term capital gain of $1. You "bought" your call option, paying zero and sold it for $1.

Choice 3: Allow your option to expire worthless. You return to the supermarket, but this time you discover that your brand of coffee is on sale at $3.75 per pound! Pleasantly surprised, you pick up 3 cans. When you check out, you have a decision to make. Should you pay $3.75 per pound, or should you exercise your option and give the cashier your rain check? In other words, should you exercise the call option that allows you to pay $4 per pound? Clearly you don't want to use the rain check. You have the right to pay $4 per pound, but why would you? You can pay $3.75 per pound instead, so you keep your call option hidden and buy the underlying asset below the strike price. Remember, you have no obligation to use your rain check. Declining to exercise your call option makes sense because:

- The market price of the underlying asset is below the call's strike price.
- That means the option is out-of-the-money and has no intrinsic value.
- You don't want to exercise an option that's out-of-the-money.

You no longer need the rain check because you have more than enough coffee to last awhile. If you want more, you can pay the strike price. Your option, the rain check, still has time remaining before it expires. It's your intention to allow it to go unused, or expire worthless. But, because the supermarket may end the sale and because you may find an opportunity to sell the rain check, you keep it. You don't expect to sell it before it expires, but it costs you nothing to take it with you when you go shopping next time, just in case the

---

3. *Someone familiar with options might have said: "I'll only pay 90 cents."*

underlying (coffee) is priced at $5 per pound again. If that happens, the option once again is in the money and has an intrinsic value.

{ *NOTE: You don't want to exercise a call option when you can buy the underlying for less than the strike price. Similarly, you don't want to exercise a put option when you can sell the underlying for more than the strike price.*

Using a put option

If your car becomes a total loss due to an accident, it's almost worthless to you. Sure, you can probably sell it to a company that salvages parts, but if you own a put option (an auto insurance policy), it's better to sell the car to the insurance company for the car's replacement value (strike price). If you have an unusual situation in which you can sell the damaged car for more than the insurance company would pay you, then you would not exercise your put option. Even though that option is in-the-money (it has an intrinsic value equal to the strike price) you would not exercise that option. Why collect money on your insurance policy when you can collect a greater amount by selling the car to a company that offers you a higher price? In other words, you have no obligation to exercise your option. It's your choice and if you can collect more cash elsewhere, you simply allow the option to expire worthless.[4]

BOTTOM LINE: When you own an option, you have three choices. You can:

- Exercise the option. (You will seldom make this choice, but if you decide to do so, please be certain it's in-the-money.)
- Sell the option (it may be either in-the-money or out-of-the-money).
- Allow the option to expire worthless when expiration arrives and it's out-of-the-money.

When using real world stock options, you have exactly the same three choices. If the strike price of an option equals (or nearly equals) the market price of the underlying asset, the option is at-the-money

Aren't options easier to understand than you expected? A short quiz follows this chapter allowing you to determine how well you understand the concepts of options and how they work.

---

4. *The option is not yet worthless because the expiration date is still in the future. But, you no longer own the car, and are in no position to use the policy.*

Quiz

1. The owner of a call option may be assigned an exercise notice obligating that investor to buy 100 shares of the underlying asset at the strike price.

○ **TRUE**   ○ **FALSE**

2. QUIZ is trading at $34.17 per share. Which of the following options are in-the-money? Which are out-of-the-money?

A. QUIZ Oct 35 call   **B.** QUIZ Nov 30 call
C. QUIZ Feb 30 call   **D.** QUIZ Dec 30 call
E. QUIZ Dec 25 call   **F.** QUIZ Feb 30 put
G. QUIZ Jan 35 put

3. IBM is $104 per share. Does the Jun 100 call have any intrinsic value? If yes, how much is the intrinsic value?

4. If you exercise one XYZ Mar 45 call option and purchase 100 shares of XYZ stock, how much cash is removed from your account to pay for the shares?

5. If you are assigned an exercise notice on 3 ABCD Oct 100 puts, how much cash is removed from your account to pay for the shares?

6. What is the primary right of the writer of an XYZ Sep 70 call option?

7. What is the procedure by which the seller of a call option can request that the option owner exercise the option?

8. You sell two QUIZ Nov 40 call options, collecting $100 apiece. Time passes and QUIZ Nov 40 call options are trading at $0.05 ($5 per contract). What happens if you buy two QUIZ Nov 40 calls?

9. XYZ is trading at 41.25 per share. You sell one XYZ Dec 40 call and collect $400. What is the premium of the XYZ Dec 40 call?

10. If you buy an option and pay $200, are you allowed to sell it for $50?

11. You buy one IBM Jan 95 call at a premium of $3.20. Two weeks later you sell your call at a premium of $4.00. Can you be assigned an exercise notice and become obligated to deliver 100 shares of IBM at $95 per share?

12. What is your profit (or loss) in question 11?

Chapter 2

Exchange-Traded Options

Once you recognize that you have been using common options for years, you understand that options are neither difficult to understand nor dangerous. What is dangerous is people buying and selling options without a clear understanding of what they are trying to accomplish. Too many investors buy calls, see their stocks rise in price and, bewildered, discover that they lose money. I don't want that to happen to you. The better you understand what you are doing when working with options, the better your chances of being a successful investor and trader.

In this chapter we'll take a closer look at options that trade on exchanges. Options for which the underlying asset is an individual stock, stock index or an ETF are listed for trading on up to six different options exchanges in the United States, plus additional exchanges overseas. It's likely that this number is going to change as new exchanges come into being and as mergers reduce the current number of players. Options are big business and options for other assets are available for trading, including currencies, bonds, commodities, etc.

Defining an option

Options are fungible, meaning they are interchangeable. Thus, whenever anyone buys or sells an option, the option must be clearly defined so everyone involved in the transaction understands which specific option is trading. But more than that, if you have a position in an option (you either bought or sold the option), that option must be clearly identifiable so you can close out your position.[1] To accomplish that, four pieces of information are necessary:

- Symbol of the underlying asset.
- Strike price.
- Expiration date.
- Option type (put or call).

To meet that requirement, those descriptive items are written in the following format:

- MSFT Jul 30 put: a put option granting its owner the right (but not the obligation) to sell 100 shares of Microsoft at $30 per share, any time before the option expires in July.
- IBM Oct 100 call: a call option granting its owner the right to buy 100 shares of IBM at $100 per share, any time before the option expires in October.
- IWM Mar 84 call: a call option granting its owner the right to buy 100 shares of the exchange traded fund IWM (Russell 2000 index) at $84 per share, any time before the option expires in March.
- BA Jan 110 put: A put option granting its owner the right to sell 100 shares of Boeing at $110 per share any time before the option expires in January.

Standardization of options

Before options were traded on exchanges, they traded in a haphazard manner. Options had random expiration dates and strike prices. Option sellers listed the contracts they had for sale in newspaper ads. If you wanted to sell an option you had previously bought (or wanted to buy an option you previously sold), it was a very difficult proposition. You (actually your broker) had to find someone willing to take the other side of your position, and that was a difficult task.

When options began trading on an exchange (the Chicago Board Options Exchange, or CBOE) in 1973 all that changed. Options became standardized, meaning they had well-defined strike prices and expiration dates. The fact that options were now fungible allowed buyers and sellers to trade with the confidence that comes with the knowledge that positions could be closed (sell an option purchased earlier or buy back an option previously sold) prior to expiration.

Strike prices

Options have standardized strike prices. Thus, when options with new strike prices are listed for trading, those strikes occur at specific intervals based on the stock price and its volatility (volatility is a major consideration when using options and is covered in Chapter 7). More volatile stocks undergo larger and more frequent price changes than less volatile stocks, and thus require a greater number of strike prices.

Puts and calls are listed in pairs. Thus, if the December 80 call option is available to trade, then the December 80 put is also available. Each stock has at least two different strike prices: one above the current stock price, and one lower. That means there is always[2] at least one out-of-the-money (OTM) call option and one OTM put option available for

---

1. There would be little interest in option trading if you were forced to hold a position until expiration.
2. If the underlying stock gaps significantly higher or lower when the market opens, it's possible that no out-of-the money options are available. When that occurs, new strike prices sometimes are added immediately; at other times new strike prices are not listed for trading until the following business day.

trading[3]. Almost all stocks have additional strike prices. Let's see how this works:

On the first business day following expiration (Monday, unless it's a national holiday), the recently expired options no longer exist and to replace them, the exchanges list options with a new expiration month. For example, let's assume that June expiration has just passed. The following Monday, the exchanges list new options for each underlying asset. IBM options that expire in August begin trading.

If IBM is priced at 103, then the exchanges list one strike price above and one below the current market price:

- Aug 100 calls and puts.
- Aug 105 calls and puts.

If the stock last traded near[4] one strike price, then a third strike is added: For example, if IBM last traded below 102, the exchanges would also list:

- Aug 95 calls and puts.

Calls and puts are always listed together. You never find a situation in which a call is listed, but the corresponding put is not listed.

IBM is a stock that generates a fair amount of trading volume. The exchanges tend to list additional options to accommodate investors who trade IBM options. Thus, even if the stock did not trade low enough for the Aug 95s to be listed, the exchanges would probably list Aug 95s and 110s anyway. They might even list 90s and 115s. There is no rule written in stone. The idea is to try to list options that attract both buyers and sellers, but not to list options that would not attract any interest from investors. There is no reason to list IBM 50s or 200s. New strike prices are clustered around the current stock price.

{ NOTE: When the new expiration month options are listed, any strike price listed for the new month is automatically added (if it does not already exist) for each expiration month (except for LEAPS, which are described later in this chapter). Thus if IBM Oct 100 is the lowest strike price for October, if the Aug 95s are listed, then the Oct 95s are listed for trading.

Non-volatile stocks offer fewer strike prices. If it's very unlikely that any specific stock moves by more than two or three points over any given one-month period, there is no reason to list more than two or three strike prices. It's the fact that a given stock (judging from its past price history) has demonstrated that it can easily undergo significant price changes that dictates the listing of additional strike prices. Look at it from the viewpoint of a potential option buyer. If IBM had little chance to increase in value from 102 to 105 over any reasonable period of time, few people would be interested in buying (or selling) options with a strike price of 110 or higher. That's the reason why more volatile stocks—those with the ability to undergo significant price changes—have a greater number of strike prices available to trade than stodgy, non-volatile stocks.

How are new strike prices added?

It's important to always have at least one call option that is out-of-the-money (strike price above stock price) and at least one out-of-the-money put option (strike price below stock price). Thus, new options are added when necessary, to satisfy that requirement. If the price of the underlying stock changes sufficiently, then new strike prices are added. For example, if IBM has August options with strike prices ranging from 90 through 115, options with new strike prices are listed for trading:

---

3. An OTM call option has a strike price that is above the current stock price. An OTM put option has a strike price lower than the current stock price.

4. Within 2 percent of the strike price on either Thursday or Friday of expiration week.

- If IBM trades as high as 115 (the current highest available strike price), the 120s (and probably the 125s) are added for trading the next day.
- If IBM trades as low as 90 (the lowest available strike price), then 85s (and probably 80s) are listed for trading the next day.
- Upon request. New strike prices are added when exchanges honor requests from customers to list specific options.

When these new strike prices are added, they are added for all expiration months,[5] unless those options already exist.

EXAMPLE —————

TABLE 2.1: CHEM Options

EXP	STRIKE
Mar	35
Mar	40
Mar	45
Apr	35
Apr	40
Apr	45
Jun	30
Jun	35
Jun	40
Jun	45
Sep	35
Sep	40
Sep	45

Adding new strike prices.

Assume CHEM, a manufacturer of specialty chemicals used for academic research, is priced at $41 per share and has the following listed options (found in Table 2.1):

If CHEM trades as high as 45, then options with a strike price of 50 are added for Mar,[6] Apr, Jun and Sep. If CHEM trades as low as 35, then options with a strike price of 30 are added for Mar, Apr and Sep (Jun 30 is already listed).

When new options are made available, the strike prices are not chosen at random. Most listed options adhere to the following pattern, but there are numerous exceptions. Some of the lower-priced stocks as well as some ETFs have options whose strike prices are only one point apart. As a general rule, the following strike prices are used:

- Every 2-1/2 points from 5, through 22-1/2.
- Every 5 points from 25 through 100.
- Every 10 points from 110 through 200.
- Every 20 points above 200.

Expiration dates

Options have standard expiration dates. One of the four descriptive terms for an option is its expiration month. Expiration day for these options is Saturday, following the third Friday of the specified month. Because that Friday is also the last day these options are available for trading, most people refer to that day as "expiration Friday" or "expiration day." As long as you understand that the third Friday[7] is both the last day the options trade and the last day they may be exercised, the technical definition of "expiration day" is not important. In general, you will seldom, if ever, want to exercise an option.

{ *NOTE: You, as an individual investor can usually fare better by selling your option rather than exercising it. But, when expiration day arrives, options that are in-the-money are not just thrown away. They are most often in the hands of market makers who accumulate them as individual investors sell out their positions. The point is that you may seldom exercise an option you own, but you can count on being assigned an exercise notice when you are short an option that is in-the-money as of the close of business on expiration Friday.[8]*

---

5. New strike prices are not added for the front month (the nearest expiration), unless there are more than five business days remaining before expiration.

6. To add the front month (March, in this example) there must be more than five business days remaining before the option expires.

7. Expiration is not the third Saturday. It is the day following the third Friday.

8. Every once in awhile, an option that's in the money by a few pennies is allowed (by its owner) to expire worthless. That means that someone who was short that option "slides" and is not assigned an exercise notice.

Each underlying asset has listed options with at least four different expiration dates. Some indexes and many individual stocks have more than four. As you might expect, the expiration months listed for trading are not chosen at random. There is a protocol that determines which new month is added (to replace the recently expired month) after expiration.

Rules determining which expiration months are listed

1. Each stock is assigned to an expiration cycle.

Those cycles are:

- Jan, Apr, Jul, Oct
- Feb, May, Aug, Nov
- Mar, Jun, Sep, Dec

2. Every underlying asset adds options with a new expiration month on the Monday following expiration.

The two nearest calendar months are always made available. For example, if February options expired last Friday, the following Monday, every stock, index and ETF offers options that expire in Mar and Apr.

3. In addition, each underlying asset has options that expire in two additional months, with the proviso that each of those months comes from its expiration cycle.

From the cycle, the two nearest months (that are not already trading) are listed for trading.

EXAMPLE

(Assuming all stocks list Mar and Apr options):
Jan cycle: Mar, Apr, Jul, Oct
Mar and Apr are the two front months. Jul and Oct are from the Jan cycle. IBM is in the Jan cycle, thus already has Jul options. Thus, Oct is the newly listed month.

Feb cycle: Mar, Apr, May, Aug
Mar and Apr are the two front months. May and Aug are from the Feb cycle

Mar cycle: Mar, Apr, Jun, Sep
Mar and Apr are the two front months. Jun and Sep are from the Mar cycle

Many underlying stocks have options with additional expiration dates. Those options have much longer lifetimes and are called LEAPS, which stands for Long Term Equity Anticipation Series. (The final "S" is part of the acronym. Thus, these options are referred to as LEAPS and not leap options.) All LEAPS options expire in Jan and may be as far as three years in the future. For example, if a stock offers LEAPS options and if that stock has options that expire in Jun, Jul, Aug and Nov of 2008, it would also have LEAPS that expire in Jan09 and Jan10.[9] Note: When LEAPS options are listed, there are always two different years available.

Do options provide too many options?

When trading options, you always have choices. Each underlying asset not only lists options with at least four different expiration dates, but also multiple strike prices. This may cause you to believe that making intelligent trading decisions is impossible. That belief will be short-lived, because I'll walk you slowly through the choices and carefully explain how you choose an option that is not only appropriate for the specific strategy under discussion, but also suitable for you and your style of investing.

How and when to exercise an option you own

Check with your broker to learn the details of how they want to be informed about your plans to exercise. Each broker has a system, but the latest time that they accept instructions to exercise options is shortly after the market closes for business on the third Friday of the month.

Most of the time it's far better to simply sell an option, rather than exercise it. However, there are situations in which exercising an option may be the better choice. Thus, the question arises: How do you exercise an option? There are two methods:

---

9. *When a LEAPS option is described, the term, "Jan," is not sufficient. Two digits are inserted after "Jan" to designate the expiration year.*

1. Instruct your broker to exercise. Each broker has a preferred method for exercising a call or put option. Some prefer e-mail to a specific address, while others prefer a telephone call. Still others may allow you to notify them via a direct link from your online trading account. (Choose this option if it's available to you.) It's your obligation to learn what your broker requires, so be certain to ask. Keep the information in a place that's readily accessible because if you ever decide to exercise an option, there's a cutoff time each afternoon, shortly after the market closes for the day.

2. Exercise at expiration. If you own an option that is in-the-money (ITM) and for some reason you failed to sell that option, you probably want to exercise, rather than allow the option to expire worthless. Note that this is not always true.

- If an option is only worth few dollars (that means a few pennies per share), it's often not worthwhile to exercise. Most brokers charge a commission to exercise an option. For example, if you exercise a call option and buy stock, unless you want to maintain ownership of the stock, you are forced to pay another commission to sell the stock. Those combined commissions can easily cost more than the few pennies per share you earn when selling the stock on the next business day. Don't overlook the risk of holding the stock over the weekend. (You have to pay three days' worth of interest on the cash required to buy and hold stock over the weekend.) The stock may open significantly higher or lower on Monday, compared with where it last traded on expiration Friday. All things considered, it's far better for you, the individual investor, to let an option expire

worthless when it's in-the-money by only a few pennies[10] and you are unable to sell it.
- Automatic exercise. When expiration arrives, if you own an option that's worth at least $1, i.e., it's in-the-money by $0.01 or more, the powers that be have decided that you probably want to exercise this option—and they automatically exercise it for you. I think this is a terrible idea, but that's the rule. The option owner is supposed to have the right, but not the obligation, to exercise, but somehow the rules change at expiration and the obligation to exercise is forced upon the option owner. However, if you know you don't want to exercise, you must notify your broker of that decision before the cutoff time. The process is identical to the process by which you notify the broker that you want to exercise, but this time you must notify the broker that you do *not* want to exercise. It's best not to find yourself in this situation, and it can be avoided if you remember to sell, or at least attempt to sell, any options that you own before the markets close on expiration Friday.

Stock splits and other adjustments

Sometimes companies make a corporate decision to split the shares of their common stock. The most common split is 2 for 1. Thus, once the split is effective, twice as many shares exist and every shareholder holds twice as many shares as previously held. Is this a bonanza? Did each shareholder double the value of his or her investment? No.

The efficient stock market makes sure that doesn't happen. For example, if the company was worth $5 billion before the split, it's still worth $5 billion after the split. There is no reason for the company suddenly to be worth $10 billion. Thus, the market price of each share is reduced. In effect, the price is

---

10. But this is not true for professional market makers. They almost always exercise an option, even when in-the-money by one cent. They do that because they have their positions hedged and there is a tiny profit to be made by exercising options that are slightly ITM. Thus, if you find yourself short such an option, you won't know if the option is going to expire worthless or be exercised until your broker notifies you next Monday (before the market opens).

also split 2 for 1. Thus, if you own 200 shares valued at $80 per share, you have $16,000 worth of stock in the company. If the stock is split 2 for 1, then you own 400 shares, valued at $40 per share, or the same $16,000. Stock splits should not make any difference in the value of your shares. In the real world, there is the perception that a stock split makes the company's shares more attractive to own, and most of the time, when a company announces a stock split, the price of the company's stock increases.

It's important to ask the question: If the stock splits, does that make any difference to the options? The answer is yes. Options are affected just as are the company's shares. In other words, if you own 10 IBM Jul 100 call options, and if the company splits its stock 2 for 1, you now own 20 IBM Jul 50 calls. Here's how you should think about such a split:

You own calls, each of which gives you the right to buy 100 shares of stock at $100 per share. Thus, each option represents the right to buy $10,000 worth of IBM stock. If the stock splits, your rights as an option owner are not affected. You still have the right to buy $10,000 worth of IBM stock for each option you own. Because the stock split cuts the stock price in half, the exercise price of the options are cut in half. The right to pay $100 per share for a stock trading at only $50 per share is not worth very much, and it doesn't make sense for the options suddenly to become worthless. Thus, each option now gives you the right to buy 100 shares of IBM stock at $50 per share, or $5,000 worth of stock. To restore your previous position, you must now be given one extra option for each option held originally. This means you now own twice as many call options, each of which gives you the right to buy $5,000 worth of stock. You are right back where you began: you own IBM call options (20 Jul 50 calls), which gives you the right to buy the same value in IBM stock as you previously had the right to buy.

That was a very lengthy way of telling you that the option splits just as the stock does. In the case of a 2 for 1 split, you now own options with the right to buy twice as many shares at one-half the price. Put owners now have the right to sell twice as many shares at one half the price. The expiration date is unchanged. In the event of a 4 for 1 stock split, you would own four times as many options and the strike price would be one-quarter the original strike price.

Unless the split is 2 for 1 or 4 for 1, a different protocol is used.[11] There are two situations to consider:

1. The stock splits evenly, i.e., 3 for 1.

- The strike price is unchanged.
- The number of contracts remains the same.
- The deliverable[12] changes to reflect the split.
- The option symbol changes.

EXAMPLE

You own five ABC Aug 40 calls and the company announces a 3 for 1 stock split. Once the split becomes effective, you still own five ABC Aug 40 call options (with a new option symbol), but each call is an option on 300 shares (the deliverable) of ABC stock. Your call options should be worth the same once the split becomes effective as it was worth the previous day. Thus, the new option price is (subject to changing market conditions) one-third the price it was yesterday.

- *Yesterday you owned five ABC Aug 40 calls. Each call gave its owner the right to buy 100 shares of ABC at a cost of $4,000, or $40 per share. The market price was $2.10. The value of each option is 100 x $2.10, or $210.*

---

11. The change went into effect September 4, 2007. Another modification will go into effect in July 2009 when all equity options trade in decimals (i.e., 22.500, not 22-1/2 strike prices).

12. The deliverable is the same items that a call option owner has the right to receive (or a put owner has the right to sell). In this example, that's 300 shares per option.

• *Today you still own five ABC Aug 40 calls. Each call represents the right to buy 300 shares of ABC at a cost of $4,000 for those 300 shares (i.e., exercising gives you the same amount of stock at the same total cost). The option premium is $0.70 and each option is worth $0.70 x 300, or the same $210.*

2. The stock splits unevenly, i.e., 3 for 2 or 4 for 3 etc.

• The strike price is unchanged.
• The number of shares remains the same.

EXAMPLE

You own five ABC Aug 40 calls and the company announces a 3 for 2 stock split. Once the split becomes effective, you still own five ABC Aug 40 call options (with a new option symbol), but each call is an option on 150 shares (the deliverable) of ABC stock. If the stock was trading at 42 yesterday, it is trading at $28 today, after the 3 for 2 split. Here is the tricky part. It appears that your Aug 40 calls are out-of-the money by 12 points (40 strike minus 28 stock price), but with this type of stock split, you must multiply the underlying (that's ABC stock) by the effective split. In other words, the stock price (as far as your options are concerned) is 28 x 1.5, or 42. Thus, the calls are two points in-the-money (with an intrinsic value of $200 each). They are not out-of-the money.

This is going to cause a problem for many investors (in my opinion). Today, you can look at the strike price and look at the stock price and know whether the option is in-the-money. With this new scheme, the underlying price must be multiplied by the correct factor (1.5 in this example) to determine whether the option is in-the-money.

BOTTOM LINE: When a stock split occurs, the option owner is unaffected and still maintains the right to buy (or sell) the same dollar amount of the underlying security.[13]

Adjustments

GE (General Electric) is a company that acquires other companies. Let's say that GE decides to make a tender offer to buy all outstanding shares of MYCO (my company) and that you have an option position in MYCO. What happens to your options if the deal is finalized?

The answer is simple. You have the same rights or obligations you had before the takeover.

• If you own five Nov 25 call options, you have the right to buy 500 shares at $25 per share.
• If you sold five Nov 25 calls and are assigned an exercise notice, you become obligated to sell 500 shares at $25.
• If you are the owner of Dec 22.5 puts, you still have the right to sell MYCO shares at $22.50 per share any time before the options expire.
• If you are short (i.e., you sold) Dec 22.5 puts, you may become obligated (if assigned an exercise notice) to buy 500 shares at $22.50 per share.

In this scenario, GE is paying cash for shares of MYCO. When the deal is finalized, the shares of MYCO can never be worth more nor less than the cash amount that GE paid. In fact, the shares no longer exist. If you still have shares (for some reason you failed to tender them to GE), GE buys them from you at the same price it paid for the other MYCO shares it purchased. Thus, if the takeover price is $28 per share, every call option with a strike price above $28 is worthless. That is true regardless of the expiration date. Every call option with a strike price of $25 is worth $3 (the intrinsic value is $3

---

13. *Obviously, if the price of the underlying stock rallies when the split is announced, then the call owner profits and the put owner loses. But that gain or loss is a result of a change in the price of the stock and is not directly the result of the announced split.*

because the stock is worth 28 and the strike price is 25). Any remaining time value in the option is lost. Call options with lower strike prices are worth their individual intrinsic values. Don't be surprised if you are assigned an exercise notice immediately.[14] The call owner exercises the call option, pays you $25 per share and immediately tenders the shares to GE, collecting $28 per share.

Similarly, all put options with strike prices below $28 per share are worthless. No one would exercise a put option to sell shares at less than $28. Put options with higher strikes are worth their intrinsic value and lose their time value.

Before the deal is finalized, the situation is different and the options can still vary in value. Why? Because another suitor may come along and pay an even higher price than GE is offering. Thus, the Oct 30 calls, which are worthless if the GE deal goes through, may become valuable if another company comes along and offers to buy MYCO at $32 per share. And don't forget that proposed mergers can fall apart at the last minute. If that happens, the market price of MYCO shares changes to reflect the disrupted deal. That means the shares are very likely to trade much lower (rewarding the owners of put options) unless there appears to be another buyer of the company waiting in the wings.

Sometimes a takeover involves only shares of stock or only cash. Sometimes it's a combination. For example, assume GE buys MYCO by paying $20 cash plus 0.20 shares of GE stock for each share of MYCO. That complicates matters for option traders, but it's not difficult to understand the situation. If you own one call option, you have the right to buy 100 shares of MYCO by paying 100 times the strike price. Because 100 shares of MYCO are now worth $2,000

plus 20 shares[15] of GE, that's what the MYCO call owner gets if the option is exercised.

Before the merger, the option owner had the right to buy 100 shares of MYCO. Now the option owner has the right to buy $2,000 plus 20 GE shares. One hundred shares of MYCO was much more volatile than 20 shares of GE. Thus, from the point of view of an option buyer, there is not much reason to buy these options because there's little likelihood of the underlying asset (cash plus 20 GE shares) undergoing a significant price change (GE is a relatively nonvolatile stock). That's another way of saying that this option is not worth much more than its intrinsic value.[16]

The good news for call owners (and bad news for put owners) is that GE probably had to bid significantly above market price to complete the takeover, and that means MYCO shares probably jumped in price. The bad news for call owners is that the value of the option above its intrinsic value is almost zero.

EXAMPLE

Calculating the intrinsic value of MYCO options, assuming GE is trading at $40 per share. 100 shares of MYCO is worth:

- *$2,000 ($20 per share) cash,*
- *plus 0.20 shares at $40 per share, or $8,*
- *total current value of 100 shares of MYCO is $28.*

Thus, the intrinsic value of the MYCO 25 calls is $3 and the call is worth about $300.

The MYCO 30 puts have an intrinsic value of $2 and are worth about $200.[17] Note that the MYCO 30 calls are worthless and remain worthless unless GE rises above $50[18] (unlikely) before the MYCO options expire.

---

14. After the deal is finalized—not when the deal is announced.

15. ($20 per share plus 0.20 shares of GE) x 100.

16. Options are usually worth much more than the intrinsic value.

17. Owners of MYCO 30 puts have the right to exercise and collect the strike price, or $3,000. The combination of shares and cash is only worth $2,800, so the put is in-the-money.

18. When GE is $50, the value of MYCO shares is $30 ($2,000 plus 20 GE shares worth $50 each). If GE trades any higher, the MYCO 30 calls go in-the-money and begin to accumulate an intrinsic value.

BOTTOM LINE: When a merger involves cash, the call owner has the right to exercise the option and receive the same cash payment received by the owner of 100 shares. When a merger involves a complex mix of cash, stock, bonds or anything else, the call owner has the right to exercise the option and receive the same mix as received by the owner of 100 shares.[19] The option owner's right to exercise the option and either buy or sell 100 shares is protected.

But the option owner is likely to have a good-sized gain or loss depending on the terms of the takeover.[20]

After the merger described above, any MYCO options still trading are adjusted such that by paying the original strike price, the call owner who exercises the option receives $2,000 plus 20 shares of GE. The put owner retains the right to exercise and, in return for collecting the strike price, deliver $2,000 and 20 shares of GE.

---

19. *And the put owner has the right to sell that same mix and receive the strike price x 100.*
20. *Call owners usually gain, because takeovers usually occur at a price substantially higher than the current market price. Put owners tend to lose.*

1. How many specific pieces of information are required to describe an option?

2. Is this scenario possible? An investor wants to enter an order to buy IBM Dec 120 calls, but discovers that the calls are not listed on any options exchange. The investor only finds IBM Dec 120 puts.

3. It's Monday morning. Last Friday the Oct options expired. Which two expiration months are available for all underlying stocks?

4. It is Wednesday, Oct 10 and the exchanges list a new option series for trading. It's the XYX Oct 65. What are the three most likely reasons these options were listed for trading today?

5. You own two ZZZ Aug 60 call options. ZZZ announces a 3 for 1 stock split. After the split is effective, what is your ZZZ option position?

6. You sold 10 GGG Mar 25 puts, collecting $50 for each. Subsequently GGG announced that it's being taken over by a competitor who is paying $29.50 in cash for each outstanding share of GGG. Is this good news for you?

7. Today is the third Friday of December and you own five FFF Dec 40 calls. The stock is trading near 40 and you have been trying to sell your calls, but there is no bid. The stock closes for the day at 40.05 and you still own your calls. What should you do? Which, if any, of the choices below makes sense?

   A. Do nothing. The options will expire worthless.
   B. Do nothing. Maybe you will be assigned an exercise notice, and maybe you won't.
   C. Do nothing if you want to buy stock at $40 per share.
   D. Quickly notify your broker not to exercise if you don't want to buy stock at $40 per share.

8. You own 10 XYX Apr 35 call options. It's Friday, April 17 (the third Friday in April), and XYZ stock's last trade of the day is $32 per share. What happens to your options?

Chapter 3

Buying and Selling Options

Options are currently listed for trading on six options exchanges in the U.S., plus many others around the world. Options are becoming more and more popular, as trading volume sets new records year after year (Figure 3.1). Trading volume is not just creeping higher, it's exploding. And the number of equity products with listed options continues to accelerate, although at a more reasonable pace (Figure 3.2). Why is this happening? Why has trading volume been increasing so rapidly in recent years?

The surging volume tells us that options play an increasingly important role in the overall investment strategy for a great many people. Much of the new option volume must be attributed to the growth in the number and size of hedge funds. As these funds grow, the amount of money under management constantly increases.

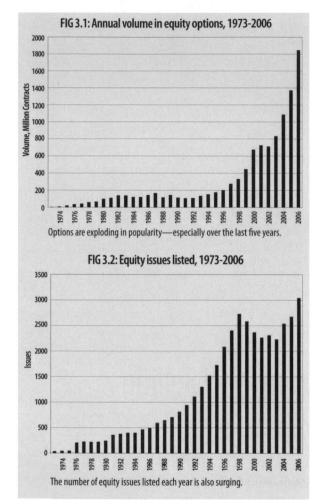

FIG 3.1: Annual volume in equity options, 1973-2006

Volume, Million Contracts

Options are exploding in popularity—especially over the last five years.

FIG 3.2: Equity issues listed, 1973-2006

Issues

The number of equity issues listed each year is also surging.

Thus, the funds use an ever-increasing number of options to implement their strategies and operate their profitable businesses. But, hedge funds are not the only contributor to the increased activity in options trading. Some traditional mutual funds have adopted an option strategy known as covered call writing. That strategy in discussed in detail in Chapters 10 through 12.

The individual investor is also trading options more than ever. Several prominent online brokerage houses advertise their options expertise in an attempt to attract new customers. New discount brokers specializing in options are appearing on the scene, hoping to capture a share of the market. When the International Securities Exchange (ISE) went public, its stock soared. The oldest and largest options exchange, the Chicago Board Options Exchange (CBOE) is preparing for its initial public offering. Trading options is one of the most exciting businesses in the world.

Because hedge funds don't disclose their methods, and because those methods are likely to be very sophisticated, there's no way for us to know exactly how fund managers use options. But, I can show you how individual investors and professional traders use options. Some of these methods are appropriate for newcomers to the options world, while others require more experience and a better understanding of how options work before they can be used successfully. We'll study the most basic of these strategies in Part II and then consider a few more sophisticated, but still easy to understand, methods in Part III.

Why would anyone buy an option?

Let's take a look at options from the perspective of an individual investor in an attempt to understand why investors want to buy or sell an option.

Let's say you have an opinion on the stock market. You don't have any specific stocks in mind, but you just know the overall market is headed higher (or lower). What can you do? One obvious choice is to buy a basket of stocks, hoping to participate in the coming rally. The problem with that idea is that you don't really know which stocks to trade and, in addition, commissions can add up (even with a deep discount broker) when you trade many different stocks.

Another choice is to buy shares of a mutual fund. The problem with that choice is that so few funds outperform the market averages that you hate to pay someone a management fee to provide below-average returns. The idea of buying shares of an exchange-traded fund (ETF) or an Index Fund occurs to you. You know these are much better items for investment purposes than traditional mutual funds. And they offer a diversified portfolio with extremely low management fees. These are reasonable choices for the average investor.

If you invest $5,000 and if the market rallies by 10 percent, you might make $500. Not bad, but that's not really much money for successfully predicting a sizeable market advance. It's difficult enough to predict market direction (this author firmly believes that very few people can do it on a consistent basis), and if you can do it, you want to earn a higher return than the average investor—as a reward for being so clever. To do that, an investor must use leverage.

You can always purchase your shares on 50 percent margin,[1] thereby increasing the amount you can earn (and also the amount you can lose). If you buy $10,000 worth of shares with your $5,000 cash, you could earn $1,000 or 20 percent. That's much better. But is it enough? Is there a way to gain even more leverage? Yes there is.

You can buy options. If you are right in your stock market prediction, you can make a very substantial profit. On the other hand, you might lose your entire investment—something that would never happen if you simply bought shares of that index fund. Let me repeat for emphasis: You could easily lose your entire $5,000 investment when you buy options. Are you willing to risk that loss? There are many investors who are not only willing, but also anxious to take that risk. And it's important for you to understand why they do so. I hope you are not among those risk-taking investors, and in these pages I discourage you from making such aggressive bets on the stock market. But it is your money, and you have every right to speculate.

When you buy options (calls in this situation because you are bullish) you have the opportunity to earn significantly higher returns. But, you must also accept the increased probability of losing

money when your bullish prediction fails to come true quickly enough. Remember, options have limited lifetimes.

As you might have guessed, buying options to speculate is not on my list of recommended strategies. It's too difficult for the vast majority of investors to earn money using this approach. But it's tempting because the rewards can be so large. Many investors, speculators and outright gamblers love to buy options. And there is nothing wrong with that, if you understand that in return for the chance for a big payday, there is a high probability of losing money.

My goal is to introduce you to the world of options and to show you how options can be used to enhance your income while reducing risk. I'm not encouraging you to gamble, but if you choose to do so, I'll help you reduce the chances of losing money.

A more detailed description of the strategy of buying options is presented in Chapter 9. The following is a condensed version. If the SPX (Standard & Poors 500 Index) is trading at 1500, and if you are correct in your prediction of a quick 10-percent advance, the index would move to 1650 in four weeks. Assume there are 36 days until the Apr options expire and you decide to buy April call options. Without going into how options are priced at this point, let's just say that you decide to buy SPX Apr call options with a strike price of 1550. Those options could reasonably cost you $950 apiece.[2] Assuming you are willing to take a chance with your entire $5,000, you buy five SPX Apr 1550 calls and pay $4,750. Remember, these options give you the right to buy SPX at 1550.

Four weeks later, the index has reached 1600 (congratulations!) and you decide it's time to sell your options. Sure, you predicted the index would rally to 1650, but there's no need to be that greedy. How much should you receive when selling your

---

1. You use your own $5,000 and borrow an equal amount from your broker.
2. How to determine a fair value for an option is discussed in Chapter 6.

calls? They are 50 points in-the-money and thus, the intrinsic value is $5,000 for each option. A reasonable price for these calls is 51.50, or $5,150 apiece. You sell your five contracts and collect $25,750 for a net profit of $21,000, or a return of 442 percent. Pretty impressive! Many investors would never hold the position as long as you, thereby earning less money. But, the point is that it's possible to make outstanding returns when using leverage. And that possibility is just too attractive to many beginners. They cannot resist the temptation. A few make substantial profits and believe it's a cinch to get rich quickly using options. Others lose their entire bankrolls—either because the rally doesn't occur, or it happens after their options expire. These investors walk away from the options world thinking that options are just too dangerous for them. It's sad. Options are versatile tools that should have a place in the investment arsenal of many investors. If you choose to gamble, if you find these potential returns just too irresistible—so be it.

TABLE 3.1: Leverage at work: profit potential when owning five SPX APR 1550 call options

P/L	SPX Price
-$4,750	1500
-$4,750	1525
-$4,750	1550
$7,750	1575
$20,250[3]	1600
$32,750	1625
$45,250	1650
$57,750	1675

This possibility is why investors buy options.

In the example we showed how a bullish investor can buy call options. Similarly, a bearish investor can buy put options, hoping to profit from a market decline.

Many stock market observers consider buying options to be a low-risk strategy because loss is limited to the cash paid for an option. While that's true, the additional truth is that losing the entire investment occurs far too often. If you buy options, it's important to understand how to limit losses. But let's not get ahead of ourselves. There's a great deal more to learn about options and how they work before you begin trading with real money.

Why would anyone sell an option?

When you sell an option, you are paid a cash premium. That cash is yours to keep, no matter what else happens. Some people shudder at the thought of selling options because they believe it entails unlimited risk. And they are right, if the sales are naked (unhedged). That risk is almost always too substantial (for most investors) to accept in return for that cash premium.

For those readers who already understand something about options, I don't advocate the sale of naked options. That means when I talk about selling one option, it always involves the purchase of another. In almost all strategies discussed in this book, I'll show you how to reduce risk to manageable and acceptable levels. But for now, it's important to know that the main reason investors sell options is their ability to collect cash from those sales. When you buy an option, your maximum gain is unlimited. When you sell an option your maximum gain is the cash collected.

---

3. This profit differs from the $21,000 figure, because this time the calls are held to expiration and lose $750 in time value.

Chapter 4

The Mechanics of Trading

Most readers are familiar with the process by which an order is entered to buy or sell stocks. Options trade in similar fashion. This chapter features a brief description of the process by which you buy and sell options.

Brokers

Before trading options, you must open an account with a broker and fill out paperwork requesting permission to trade options. Many brokers accept online applications, simplifying the process. Before your broker grants permission to trade options, they provide an excellent educational pamphlet entitled *Characteristics and Risks of Standardized Options.* Don't just toss it away. It contains useful information.

If you are new to the options world, your broker places a limit on the type of orders they accept from you. The rationale behind such limits is that the more risky strategies should only be available to experienced traders. Unfortunately, these limits make it impossible for an individual investor to adopt some of the more conservative strategies. These limits are a hindrance, but it's for your own safety (as well as theirs).[1] This policy was adopted for the right reasons, but it often has the opposite effect by forcing investors to choose between less conservative option strategies and avoiding options.

If you do your homework, you may find a broker who allows customers to enter any type of order. Please be careful. When using that type of broker, it's a Catch-22. More good option strategies become available to you, but it also becomes possible to enter orders for option plays that are risky for rookies. If, after understanding the content of Chapter 8, you feel you have the ability to manage market risk successfully, then this type of broker may be a suitable match.

I don't want to recommend one specific broker, but it's to your advantage to use a deep discount broker when possible. The good news is that there are a number of such brokerages worthy of your business. Be aware that new brokers—offering reduced commissions for options traders—are appearing more frequently, looking to grab market share in this lucrative business. When opening an account, it's a good idea to consider a positive recommendation from someone you know and whose opinion you trust. If you don't know where to get started, consider examining *Barron's* at your local library for a list of recommended online brokers. The list is updated annually.

The traditional way to buy and sell stocks was to use the telephone to place an order with your broker. Today, it's much more efficient—in terms of saving both time and money—to trade online. If you have the confidence and experience to trade online, I recommend it.

Some readers may feel the need to work with a full service broker, despite the higher costs. There's nothing wrong with doing that, but be certain your individual broker understands options and that you gain something of value in exchange for paying those higher costs. Remember that you can and should negotiate commissions. There's no need to pay their published rates. And once you gain the confidence to handle option transactions alone, it's time to move on to that deep discounter and cut your expenses.

You may be surprised to discover that your broker is one of those behind-the-times people who fails to understand that options are tools to help you reduce risk. If your broker is not enthusiastic about options trading, then I strongly suggest that you find another broker. The sad truth is that too many brokers never learned to use options and thus cannot help clients adopt profitable strategies. Some brokers may have had a few clients who traded options, and if those clients, left to their own devices, lost money with options, the broker could easily reach the conclusion that trading options, and not the broker's own inability to help clients, was to blame. Such brokers develop and maintain a negative image of options and tend to steer their clients away from using them. I suggest you devour the material in this book and draw your own conclusions. Your broker may have your best interests at heart, but unless he or she understands options, you should seriously consider using a different broker.

Several brokerage firms are option specialists. Each has something useful to offer. Learn the advantages of using a few of them by asking your friends who trade options, and choose a broker who provides something of value to you. Some have extremely low commissions, which is great if you are knowledgeable and unlikely to require excellent customer service. Others offer an extremely user-friendly trading platform, making it easy to enter your option orders. And

---

1. *Brokers don't want their customers to go broke and close the account when owing money to the brokerage house.*

others offer outstanding software that allows you to analyze complex positions. That's appealing to many, but if you have no intention of owning complex positions, then the software may be overkill. Ask if your prospective broker provides all the information you need at tax time—in a format that simplifies the process of filing your tax returns. Don't overlook the timesaving importance of tax information if you are an active trader (hundreds or thousands of trades per year). The point is: there are many excellent brokers available and you should be able to find one who allows you to trade comfortably and who fills your needs at a reasonable cost.

When your broker accepts your order and sends it to an exchange where it can be executed, the broker is obligated to attempt to fill your order at the best available price. To that end, the broker routes (sends) your sell order to the exchange displaying the highest bid price, or sends your buy order to the exchange with the lowest asking price. Some brokers allow you to send your order to the specific options exchange of your choice, but if your broker offers "smart routing" you needn't be concerned about where the order is sent.

Sadly, some brokers insist on sending orders to one specific options exchange, resulting in problems for their customers. If your broker insists on sending your order to one specific exchange, it's not unusual for that order to go unfilled, despite the fact that the identical option is available on another exchange at the price you are willing to trade.[2] If your broker insists on this, please open an account elsewhere. Before you open your account, ask the broker if they send each order to the exchange displaying the best price, or only to their preferred exchange.

The option markets

For readers who are not already familiar with the language of investing, some of the important terminology is listed below.

Bid. The current highest published[3] price anyone is willing to pay for each specific option. Bid prices for options change frequently, depending on the price of the underlying asset, as well as other market factors.

Ask. Also referred to as the "offer price." The current lowest published price anyone is willing to sell each specific option. As with bid prices, the ask price changes often.

Bid-ask spread. The difference between the bid price and the ask price. Narrow, or tight bid-ask spreads are beneficial to you, the individual investor.

NBBO. Acronym for National Best Bid or Offer. Highest bid and lowest offer on any exchange. Your broker is supposed to guarantee that you never receive a fill at a price that is worse than the NBBO.

Fill. Notification that your order has been executed. Sometimes you may receive a partial fill if you buy or sell some, but not all, of the options represented by your order.

Market maker. A professional trader who makes a firm bid and offer at all times and who stands by (either in person in the trading pits on the floor of the exchange, or via computer) to purchase any option you want to sell or sell any option you want to buy. When you enter an order, it's not necessary

---

2. *If you don't believe this is possible, consider this: Broker A sends a buy order to one exchange, refusing to send it to another. Broker B sends a sell order to a different exchange, also refusing to send the order elsewhere. Despite the fact that one customer is willing to buy at the same price that another is willing to sell, it's possible that one of those orders will not be filled. It's highly unlikely that both orders go unfilled because someone will want to either buy or sell that option at the locked price.*
3. *Often market makers don't display their best bids. Thus, you may sometimes sell your option at a price higher than (or buy your option at a price lower than) the best published bid (or offer).*

to trade with a market maker, nor is it necessary to pay the asking price (nor sell at the bid price). Many times, by matching your order with that of another individual (or professional) trader, your order can be filled—and the market maker does not participate in the trade.

Market order. An order to be filled as quickly as possible at the best possible price at the time the order reaches the trading floor. Not too many years ago, the time required to fill a market order was much greater than it is today. Today, the order is electronically transmitted to the pit and you usually receive a fill within a second or two. When trading options, it's often a bad idea to enter a market order because it's an invitation to receive a fill at a very poor price. It's worth the effort to try to get a better price, rather than just paying the market price. Unless there is some special reason why you simply must buy or sell this second, no matter what the price, it's preferable to enter a limit order. And if unfilled, you can quickly change that order in an attempt to get filled.

Limit order. An order that can only be filled at a specific price (or better). Thus, when using a limit order to buy, the limit price is the maximum that the customer is willing to pay. When using a limit order to sell, the limit price is the minimum the customer is willing to accept. Whereas a market order is always filled, that's not true for a limit order. If, for example, you want to sell an option, but are not willing to accept less than $1.20 per contract, then you enter a limit order to sell at $1.20. Such an order always implies "or better." That means your broker attempts to get a higher price when possible, but accepts $1.20 as the minimum. If no one is willing to pay that price, then the order remains in the trading pit where anyone may buy it at a later time (unless you cancel the order). Part of the time, but not always,

limit orders are filled, even if not immediately. Similarly, when you want to buy an option, but are unwilling to pay the asking price, enter a limit order in an attempt to buy at a lower price.

Spread (or combination) order. Spread orders are discussed in Part III. A spread is an order that consists of more than one different option—one of which is bought, and the other is sold. When entering a spread order, please remember to use a limit order.

Order entry

When you enter an order, many brokers require that you provide specific information. I don't understand why that requirement exists because brokers' computers can quickly and accurately determine this information. Nevertheless, here is the terminology as it is used today.

When you buy an option, there are two possibilities:

- **Buy to open.** You open a new position (you don't own any of these specific options) or add to a current position.
- **Buy to close.** Purchase an option you sold previously. You close (eliminate) or reduce a current position.

When you sell an option, there are two possibilities:

- **Sell to open.** Establish a new position or add to an existing position. You are short this option.
- **Sell to close.** Eliminate or reduce an existing position. You previously bought this option.

Trading options is neither complex nor difficult. But it's important for you, the investor, to understand what you are trying to accomplish. That's why the individual strategies are described in great detail.

1. When you enter a market order to buy a put option, you may expect to receive a fill at the bid price.

○ **TRUE** ○ **FALSE**

2. Trading options online is usually less expensive than trading options via the telephone.

○ **TRUE** ○ **FALSE**

3. Why is it best not to use market orders when trading options?

4. Which publication provides good information about online brokers with an annual rating?

5. You enter a limit order to buy three XYX Feb 80 calls at $3 each. Your broker gives you a fill, telling you that you paid $3.20 for each option. Is that OK?

6. You decide to buy five HIJK Mar 45 calls. The NBBO is $2.10 to $2.25. Your broker enters your order and immediately reports that you bought five calls at $2.30 on the American Stock Exchange (AMEX). Are you pleased with your fill?

7. You own three JKLM Nov 25 puts. You decide to sell them. How is your order designated?
A. Buy to open
B. Buy to close
C. Sell to open
D. Sell to close

8. It's to your advantage when your broker sends all of its option orders to a single exchange.

○ **TRUE** ○ **FALSE**

Chapter 5

The Options Clearing Corporation

In 1973 the Chicago Board Options Exchange (CBOE) became the first exchange to list options for trading. At the same time, the Options Clearing Corporation (OCC) came into being. The existence of a clearing firm is necessary because it's responsible for the matching of all buy and sell orders that occur in the marketplace.

Clearing provides smoother and more efficient markets, because each party in a transaction makes transfers directly to the clearing corporation, rather than to the other individual with whom the trade occurs. Thus, the OCC acts as an intermediary and assumes the role of both buyer and seller in order to reconcile orders between transacting parties. An option buyer never has to be concerned whether the option seller has the financial wherewithal to meet the obligations imposed by the contract. And that's important. Imagine what would happen if you owned a call option and were required to find and notify the seller before you were allowed to exercise an option. And if that other party refused to sell you stock at the strike price (assuming you exercised a call option), what would you do? Sue? That takes time and money. Fortunately the OCC makes sure that's never a problem. The OCC assumes responsibility and guarantees that all obligations are met.

The OCC began as a clearinghouse for listed equity options and has grown into a global entity that clears a multitude of sophisticated products. Today, the OCC is the world's largest equity derivatives clearing organization and operates under the jurisdiction of both the Securities and Exchange Commission (SEC) and the Commodities Futures Trading Commission (CFTC). It clears transactions for options on common stocks, stock indexes, ETFs, foreign currencies, interest rate composites, single-stock futures, futures and options on futures.

Exercise and assignment

As an investor who buys or sells options, you never have to be concerned with the workings of the OCC. But, for those who are interested in details, the OCC plays a vital role when someone exercises a put or a call. The first step taken by the OCC is to verify that the person who exercises an option actually owns the option and has the right to exercise it. Mistakes occur and someone could easily make an error and attempt to exercise (for example) XYX Nov 80 calls when the investor owns the Nov 70 calls instead.

Once it's verified that the customer has the right to exercise one or more of these options, the OCC randomly chooses the account of one customer who has a short position in that specific option. That customer is assigned an exercise notice and must honor the terms of the contract. The process is a bit more detailed than this simple explanation,

but if you are assigned such a notice, it's a done deal and there is nothing you can do about it.

Being assigned an exercise notice is something that many new option traders fear. But, there is no reason for that. One of the most popular option strategies (covered call writing) involves selling call options. If a person who adopts this strategy is assigned an exercise notice, this is a good result. It affords the investor the maximum profit available. You can't do better than that, and being assigned an exercise notice should be a rewarding experience, not something to dread. That does not mean it's always good to receive an assignment notice. It's not. As we discuss each strategy, if appropriate, we'll discuss whether being assigned an exercise notice is something that should be a concern.

{ NOTE: The assignment process occurs overnight, when the markets are closed. Thus, if you have a short position in a specific option, but buy back those options in a closing transaction, the result is that you have no remaining position at the end of the trading day. Under such circumstances, you cannot be assigned an exercise notice. Similarly, once you have received that assignment notice, you cannot purchase that option the next day in an attempt to cancel the assignment. It's too late for that.

Modernization of the options industry

Some standards have been in place since options first began trading on an exchange. The industry has grown enormously and some changes are necessary.

Symbology

The method used to assign a symbol to each option series has been in place since options first began trading on an exchange in April 1973. Today, many organizations that support trading in listed options are restricted in their ability to identify and process exchange-listed option contracts and thus, that symbology is about to get an overhaul. There are several good reasons behind the changes, which are supposed to be in effect by July 31, 2009. One driving force behind the change has been the introduction of options that expire on a weekly, rather than a monthly basis. There are also options that expire at the end of the calendar quarter.[1] Thus, during September, an index might list options (not all are trading simultaneously) that expire after the first week, the second week, the third week, the fourth week, occasionally the fifth week, and month end. A different symbol is required to describe each.

The four pieces of information currently used to describe an option (Chapter 2) will be changed.

EXAMPLE

Consider a Microsoft call option that expires on Feb 19, 2009 with a strike price of 47 ½.
- *The current symbol is: MSFT Feb 47½ call*
- *The new symbology requires:*
  MSFT090219C00047500

The new symbology includes:
- *The stock symbol (one to four letters). "MSFT" in the example above.*

- *The expiration year (two digits). "09" represents the year 2009.*
- *The month (two digits). "02" represents February.*
- *The day (two digits). "19" represents the day of the month.*
- *Option type; i.e., call or put. "C"*
- *Strike price (five digits). "00047" represents the integer portion of the stock price.*
- *Strike decimal (three digits). "500" represents the decimal portion of the strike price.*

The new symbology looks complicated but it will make things easier for the industry.

Stock splits and adjustments

How options are affected by stock splits and adjustments was discussed in Chapter 2. Changes were made in two stages. The first stage was implemented in September 2007, and the second stage will be implemented when the new option symbology takes effect. The discussion is Chapter 2 is current as of 2008, but note that additional (minor) changes become effective in July 2009.

---

1. *To date, only a few of the most popular indexes have quarterly options.*

Chapter 6

What Is an Option Worth?

The purchase and sale of options takes place in an open marketplace, and in many respects the process is identical with the trading of individual stocks. Most people understand, in general terms, how the price of a stock is determined. In theory, a person could learn everything there is to know about an individual stock. Taking that information into account, people who want to buy the shares gather in the trading pit[1] on the floor of the stock exchange and announce[2] a price they are willing to pay for those shares. Those who want to sell announce a price at which they are willing to offer shares for sale. The auction market continues until buyers and sellers agree on a price and a transaction takes place. This is a continuous process and the price at which shares change hands is constantly moving higher and lower. The

---

1. *These days, many "gather" via computers and trades are executed electronically.*
2. *It's the broker who represents buyers and sellers who enters the pit where the stock is traded to announce bids and offers.*

price at which trades occur is simply an agreement between buyers and sellers that the current price is acceptable for both, based on the available information. At any given time, price is primarily based on supply and demand. An increasing number of buyers tends to push prices higher, and a preponderance of sellers tends to push prices lower.

To a point, options also trade that way. But option trading involves much more. Options are derivative products and their value is derived from the value of the underlying stock, index or ETF. As the price of the stock (let's assume we are referring to stocks, but the discussion applies equally well to different underlying assets) changes, so does the price of its options. Supply and demand play a role in the market price of an option, but in the options world, prices are driven by much more than the stock price, and option traders must consider more variables than stock traders. Thus, it's important to understand how an option is valued and which factors drive the price higher or lower.

Theoretical value of an option

The value of an option can be calculated using a complex mathematical formula. The 1973 pioneering work of Fischer Black and Myron Scholes produced a formula that can be used to determine the fair market value of a European-style call option when the underlying stock does not pay any dividends (European options can only be exercised on expiration day).[3] Robert Merton extended the idea by allowing for dividends. The 1997 Nobel Prize in Economics was awarded to Scholes and Merton (sadly, Black died in 1995) for this work.

The Black-Scholes model has been modified many times over the years, but the basic equation

is still used to determine the fair market value of an option. Most readers will choose to determine the fair value of an option without bothering to understand the mathematics behind the equation. Fortunately, there's no need to solve the Black-Scholes equation every time you calculate the fair value of an option. Special calculators are readily available online[4] that do the math for you. (Some brokers also provide an online calculator for customers). The good news is that these calculators work for both American- and European-style options. All you have to do is plug in the known variables, such as stock price, strike price, option type, interest rates and dividend. You must also estimate a value for volatility, which is described in more detail in the next chapter.

If the value of an option can be calculated, it's important to know which specific factors affect that value and must be considered. They are:

- Stock price
- Strike price
- Time remaining before option expires
- Option type (put or call)
- Interest rates
- Dividend
- Volatility

Stock price. Because the value of an option is derived directly from the value of the underlying stock, it's easy to understand why the stock price is important in the valuation of an option. A call option gives its owner the right to buy stock at a specified price. Isn't it reasonable for investors to be willing to pay a higher price for call options when the stock price moves higher? Intuitively, doesn't it seem reasonable that investors who are considering buying a call option with a strike

---

3. All options previously discussed in this book can be exercised any time after they are purchased. Those are American-style options. The difference between American- and European-style options is covered in Part III.
4. There is no point in listing multiple web sites, because the Internet constantly changes. Use a search engine to find an online option calculator. There is also a good one at www.cboe.com/LearnCenter/optioncalculator.aspx.

price of $40 per share should be willing to pay more for the option when the stock is $39 than when it is $35? After all, when the stock is $39, it only has to increase in value by $1 per share before the option goes in-the-money and starts to accumulate intrinsic value. When the stock is $35, it must increase in value by a larger amount before the option goes in-the-money. It's much more likely that a stock trading at $39 will move above $40 than a stock trading at $35. Thus, when the stock is trading at the higher price, the option is worth more. The trend continues—the higher the stock price, the more each call option is worth. We'll discuss the direct relationship between an option's price and the stock price when we discuss "the Greeks" in Part III. But for now, the important point is to understand that calls increase in value as the stock rises.

A put option gives its owner the right to sell stock at a specified price. Thus, the lower the stock price, the more a put is worth. If you are considering buying a put option that gives you the right to sell 100 shares of XYZ at $40 per share, you should be willing to pay more for the put option when the stock is $42 than when it is $46. If the stock is trading at $42 per share, it's much more likely to drop below the strike price than when the stock is trading at a higher price. Thus, the put option is worth less when the stock price is higher and more when it is lower.

Strike price. When you want to buy stock, your goal is to buy it as cheaply as possible. The lower the strike price, the less you must pay if you exercise an option.[5] Thus, the lower the strike price, the more a call is worth. This should be easy to understand. The right to exercise an option with a strike price of $20 allows you to pay $2,000 for 100 shares of stock. Surely that option is more valuable than a call with a strike price of $25

(which allows you to pay $2,500 for that same 100 shares of stock). This is something clearly visible in any table of option data. Unless the calls are so far out-of-the-money that they are essentially worthless, as the strike price of the call decreases, the market price (premium) of the call increases. Calls with the lowest strike price are always priced higher than the rest of the calls.

Similarly, the higher the strike price of a put option, the more it is worth. When you own a put option, you want to sell stock at the highest possible price. Because puts give you the right to sell stock at the strike price, the higher the strike, the more the put is worth.

When deciding which strike price to buy or sell (this topic is covered in great detail as we study each individual strategy), the inexperienced speculator who loves to buy options prefers to pay a small amount of money when buying options, and tends to purchase out-of-the-money calls and puts. By doing so, the speculator hopes to reap a huge bonanza—as if the option were a mini-lottery ticket. Unfortunately, that inexperienced investor usually makes two serious mistakes: buying options with little chance of becoming profitable and paying far too much for those options. This important point is discussed further in the next chapter.

Time. Options are a wasting asset and lose value as time passes. The loss of value is not linear.[6] Instead, time decay accelerates as expiration day approaches.

When you own an option, you make money if the stock undergoes a favorable change in price, but only if the change occurs quickly enough to offset the effects of time. The longer the lifetime of an option, the more opportunity there is for that favorable price change to occur. Thus, the more time remaining, the more an option is worth.

The astute reader might ask: If more time increases the chances of the stock moving in the

---

5. *Remember, you can sell any options you own and it's not necessary to exercise.*
6. *The value of an option does not decrease by the same amount every day.*

right direction, doesn't it also increase the chances the stock will move in the wrong direction? Yes, it does. Another reasonable question is: If the stock has an increased chance to move in the wrong direction, why doesn't more time make the option worth less? To understand why the opportunity of a favorable move is far more significant in determining the price of an option than the possibility of an unfavorable move, one must examine the reasons that investors purchase options.

The main reason investors buy options is to gain leverage. That means controlling 100 shares of stock for a relatively small amount of money with the hope of turning that small investment into a much larger pile of money. If the stock moves against you, it's not good, and the value of the option decreases. Consider this: If an option is worth $200 and the stock makes a winning move, the option might be worth $600. If the stock moves in the wrong direction, the option price might drop to $100. If the stock moves far enough in the wrong direction, the option can become worthless, but it can never be worth less than zero. But, if the stock moves in the right direction, the potential gain is huge.[7] With leverage, there is much more to gain than there is to lose. And it's the possibility of that substantial gain that attracts buyers. Thus, the potential profit drives the option's price, not the potential loss. And more time provides a greater opportunity for a favorable price change.

Option type. Calls are expected to increase in value as the price of the underlying increases, and puts are expected to increase in value as the price of the underlying decreases. At least that's what's supposed to happen. In the real world, part of the time the other factors listed here can overwhelm the effects of a change in the stock price and can lead to results that leave the options novice bewildered. See the discussion on volatility in the next chapter for more on this topic.

Interest rates. One of the reasons investors buy call options is that it requires less cash than buying shares of stock. The cash saved by buying calls can be invested to earn interest. The higher the interest rate, the more an investor is willing to pay for the call option. Interest rates play a minor role in determining the theoretical value (also called fair value) of an option—and that's especially true for options with short lifetimes (and those are the options that most readers will be trading). One point to remember is that if you trade LEAPS[8] options, interest rates are more important.

Higher interest rates decrease the value of put options.

Dividends. When a stock pays a dividend, its price drops by the amount of the dividend and the stock trades "ex-dividend," which means without the dividend. The larger the dividend, the lower the stock price. Thus, calls are worth less (than if the stock did not pay a dividend) and puts are worth more when a stock pays a substantial dividend. Those dividends are priced into the options. Thus, if a stock closes for the day at $30.50 and opens the next morning at $30.10 after paying a 40-cent dividend, the options are priced as if the stock is trading at the same price it was yesterday, except for the one day's time decay. In other words, the options "knew" the stock was going to open 40 cents lower, and as far as the options are concerned, the stock price is unchanged.

---

7. *In theory, there is no limit to how much a call can be worth because the stock price can continue to rise. A put cannot be worth more than the strike price because the price of the stock cannot go below zero.*
8. *LEAPS are long-term options that are described in more detail in Chapter 2. More time in the life of an option translates into a more significant effect of a change in interest rates.*

Volatility. This is truly a situation in which the best, or most important, is saved for last. Volatility is a major factor in determining the price of options in the marketplace, and the discussion is so vital to your understanding of how options trade in the real world that the entire next chapter is devoted to the topic of volatility and its importance in the options universe.

Of the seven items listed above that play a role in determining the theoretical value of an option, six are known and only one (volatility) is unknown and must be estimated. Volatility, as defined in the options world, is an estimate of how volatile the stock is going to be in the future— specifically, between the current time and expiration day. Because the future is unknowable, volatility can only be estimated. When different traders use different volatility estimates, they arrive at very different estimates for the value of an option. That's why some people become anxious option buyers when they believe the premium is low. At the same time, others are eager sellers because they believe the premium is too high. That difference of opinion is one of the factors that keeps the options markets interesting.

You calculated the theoretical value of an option. Now what?

Let me stress that it's not necessary to use a "calculator." Most individual investors who dabble in options don't bother. But, knowing the approximate fair value of an option can give you an edge. It helps you decide whether it's reasonable to open an option position that you are considering or if it's prudent to allow the opportunity to slip away. Any time you can get an edge, it's to your benefit.

If you are a serious student and want to learn as much as possible about options and how to use them profitably, then learning to estimate the fair value for an option is worth your time.

Once you have chosen an estimated volatility for the underlying stock, you can use a calculator to

determine the fair value of an option. You simply plug in the numbers and read the results.

It's important to understand that the option value you read on your calculator is not going to be identical to the value calculated by others. In fact, it may be very different. Thus the question: how much confidence should you place in your value? Answer: as much confidence as you have in your volatility estimate. That means part of the time you cannot be very confident. And this is especially true for those of you who have little experience trading options. That brings up this obvious question: If you cannot be certain how accurate the calculated value is, why spend time learning how to estimate an option's value?

Most of the time trading in options is a straightforward, orderly process. There are buyers and sellers of calls and puts, and option prices change only when the underlying stock changes price. But sometimes distortions occur. If there are a large number of option buyers, prices rise. And that holds true for both puts and calls. Why may there suddenly be an influx of orders to buy options? Because option owners can earn big profits when the stock undergoes a significant price change. When such change has a good chance of occurring—for example, when the company announces its quarterly earnings report, or perhaps when the FDA announces the success or failure of a company's new drug, or perhaps because there are rumors of a possible takeover of the company—that's when people flock to buy options. And because that happens, prices rise. The reason this is important to you is that you must decide if the prices are too high (if you are considering buying options), or if the prices are high enough for you to take advantage of those prices by selling options.

By doing the math and using the calculator, you can determine whether options are reasonably priced at the time you want to make a trade. The calculated result is not the final word.

You can use your judgment in each situation. In other words, if you like the trade and the option price is reasonable, go for it. If the trade is borderline, i.e., it barely meets your minimum criteria, then it may be best to avoid making the trade unless you are trading the option at a price that is better than its fair value.[9]

BOTTOM LINE: If you consistently pay more than options are worth when you buy them, or if you consistently sell options for less than they are worth, then your overall performance is going to be hindered. Having a theoretical edge increases the probability of having a winning trade. On the other hand, if you tend to sell options when they are trading at prices higher than their reasonable fair value, or if you make a habit of buying options only when they are trading at less than their reasonable fair value, the probability of earning good profits over the long term is enhanced. You can get by without doing the calculations, but, as previously mentioned, it can give you an edge.

---

9. *Higher if you are a seller and lower if you are a buyer.*

1. Are the following true or false? When calculating the fair value (theoretical value) of an option:

A. The Black-Scholes (or a modification) model is used.

○ **TRUE**   ○ **FALSE**

B. Interest rates are a very important factor.

○ **TRUE**   ○ **FALSE**

C. Most of the inputs are unknown and must be estimated.

○ **TRUE**   ○ **FALSE**

2. How does an increase in the stock price affect the value of a call option? A put option?

3. Do you agree? When buying or selling options, it's not necessary to pay attention to the theoretical value of the option because the current market always represents a fair price.

4. A company unexpectedly announces a dividend increase from $0.25 to $0.50. Assuming the price of the stock is unchanged, who gains from that announcement—the put owner or the call owner?

5. All option traders must calculate the fair value of an option to make money.

○ **TRUE**   ○ **FALSE**

6. The theoretical value of an option can be accurately calculated. Thus, all traders agree on the fair value of an option.

○ **TRUE**   ○ **FALSE**

Chapter 7

Volatility

Volatility is the property of a stock that describes its tendency to undergo price changes. More volatile stocks undergo larger and more frequent price changes. Volatility, as it is used in the options universe, is a measure of the *absolute* volatility of each individual stock and is unrelated to the volatility of other stocks, or groups of stocks.

However, outside the options world, volatility is described by the term beta. Beta provides a very different measurement of volatility, and you should know its definition, because it's a term that is often misused by investors. Beta is a measure of the *relative* volatility of a specific stock, when compared with the volatility of a large group of stocks (often the Standard & Poor's 500 Index).[1] A beta of 1.0 means the stock has the same volatility as the index. Stocks with beta values of less than 1.0 are less volatile than the index, while stocks with beta values greater than 1.0 are more volatile.

---

1. *This index is frequently considered to be representative of the stock market as a whole.*

Beta is of interest because it provides investors with an estimate of how much price movement to expect from an individual stock when the S&P 500 Index moves up or down.

Let's use an example from the perspective of an option buyer to illustrate why option volatility is very different from beta.

EXAMPLE

You like the short-term prospects of Tool Works, Inc. (TOOL). The stock is currently trading at $33 per share and you want to buy the Oct 35 call, which expires in six weeks. The current bid for the TOOL Oct 35 call is $0.70 and the current offer is $0.90. Question: Is $90 per contract a reasonable price to pay for TOOL Oct 35 calls?

The correct answer to this question is: "I don't know. I need more information."

If you examined the day-to-day price changes for TOOL over the past three years and noticed that the average daily price change was 3 cents and that the largest such change was 12 cents, would you be interested in paying $0.90 for the option?[2] With the stock trading at $33, it requires an increase of $2 per share for the option to go into-the-money. That's a huge move for a stock that moves, on average, only 3 cents per day. If you like this stock and want to own it, it's much better to simply buy some shares, rather than to take the huge gamble on the Oct 35 call. It's extremely unlikely you can make any money when buying this call. (In fact, the price is so high that selling the call and collecting $70 per contract may appeal to you. Chapters 10 through 12 detail the strategy of buying stock and selling calls.)

It should grab your attention if, when examining TOOL's price history, you discovered that the average daily price change is 25 cents and that TOOL moved more than $2 in a single day 15 times over the past three years. If the stock is that volatile, then there is a reasonable chance the stock could trade a few dollars higher (or lower) sometime during the next six weeks. In fact, there's a reasonable chance that TOOL could jump $2 in only a few days. Under those conditions, paying $90 per contract seems reasonable.

When venturing into the world of stock options, the only volatility measurement that matters is that of the individual stock as a stand-alone item. Its comparison with other stocks or indexes is unimportant, and thus, beta is not relevant. It doesn't matter if the stock is more volatile (or less volatile) than the average stock because you are buying an option based on the likelihood of this specific stock undergoing a sufficiently large price change during the option's lifetime. You are not concerned with the entire market moving higher or lower. When you buy or sell options, the important consideration is how much and how quickly the price of your individual stock (or other underlying asset) changes—and that's not what beta measures.

Calculating the volatility of an individual stock

When taking a measurement several times, the nearer each measurement is to the average, the more confidence you have in the average. A standard deviation is a measure of how much variation there is in a group of measurements. In other words, when the standard deviation is small, the confidence level is high that the average measurement is very near the actual measurement. If the measurements vary widely, then your confidence in the average is reduced. By definition, 68 percent of all measurements

---

2. Ninety dollars per contract is the same as paying $0.90 to buy the option because there are 100 shares per contract and that quote of $0.90 is the per-share price, not the per-contract price.

fall within one standard deviation of the average measurement and 95 percent of all measurements fall within two standard deviations of the average.

The standard deviation is the most commonly used measure of how much the values in a set of numbers vary. If the data points (in our example, that's the stock's daily closing price) are near each other, then the standard deviation is small. If many data points are distant from each other, then the standard deviation is higher. When it comes to stock prices, we are not interested in the accuracy of each data point. Because each piece of data is the closing price for the stock, it's a known quantity, and thus is accurate. But, we can use the standard deviation to show us just how volatile the stock is. When the standard deviation is small (for example, when the average daily price change for TOOL is 3 cents per day in the example above), then the volatility is low. When the standard deviation is large (TOOL moves an average of 25 cents per day, in the example above), then the stock is more volatile.

When a stock is described as having a volatility of 30, 68 percent of the time, the price of the stock is within 30 percent (one standard deviation) of its starting price one year later. It also means that 95 percent of the time, the stock moves less than 60 percent (two standard deviations) in one year. Looking at it from the opposite point of view, 5 percent of the time, or one of every 20 years, on average, a stock whose volatility is 30 can be expected to move more than two standard deviations, or 60 percent.

Volatility types

There is more than one way to talk about volatility. Historical volatility is calculated by measuring the actual price movements made by the stock in the past. When buying or selling options, you want to know the volatility the stock is going to have from the time the option is purchased (or sold) until the expiration of the option. That volatility can never be known because the time frame is the future. Thus, a volatility estimate must be used. Although it's never going to be a perfect estimate, the past volatility of a stock usually provides the best guess as to its future volatility.

However, the volatility estimate used to calculate the fair value of an option is based upon more than the historical volatility of the underlying stock. It must also consider events that occur during the lifetime of the option— events that may have a significant impact on the stock price. An example of such an event is the company's quarterly earnings announcement. General market news can also move markets. For example, when the U.S. Federal Reserve unexpectedly announces a change in interest rates, the stock market often reacts by undergoing a significant move in one direction or the other. When markets are calm, volatility estimates are reduced. When markets are very volatile, all volatility estimates are raised.[3]

The term used to describe the estimated future volatility is forecast volatility. Sometimes it is simply referred to as estimated volatility.

When we look at option prices, we use a different term, implied volatility (IV). Unlike the other types of volatility, this one is a property of the option (rather than of the stock). Implied volatility is the real-world estimate of the future volatility of the stock. In other words, when the implied volatility is used in the option pricing model, the calculator generates a theoretical option price that equals the actual price in the marketplace.

Volatility is important to option traders because it's a vital factor in determining the price of options

---

3. That makes sense. After all, if the markets have been moving higher or lower by more than 1 percent every day for the past week, investors are willing to pay more for options—hoping market volatility continues. Conversely, option sellers demand a higher premium to compensate for increased risk.

in the marketplace. Option buyers make money when stocks undergo significant price changes (if the change is in the correct direction). Because volatile stocks are much more likely to undergo large price changes, option buyers pay a much higher premium for options of volatile stocks. As a result, the options of similarly priced stocks often have vastly different option prices.

The importance of implied volatility (IV)

To give you a much better picture of how important the volatility component of the Black-Scholes model plays in determining both the theoretical price of an option and its price in the real world, consider a call option with a lifetime of six months. The stock price is 40, the strike price is 40 and the interest rate is 5 percent:

- When the implied volatility is 20, the fair value of the option is $2.72.[4]
- When the implied volatility is 30, the fair value of the option is $3.81.
- When the implied volatility is 50, the fair value of the option is $5.98.
- When the implied volatility is 90, the fair value of the option is $10.24.

Note how much these option prices differ. It's obvious that the options of volatile stocks command much higher premiums than the options of less-volatile stocks. But, there is another important (and practical) lesson to be gathered from this information. When a company is about to announce its earning results for the current quarter, and especially when there is much speculation about those results in advance of the news release, it's natural for speculators to buy puts and calls on that company. After all, if the company announces unexpected results—reasonable when there has been uncertainty about how the company's business is doing—then there is a strong possibility that the stock will gap[5] much higher or lower. Because option rookies don't understand the fine points of buying options, those novices anticipate making a large profit if the stock undergoes a significant price change. These speculators are often disappointed by the results. Let's consider why that happens—so that it never happens to you.

Most speculators prefer to buy out-of-the-money (OTM) options because those options cost less per contract than at the money (or in-the-money) options.[6] The lower price allows buyers to use their investment dollars to purchase more options and gives them the opportunity to make a killing. They fail to recognize that many other investors have the same idea and buy those options before news is released. Because there's increased demand for those options, the market makers (or other investors) who sell those options raise prices. There are two reasons for that:

- By raising prices, there is the hope that more sellers are attracted to the marketplace, allowing market makers or option specialists to repeatedly earn small profits. If specialists can buy at the bid price and sell at the ask price, they not only make money, but they don't accumulate positions that must be hedged.[7] The more often they can buy and sell, the easier it is to avoid taking on risk.

---

4. *If 20 is the estimated volatility, then the Black Scholes model tells us that $2.72 is the option's theoretical value.*
5. *Trade at a price very different from the previous price.*
6. *If you don't remember why OTM options cost less, refer back to Chapter 6 and the discussion about how the strike price affects the value of an option.*
7. *Hedging is the process by which risk is reduced. Professional option traders, including the market makers and specialists, do not simply take the other side of trades with individual investors and hope for the best. They buy and sell other options as well as the underlying stock with the intent of owning positions with as little risk as possible.*

This buying and selling for small profits is referred to as "scalping."

- When there are only buyers and no sellers, and the market makers continue to sell options without the opportunity to buy options to offset risk (hedge),[8] they rightfully demand higher and higher prices for the options.

It's important to understand this scenario because when speculators buy options, they seldom pay attention to price. Many incorrectly assume that if an option is actively trading that the current price is reasonable. Because they have no idea how options are priced, they enter the market (via orders with their brokers) and pay whatever price is asked of them. Please don't allow that to happen to you. If you decide to gamble and pay a very high price (i.e., buy options with a very high implied volatility) for an option, you must be aware that your chances of earning a profit are *significantly* reduced. The problem with most under-educated option buyers is that they have no clue that the odds of success are stacked against them.

Thus, there's no reason for market makers to sell the same options at the same price when there are many buyers and few sellers. Some believe there's a conspiracy and that market makers are cheating them because prices keep rising. But that's an unfair conclusion. When a professional trader makes a two-sided market (bid and offer) he or she never knows whether the next order, or batch of orders, arriving electronically is from buyers or sellers.

No one in the investment world continues to sell a product that is in great demand at the same price. After all, they are not Wal-Mart. In the investment arena, an increase in demand results in higher prices. No one complains when

a constant demand for shares drives the price of a stock higher, but many feel that options should be treated differently. Remember, one reason for ever-increasing prices is an attempt to attract investors to sell options to the horde of buyers.

When the stock price remains essentially the same and option prices are rising, that means implied volatility of the options is increasing. The bottom line is that these option-buying speculators are often unaware of the implied volatility of the options they buy, and that leads to many unhappy speculators. In the discussion above we noted how the price of a six-month option with a 40 strike price varies considerably as the volatility of the underlying stock increases. That is not only a theoretical discussion. In the real world, if the implied volatility goes from 20 to 30, the option price increases as indicated above (from $2.72 to $3.81). Let's take a look at another example to see why this is true.

EXAMPLE

Assume WOW is announcing earnings after the market closes for trading today. Because it's the last time to buy WOW options before news is announced, there's a great deal of interest in the options. In this scenario, it's common for the options to trade with a pumped IV, as buyers, who hope to be rewarded if WOW makes a big move tomorrow, bid up[9] the prices of both calls and puts. This stock is appropriately named because it has occasionally produced significant earnings surprises over the past several years, and that adds to the desirability of owning options.

WOW usually trades with an implied volatility of 40. The Nov options expire in 21 days and WOW is trading at $50 per share. Let's look at the Nov OTM options because these are most attractive to

---

8. *Modern market makers avoid risk as much as possible, but it's not always possible to hedge all risk.*
9. *If they cannot buy options with their current bids, they keep raising those bids.*

Table 7.1: WOW options prices before and after news

STOCK	DATE	STRIKE	IV	TV
50	Oct 28	55	40	$0.45
		55	50	$0.79
		55	60	$1.19
		55	70	$1.63
		60	40	$0.06
		60	50	$0.19
		60	60	$0.41
		60	70	$0.65
54	Oct 29	55	40	$1.65
			35	$1.40
		60	40	$0.36
			35	$0.24

WOW IV gets crushed after news is released.

IV = Implied Volatility   TV = Option theoretical value
Oct. 28 is 21 days prior to the November expiration

speculators. The data are presented in Table 7.1.

Late in the afternoon, Player A decides to buy some WOW Nov 55 calls. There has been a lot of interest in these options and the IV is quite high (70). Our player pays $1.65[10] for some calls.

Player B is a bit more experienced and knows that many players tend to buy options near the close of business and that buying pressure increases option prices. Of course, when buying early in the day, there's always risk that the stock trades lower

(decreasing the value of calls). But Player B, being bullish, is willing to take that chance and buys Nov 55 calls when the IV is "only" 60. Thus, B's purchase price is $1.20.

The market closes for the day and our players receive some good news. WOW announces better-than-expected earnings and opens 8 percent higher the next morning, trading at 54. Our players are happy, expecting a nice payoff for that four-point jump in the stock price. But something strange happens (from the point of view of our players). There are few option buyers. Everyone who wanted to own these options bought them yesterday, and those people are now sellers, hoping to lock in their overnight profits.

Here's what happens as the markets open for trading: News has been released and no further news announcements are anticipated prior to expiration. Thus, market makers drop the volatility estimate for the underlying stock.[11] In addition, there is a preponderance of sell orders. As a result, the computers that calculate the bid and ask prices for the options[12] produce prices that are substantially lower than yesterday's. As seen in Table 7.1, a fair price for the Nov 55 call is $1.65 when IV is 40. That means Player A is lucky to break even and Player B, who was smart enough to shop early, has a small profit. But it's a small payoff—especially considering the risk (possible loss of all, or almost all[13] of the $120 paid per call).

---

10. Even though options trade in penny increments, let's use round numbers for the trades.
11. As they should with no special news anticipated. IV can readily drop to its normal level.
12. In today's world there are so many different options to price that price changes cannot possibly be done manually. Thus, the market makers establish a set of parameters, including the crucially important volatility, and allow the computer to establish bid and ask prices as the price of the underlying stock changes. The parameters can be changed during the trading day, if conditions so warrant (and yesterday, the volatility estimate was raised repeatedly).
13. If the stock gapped down (instead of up) by 4 points (to 46) the Nov 55 call is worth $0.05 when IV is 40.

As is often the case, Player A may feel cheated and frustrated and refuse to sell the options without making money. After waiting an hour, Player A finds WOW is trading near $54, there are still more sellers than buyers, and unfortunately, the IV has dropped to 35. Just as option prices (and IV) rose when buyers predominated, so prices (and IV) decline when there are too many sellers. With the stock still trading at 54, and with the IV now 35, player A discovers that the options he owns are no longer trading at $1.65. Instead, the price is $1.40. Disgusted, Player A takes the loss, decides that options are a rigged game and never again trades options. That unhappy outcome can be avoided.

Time premium in the price of an option

You now understand that the volatility of a stock plays a vital role in determining option premium (option's price). There are now two additional terms to add to your option vocabulary: intrinsic value and time value.

An option's premium is the sum of two parts:

- Intrinsic value
- Time value

The intrinsic value is the amount by which the option is in-the-money. The remainder of the option's premium is the time value. For example, if IBM is priced at $105 per share, and if the May 100 call is $9.30, then the intrinsic value is $5 ($105 minus $100) and the remaining $4.30 is the time value. Most of that time value is related to the stock's volatility, but a small part is associated with interest rates.[14] As we have seen, the more volatile the stock, the greater the time premium in the option.

Avoiding pain

Some investors always gamble and bet that a specific company is going to announce surprising news—either good or bad. And one way to gamble is to buy calls or puts just before news is released. But, as our example (WOW Nov 55 calls) shows, it's important to pay attention to the price paid for an option. Sometimes the price is so out of line that the prudent investor chooses not to play. Of course, the prudent investor does not adopt this speculative option strategy in the first place.

Take a look at the Nov 60 calls in Table 7.1. The only way to earn a profit from the four-point stock price increase is to buy the options when the IV is near 40—and that's impossible because almost no one sells options at such low prices ($0.05 or $0.10) prior to the release of important news. But there are plenty of speculators who do pay $0.65 with high hopes. Imagine their anguish: paying $0.65 for a call option, seeing their stock gap higher by $4 (that's 8 percent) and discovering that the option's price is cut almost in half ($0.36 theoretical value) only one day later.

Does this mean you should never play? I cannot answer that for you, but I never buy options under these circumstances. If you choose to gamble, please don't chase options that are too far out-of-the-money. Those are the very options that are priced unreasonably. Don't misunderstand—it's possible to have an occasional large payday when buying such options. But the odds of making money over the long term are poor if you use this strategy.

BOTTOM LINE: It's very much against the odds of success to buy options when IV is much higher than its average. You can use a calculator to determine the current IV of the options, and you can use the Internet to find historical volatility levels for each individual stock.[15]

---

14. *Call buyers save cash by buying options instead of stock. Thus, some of the interest they earn on that savings goes into the value of the option.*
15. *One such site that provides free data is: http://www.optionstrategist.com/free/analysis/data/index.html*

General investment reminder

Investors usually ignore volatility when compiling a list of stocks they are considering owning. I suggest that you do take volatility into consideration, especially if you adopt any of the option strategies described here. If you are a conservative investor whose goal is to increase annualized returns, then less volatile stocks are appropriate. If you are an aggressive investor hoping to earn substantial sums, and if you understand there is more risk involved with such investments, then you can consider more volatile stocks. I am not suggesting that you buy volatile stocks. Please continue use the same criteria currently used to develop your list of potential stocks to own. When you have that list, consider those with higher volatility when ready to adopt an option strategy.

Of all the variables that go into calculating the theoretical value of an option, volatility is not only the most important factor, but also the most difficult factor for the investor to determine, because the time frame is the future. Use historical data as a guide when making your estimate for future volatility.

1. A stock has a beta of 1.25. That means its options trade above their fair value.

○ **TRUE** ○ **FALSE**

2. When calculating the historical volatility of a given stock, the stock's daily closing prices are used.

○ **TRUE** ○ **FALSE**

3. Most investors who buy out-of-the-money options just prior to a news announcement pay a reasonable price for those options.

○ **TRUE** ○ **FALSE**

4. Consider a stock whose historical volatility has been 20.

A. How often should you expect this stock to rise or fall by more than 20 percent in one year?

B. How about 40 percent?

5. If all this discussion about volatility makes you uncomfortable because it's just too complex, then it's OK to ignore this topic.

○ **TRUE** ○ **FALSE**

Chapter **8**

The Importance of Risk Management

We have covered a lot of territory concerning options—far more material than most people who get involved with options ever bother to learn. That's to your advantage because understanding options and how they work puts you in a good position to begin using options successfully. It's not a guarantee of success, but it shifts the odds of success further in your favor.

There is one final topic that must be discussed before moving on to trading strategies: risk. Risk is a concept that most investors tend to ignore because they are unsure how to deal with it.

Here's my basic premise when trading options:[1] It's easy to make money using options when you adopt conservative strategies, such as those

---

1. *Compared with buying and holding a stock portfolio.*

described in this book. The difficult part is keeping that money.

If you believe that profits come with little effort, if you get overconfident, if you begin to invest ever-increasing amounts of money and trade larger positions than your financial condition warrants, if you believe the markets are always friendly, you will find, to your great disappointment, that it's also inevitable that you lose money—at least part of the time. There is nothing wrong with taking losses. It cannot be avoided. You cannot expect to earn a profit from each and every investment. That's life in the investment world.

It's crucial to your long-term success as an option trader to be certain that those losses are nothing more than a sting. Do not allow them to hurt you. To accomplish that, you must manage your risk and keep losses under control. I'll do what I can to help you understand that point, but it's going to be up to you to stay within your comfort zone and not to expand that zone rapidly just because you begin making money.

To trade within your comfort zone, you must find both the risk and the potential reward for each specific trade to be acceptable. More than that, you must believe the risk and reward for your entire investment portfolio is within your comfort zone. This may seem obvious, but if you are doing well and making money, it's very easy to forget. When things are going well is the time when it's most important to pay attention to how much money you might lose if the stock market suddenly converts your positions into losers. Don't believe this cannot happen—it not only can, it will.

Money management is related to risk management. When I speak of risk, I'm referring to the relative amount that can be earned or lost from a specific trade. I can't tell you exactly how to manage your money because I can't know how much capital you have in your trading account, nor can I know if you are averse to taking risk or if you are aggressive and willing to risk significant losses in return for the opportunity to earn large profits. Thus, I cannot recommend that if you adopt a specific strategy that it's appropriate to trade 1-lots,[2] 5-lots or any other number of contracts for a specific position. I can only tell you that the size[3] of your positions and the total money at risk is something you must decide for yourself. And that's money management.

For some investors a potential loss of $1,000 is devastating, for others it's almost insignificant. It's vital that you manage your money so that not too much of it is at risk for any individual position and that you are never in danger of losing a significant portion of your investment portfolio. There is no formula that suits everyone. Managing your money is something you must do for yourself. My objective is to be certain you understand the importance of doing so.

Investors who have experience owning stocks or mutual funds understand that a severe market correction can result in large losses. But, they are never concerned with losing all, or almost all, of their account value, as long as they are not trading with borrowed money (margin). When people begin trading options, it's difficult for many to recognize that trading a bunch of options that are worth only $100 or $200 (or even less) apiece can result in a significant loss. Because of that potential blind spot, it's essential to stress the importance of managing your overall risk.

The methods discussed in Part II are three very basic option strategies. One is especially conservative and any potential loss is very limited. If you are very risk averse, collars may be the strategy for you. The other two strategies involve more risk but are popular strategies because they

---

2. "Lots" is a common option term referring to the number of contracts. Thus, a 5-lot involves the purchase or sale of 5 options or 5 spreads.

3. This term refers to the number of options you buy or sell.

involve *less* risk for investors when compared with owning individual stocks or mutual funds. If you are currently a buy-and-hold investor, then adopting the methods in Part II will reduce your risk of loss.

The methods in Part III expand the way in which you can use options. The strategies are all limited loss strategies. If you have the proper money management skills and avoid trading 100-lots when 10-lots is the appropriate size for your comfort zone, then there is little chance that a major loss will occur. You will lose money part of the time, but if disasters are avoided, you will do fine over the long term. It's up to you to manage your money and my part is to show you how to skillfully adopt the strategies.

When you begin trading with real money, it's an intelligent decision to trade only a few contracts at one time, even if you have the investing experience and the financial ability to trade larger quantities. You can easily increase the size of your positions after you become comfortable trading the option markets. However, this is only for investors who have the financial wherewithal to trade larger positions. It is not a good idea for someone with an account that totals $5,000 or $10,000 to suddenly trade positions that may result in a loss of their entire trading account. Understanding the risk of a position in dollar terms is the basis of good money management. It's one thing to have a position that may, if you are very unlucky, lose $10,000 when you trade in an account worth $100,000. But, it's a far different matter to own that position when your account is worth a total of $10,000.

Some investors who have been making money trading 3-lots suddenly decide that it's time to make some real money and start trading 30-lots. All I can say is please avoid this trap.

Long-term success

Your long-term success as an option trader is not going to depend solely on how much money you make from each trade or on how much of a return you are able to earn on your investments. The fact is that it's not difficult to make money when using options, as long as you avoid risky methods. For most people, that translates into having more winning trades than losers. It also means that when you do lose, your losses tend to be smaller. You may ask: That all sounds good, so what's the problem?

The problem arises (and it's a real problem) when investors become overconfident. They believe that they are very talented traders, that they always make good money, that options really do help them make lots of money (with little effort), and that risk is under control because they are using limited-risk strategies. Don't fall into that trap. Risk is under control when you have a firm grasp on the potential monetary risk and reward of your entire portfolio.

You may feel this chapter is totally unnecessary, and for the careful investor, perhaps it is. Options are fun to trade. Option strategies reduce risk, but the key to success is not to trade more than your bankroll (and your trading acumen) allows. Please stay within your comfort zone.

Part II

The Basic Conservative Strategies

Chapter 9

The Basic Conservative Option Strategies

So far, we have spent considerable time discussing information *about* options. It's time to begin reaping the benefits of having a thorough understanding of what an option is and the mechanics of how to trade them. You are now far more knowledgeable than the vast majority of traditional options rookies. Too many options newbies jump right in by making trades, never really understanding what they are attempting to accomplish, other than to "make money." Congratulations on avoiding that pitfall.

This section thoroughly explains basic options strategies—not because they are the best possible ways to trade options (although they are good strategies), but because if you come away from Part II with a clear understanding of how these strategies work, then you are ready to grasp the concepts behind more advanced option strategies.

We begin from the perspective of an individual investor whose stock market experience has been limited to owning individual stocks or mutual funds. If this is your background, and if you have not previously traded options, then the three basic conservative strategies are an excellent place for you to gain your first experience with options. Why? Because these methods involve buying stock,[1] something with which you are already familiar, and that makes it easier for you to remain in your comfort zone while expanding your investment horizons.

For many years, mutual fund investors were unable to use options. Although that's still true for the owners of most traditional mutual funds, in today's investment world there's a new kid on the block, the exchange traded fund (ETF). Many of these ETFs, the 21st century version of the traditional mutual fund, have listed options. That means you can use the option strategies described throughout the book when the underlying asset is one of the many ETFs whose options trade on an exchange. If you are more comfortable owning a diversified portfolio rather than individual stocks, that's now possible.

The three basic conservative option strategies

These strategies are:

- Covered call writing. Using stocks you already own (or buying new stocks), you hedge (reduce the risk of owning) those positions by writing (selling) one call option for each 100 shares of stock. That means you are selling someone else the right to buy your stock at an agreed upon price.
- Collars. You establish a collar position by buying stock and selling a call option, just as with covered call writing. Then you also buy a put option, protecting yourself against the possibility of a large loss, in case the stock

undergoes a severe price decline. This is the most conservative of the basic strategies, because it has the least profit potential but offers the most safety. Collars can protect almost the entire value of your investment.[2]

- Cash secured, or naked, put writing. You sell a put option, accepting an obligation that may require you to buy stock at a later date. You may never be forced to buy that stock, but you must be prepared to do so. If you have cash on hand (in your account) to make that purchase, then you are "cash secured."

These basic strategies are not only for newcomers to the options world. Many experienced investors adopt these strategies and find them so satisfactory that they never consider adopting different methods. And that may also be how you feel. I used these strategies for many years as my *only* option strategies. Later I began using other methods; we'll discuss those in Part III. One of the basic tenets of using options (or any investing method) is that you, the individual investor, should adopt methods that make you feel comfortable with your holdings. Some investors are extremely conservative, while others are high rollers who take big chances. It's important that you sleep well at night and that means using methods that fit your comfort zone.

Choosing stocks

When choosing stocks to buy, your obvious goal is to find stocks whose value increases over time. This is not an easy task, or everyone would make a fortune in the stock market. It's important not to make snap decisions when buying or selling specific stocks, especially when the decision is based upon someone else's recommendation. If some analyst upgrades or downgrades a stock, or if someone gives you a hot tip, it's prudent to conduct your own research and make your own

---

1. *In two of the three strategies you do buy stock. In the third, you may become obligated to buy stock.*
2. *You can protect the entire investment, for a price.*

decision whether it's reasonable for you to trade the shares before becoming a stockholder. But the methods you use to make the stock-buying decision are not part of our current discussion. The important point to remember is: There is no reason to change those methods just because you are learning to use options. Remember also to consider a stock's volatility history as another characteristic of stocks that can determine if the stock qualifies as an addition to your list of potential investments (see Chapter 7).

We are not too many years removed from the technology bubble that cost a great many investors a substantial portion of their savings. If you are among those who want to return to the stock market but have not yet done so because of your fear of sustaining significant losses, this section is for you. If preservation of capital is your top priority when investing, and if making money is a goal, but a secondary one, then these three basic strategies can help you achieve your investment objectives. Two of these methods provide limited insurance against loss, but they increase your ability to earn a profit from your investments. The third strategy allows you to invest in the stock market with a great deal of confidence, and depending on the deductible you choose for your "insurance policy,"[3] it can protect almost the entire value of your portfolio.

Let's take a detailed look at these investment techniques one at a time. It is my intention to leave you with an excellent understanding of each strategy, how to apply the strategy, and how to know if the specific strategy is suitable for you and your investment philosophy. A thorough discussion of the risks and rewards associated with each strategy is included.

Before getting started, let's consider one basic option strategy. I must repeat the warning of Chapter 3: I don't recommend this strategy. The chances of making money on a consistent basis are very small, unless you are very talented in determining which stocks to buy and when to buy (or sell) them.

Buying options

Buying options is the single strategy that attracts more investors to trading options than any other because it occasionally produces a jackpot. Buying options is similar to buying a mini-lottery ticket,[4] and the possibilities are too tempting for many to ignore.

It's not that buying options is a bad strategy, but it's difficult to be a successful. That requires skills that most traders lack. There are two good features about buying options: losses are always limited to the cost of the options and there's an opportunity to earn a large profit from a small investment. Unfortunately, too many investors who buy options lose their entire investment because they are unwilling (or don't understand how) to accept a small loss and thus, they hold their options until they expire (worthless, most of the time).

In this author's opinion, it's wrong to encourage investors, especially investors with little option trading experience, to adopt a strategy with little chance of success. If you occasionally speculate, there's nothing wrong with that. But the recommendation here is that you are better served using strategies that increase your chances of making money. Isn't that the reason you picked up this book in the first place—to learn to use options to *make money*? The fact that options can be used to reduce risk (while earning that money) is a huge bonus and it's intelligent to take advantage of that risk-reducing characteristic of options.

Succeeding as an options buyer: the requirements

As an option buyer, you have more losing trades than winning trades. To succeed the average profit must be significantly larger than the average loss.

Predicting direction

When you buy puts or calls, you are predicting in which direction the underlying asset moves. If you are wrong, you have no chance to earn a profit.

---

3. *The put you purchase when using collars acts as that insurance policy.*
4. *I'll concede that you have a much better chance to make money buying options instead of lottery tickets.*

Keep in mind that predicting direction is difficult at best. Most professional money managers do a poor job.[5] Although they are very good at collecting management fees from their customers, the majority cannot outperform the market on a consistent basis.

In contrast, when you sell an option, you win most of the time because you only need the stock not to move too far in the wrong direction. In other words, when you sell calls, you profit when the stock declines, holds steady, or increases by a small amount. Thus, it's much easier to make money by prudently selling options. When selling options, I prefer to buy another option as insurance against a large loss. You'll see how that works in Part III.

One advantage to buying options is that profits can be unlimited. It's a popular strategy because there's always the chance to earn that large profit. Option sellers have no such paydays. When you sell options (or option spreads) profits are limited.

Timing

If predicting direction is not difficult enough, the option buyer must also be right on timing. Options are a wasting asset and lose value day after day. Thus, it's important for the stock to make its move before the option becomes worthless. Needing the ability to time the market makes it more difficult to make money when buying options.

Size of move

Depending on the option you buy (OTM, ATM, ITM) the underlying asset must not only move in the right direction within a limited time period, but the move must be large enough to compensate for the extrinsic value of the option (same as time premium—it's the option premium less its intrinsic value). For example, if YYZ is trading near 29 and you decide to buy YYZ

calls with a strike price of 30 and which expire in 30 days at $1.00 per option, you don't make any money when the stock slowly rises to 31 on expiration day.[6] If the stock reaches 31 earlier, you may choose to sell the call and earn a profit. Unfortunately, the stock (in this scenario) takes too long to increase in price and you cannot earn money. It's very disappointing to see your stock move from 29 to 31 in a short time period and discover that you didn't profit from correcting predicting the price rise.

Premium paid

In Chapter 3 there is an example of a successful trade in which an investor buys 5 SPX call options and the market makes a favorable move. That profit potential is the lure. If you have a track record of successfully predicting whether the market is rising or falling, and if those market moves are large enough, you may do very well as an option buyer. If you have those skills, use them. Take full advantage. Most investors cannot do it, but enjoy trying. They believe their track record is much better than it is. Options can be used to gain leverage.[7] But they can also be used to reduce risk. I believe in playing options on the conservative side and using options as risk-reducing investment tools. But you must choose your path—the path that fits your skills and comfort zone.

We'll discuss buying options as insurance, to protect one position or an entire portfolio. When you buy options for that purpose, you are not predicting market direction. You are protecting your portfolio against an unforeseen event. One of the three basic conservative strategies involves buying put options as an insurance policy.

---

5. *Mutual funds are run by highly paid professional managers and the majority cannot outperform the market averages. That's one reason why smart mutual fund investors have switched to buying index funds. Those investors got better performance and pay lower fees.*
6. *The option is worth $1, and that's the price you paid. You break even, ignoring commissions.*
7. *Leverage represents the possibility of making a very high return on an investment.*

Chapter 10

Covered Call Writing: Preparing to Trade

I'm sure you're more than ready to get into specific strategies for using options to make money. We've spent a great deal of time on background information because it's very important for long-term profitability. By knowing the answers to the most basic questions before you commit your money, you avoid the pitfalls of many novices— and that means reducing unnecessary losses during your first few trades.

We'll take a step-by-step approach to learning several easy-to-understand, risk-reducing options strategies. We begin with three basic conservative option strategies, each of which is widely used by investors. Most people who want to learn about options already have some investing experience and are familiar with buying and selling stock. Because each of the three basic conservative option strategies makes it both safer and more profitable to own stock, learning these strategies is the best way to ease into option trading. This is not the traditional path taken by most options students, but I believe it's the easiest way for you to get a firm grasp on how to use options to make money, while at the same time reducing the risk of owning stock.

Traditionally, the only way to invest in the stock market was to buy stocks or shares of mutual funds. Today, options provide an opportunity to participate in the ups and downs of the stock market without owning shares of anything. We'll begin with option strategies designed for investors who own, or are willing to own, stocks. The concept of making or losing money when owning shares is easy to understand. The owner profits if and when the shares rise in price and loses money when the shares decline. But options are not stocks—they are a derivative product, and the pricing of derivatives is not as straightforward as the pricing of stocks. That's why we begin with strategies designed for stockholders, allowing you to use options under conditions that are already familiar.

The best way to learn about options and understand how they work is for the investor to own a real option position. Many people begin their trading careers by simply buying options, a strategy that has the benefit of limiting risk, but which gives the investor a very small chance of earning a profit. It's fine to limit risk—the importance of which is emphasized many times in these pages—but why would anyone want to begin trading options with a strategy that's likely to lose money? Instead, I'll show you how to get started with options by adopting strategies that increase your chances of earning a profit. Once you are familiar with those basic strategies, we'll move on to methods that don't involve stock.

The first of the three basic conservative option strategies consists of owning stock and selling a call option that gives someone else the right to buy your stock. In option jargon, the strategy is known as covered call writing, or CCW. This basic and somewhat conservative strategy is very popular among individual investors, many of whom use it as their primary investment vehicle.

By adopting CCW, you, the individual investor, learn first-hand how writing (selling) call options makes it possible to earn extra profits from stock ownership. It doesn't always provide *optimum* results, but it does boost earnings most of time. As you monitor your position and watch the weeks go by, you'll gain an understanding of how options are valued in the marketplace. You'll notice how option prices behave as your stock rises and falls and how the passage of time plays a vital role in the pricing of options. We discussed the theory of how options are priced earlier (Chapter 6), but it's easier to grasp the concepts as you watch your own money at work. If you have the ability to monitor your positions online, rather than relying on the newspaper, you have a great advantage. Today, few newspapers publish option prices, and often those prices are stale.[1]

{ *NOTE: Some of you have the time and desire to watch positions frequently—daily or even hourly. If it's not feasible for you to spend that much time on your investment portfolio, don't be concerned. For the majority of readers who are employed full time, checking your portfolio throughout the day is not necessary. Once per day is more than adequate to keep an eye on how option prices change over time. Even a weekly perusal of your positions allows you to absorb important information about the pricing of options and the effects of time.*

---

1. *When newspapers published option prices on a daily basis, they used the last price at which an option traded. Sometimes, those prices were hours old, if the option was one that traded infrequently. If you can access your brokerage account online, you can see up-to-date prices for your options, based on the market bid and ask quotes. You can also get the latest quotes at cboe.com.*

I begin with covered call writing for several reasons:

- It's an easy-to-understand strategy.
- It provides an opportunity to reduce the risk of continuing to hold stocks you already own.
- It increases your likelihood of earning a profit.
- It allows you to observe how the market price of an option changes as time passes and as the price of the underlying stock changes.
- Selling options (when done prudently)[2] is more likely to show a profit when compared with buying options.

Message to readers new to the three basic conservative strategies: When learning about CCW, please be aware of your overall investment philosophy. Some investors are very conservative and want to eliminate (as much as possible) the chance of losing money when investing. Others are extremely aggressive and prefer to roll the dice and don't care if they lose everything, as long as they have the chance to make a killing. If you keep your goals clearly in mind, you can find at least one option strategy that makes it easier to accomplish your objectives. Some of you who are currently aggressive, risk-taking investors may be surprised to find that potential rewards available from adopting conservative methods are sufficiently attractive that you become more conservative investors. There's no point in taking more risk than necessary.

As you take a careful, detailed look at covered call writing, you'll discover that the risk/reward profile of the strategy varies significantly depending on the type of stock you own as well as on the specific option you sell. CCW is a versatile strategy, and when it comes to selecting an option to write, there are usually enough choices to accommodate both the very conservative and very aggressive investor. Some readers may be tempted to write the call option that provides the chance (albeit a tiny chance) to maximize potential profits. That's understandable. You should resist that temptation. Just because a huge return is possible doesn't mean it's a likely outcome. If you write a call that offers a more modest return, the probability of earning that return increases. You'll see how that works when we look at our first example.

BOTTOM LINE: It's important to adopt trading methods that allow you remain in your comfort zone. That means having no anxiety over your investment portfolio. You can modify your investment philosophy, if necessary, any time. As you begin to use options, reinforce your good investing habits. Learn new strategies that help you achieve your goals—with reduced risk. When you become comfortable using these methods, that's the time to consider modifying your investment philosophy.

Covered call writing is not for everyone. As we discuss the strategy's benefits and risks, you can determine if it's suitable for you. Let me make this important point up front: If you are the type of investor who feels that the best possible result must be achieved with every investment, then this method will not work for you. CCW provides better results most of the time, but sometimes you can earn a larger profit by simply holding stock and not adopting any option strategy. That's the nature of the game. With CCW, you make money more often and lose money less often, but you must give up the possibility of making a killing. If you are searching for stocks that double and double again in a short period of time, then this is not an appropriate strategy.

Covered call writing defined

The term, "write," is equivalent to the term, "sell." When you sell a call option, there are three possible phrases to describe the sale:

2. We'll stay away from the extremely risky option-selling strategies.

- **Closing.** This occurs when you sell an option you already own.
- **Opening.** A transaction in which you are initiating a new position or adding to an existing position
  - o **Covered.** This is an opening transaction. You don't own the call option that you sell, but you do own a sufficient number of shares of the underlying security (100 shares per option) so that your broker can deliver (transfer the shares from your account in exchange for cash) the shares if you are assigned an exercise notice. Remember when you sell a call option you agree to accept an obligation to deliver 100 shares of stock per option. You may never be called upon to fulfill that obligation, but until that option expires or is repurchased, the obligation remains in effect. Thus, *covered call writing is the sale of call options when your account holds sufficient shares of the underlying security to make delivery.*
  - o **Uncovered (Naked).** This is an opening transaction. Not only don't you own the option, but you don't own any (or you don't own enough) shares of the underlying stock to fulfill your obligation. If you are assigned an exercise notice, you sell the shares short.[3] Short selling is not something to fear, but many newcomers to the world of investing do fear it. Short selling is not allowed in IRA or other retirement accounts. Therefore, selling naked calls is not allowed in those accounts. Selling naked call options is not recommended for any but the most experienced option traders and is too risky for the majority of those.

Why consider writing covered calls?

Before adopting any strategy, it's important to understand the rationale behind it. Thus we must ask:

- What do you have to gain?
- What do you have to lose?
- Can this simple strategy make a significant difference in the profitability of your investment portfolio?

Review: In return for paying a premium, the call buyer gets the right to buy 100 shares of your stock at the strike price, but only for a limited time. In return for the receiving the premium, you accept an obligation to sell 100 shares at the strike price—but only if the call owner exercises the right to buy your stock before the option expires. You have no role in the exercise decision. The option owner determines if and when the option is exercised.

{ *NOTE: The following are crucial concepts to understand, and bear repeating: Each person has different investment goals and different tolerance for risk. When writing covered calls, a critical decision must be made when you choose which call to sell. **There is no "best" call to sell.** Many individual investors are likely to discover that there is more than one suitable choice. Our first example outlines the advantages and disadvantages of each possibility and provides insight that will make it easier for you to make your own real-world decisions—a choice that will fit your investment style. For example, some investors prefer selling near-term options (options that expire within a month or two), while others prefer writing longer-term options. You will discover your own comfort zone.*

Some options make better choices for conservative investors—people who prefer

---

3. You borrow the shares from your broker and sell them. At some unspecified future date you buy back the shares to cancel the short position.

to concentrate on safety rather than earnings potential. Aggressive investors, willing to sacrifice some of the safety available to covered call writers in exchange for the possibility of making more money, usually choose different options to write. And there's always the middle ground for investors who are concerned with both reducing risk *and* making money. Again, there's no right or wrong decision and there's a good chance that more than one choice is appropriate for you.

Is covered call writing worth the effort?

Covered call writing is a good method for investors who are familiar with stock trading to learn about options, because it fits right in with methods for trading stock, and it's the gateway to the world of options. But, does it help your portfolio grow? Is it a good method for making money? Fortunately statistics are available to help provide an answer to those questions. The bottom line is that it's more profitable most of the time, but in wildly bullish markets you earn more money by simply owning stocks.

BXM, the buy-write index

The Chicago Board Options Exchange (CBOE) publishes data for BXM, the Buy-Write[4] Index. BXM is a benchmark index created to compare the performance of a hypothetical portfolio that is completely invested in covered calls. This is not an index that anyone should attempt to mimic in the real world because it was created as a benchmark against which to compare the performance of a diversified stock portfolio (S&P 500 Index). Data for this index is available dating back to June 1988.

BXM is based on the following investment strategy: (This description is presented to show you how the BXM works. Please don't bother to copy this investment methodology because it requires too much effort. Besides, you can invest directly in BXM if you want to do so.)[5]

- Buy and maintain ownership of a portfolio of stocks that mimics the S&P 500 Index.
- No need to own all 500 stocks if portfolio has high correlation with index, but the BXM is measured from a portfolio that exactly matches the index.
- Write near-term S&P 500 Index (SPX) call option early in the morning[6] on the third Friday of each month.
- Always sell the near-term option. The strike price is always just above the current index level (the first out-of-the-money call option).
- The call is held through expiration and is cash settled.[7]
- The strategy used for BXM does not allow for any adjustments. The position must remain unchanged through expiration.
- Every month, a new one-month call option is written, based on the identical strategy.

What does BXM tell us about adopting a covered call writing strategy? The comparison is illustrated in Figure 10.1.

In Figure 10.1 the performance of BXM is compared with SPTR, the Standard & Poor's Total Return Index. SPTR performance is based on periodic reinvestment of all dividends. The data shows that the option-writing strategy performed

---

4. *A buy-write is a single transaction in which you buy stock and write a covered call. The subtle difference between a buy-write and writing a covered call is that the buy-write is a single transaction. Thus if you already own stock and write calls later, that transaction is writing a covered call.*

5. *BXM futures are available.*

6. *Options on the SPX (S&P 500 Index), unlike stock options, expire at the opening of the market on the third Friday of the month, not at the close.*

7. *In Part III we'll talk about cash-settled options. For now just understand that you don't have to deliver your portfolio of stocks if the option is in-the-money and you are assigned an exercise notice. You keep your stocks and deliver the cash value of the option.*

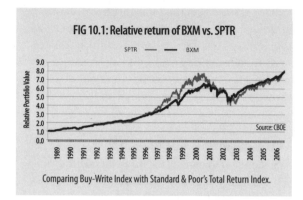

FIG 10.1: Relative return of BXM vs. SPTR

SPTR —— BXM

Source: CBOE

Comparing Buy-Write Index with Standard & Poor's Total Return Index.

on a par with the Total Return Index over the 18.5 years for which data is available.

But a closer examination of Figure 10.1 shows that SPTR performed extremely well during the four very bullish (bubble-building) years of 1995 through 1998 (see Table 10.1). BXM returned very handsome profits during those four years (more than 20 percent), but when compared with the greater-than-30-percent return of the SPTR, it pales in comparison. This shows that writing covered calls indeed limits profits. When the market is wildly bullish, covered call writing underperforms a simple buy and hold strategy. However, the markets are seldom so bullish.

On average, BXM outperformed SPTR during all the other years (see Table 10.2) by an average of more than 1.6 percent per year. Note that during the most recent four years, SPTR has outperformed BXM. Considering the fact that writing covered calls requires time and effort, is CCW a worthwhile strategy? The answer depends on you, your investment goals and your outlook for the American stock market. To me, it's reasonable to conclude that writing covered calls is worthwhile because it provides better returns more often—and does so with reduced volatility, i.e., reduced fluctuation in the value of your portfolio. It's true that those who adopt this method earn less when the market is very strong, but over the long term a

string of very bullish years is a low probability event.

CCW is appropriate for many investors. Unless wildly bullish, it's probably appropriate for a portion of your portfolio. But please don't forget the main purpose in learning about covered call writing: it is your entrance into the world of options.

CCW significantly reduces portfolio volatility and for many investors, that's important—or at least, it should be important. The BXM provides superior risk-based returns. That means for a given level of risk, BXM provides higher returns than SPX (or SPTR). To earn equal returns, the investor who owns a diversified stock portfolio must take greater risk than the covered call writer. Feldman and Roy's study showed that for the 16-year period studied, the standard deviation of the BXM portfolio was 10.99 percent and for the S&P 500 portfolio (without selling any calls) was 16.50 percent.[8] That's a significant reduction in volatility.

TABLE 10.1: BXM vs. SPTR, 1995-1998

YEAR	BXM	SPTR
1995	20.93%	37.05%
1996	15.50%	22.96%
1997	26.64%	33.36%
1998	18.95%	28.58%
AVG	20.51%	30.49%

During the market's bubble-building years, BXM returned more than 20 percent. That outstanding return was dwarfed by SPTR's better-than-30-percent return.

TABLE 10.2: BXM vs. SPTR, 1988-2006 (ex 1995-1998)

YEAR	BXM	SPTR
1988	8.13%	6.33%
1989	25.01%	31.69%
1990	3.99%	-3.10%
1991	24.39%	30.47%
1992	11.52%	7.62%
1993	14.10%	10.08%
1994	4.50%	1.32%
1999	21.17%	21.04%
2000	7.40%	-9.10%
2001	-10.92%	-11.89%
2002	-7.64%	-22.10%
2003	19.37%	28.68%
2004	8.30%	10.88%
2005	4.25%	4.91%
2006	13.33%	15.79%
AVG	9.79%	8.17%

BXM outperforms SPTR most of the time.

---

8. Feldman, Barry, and Dhruv Roy, "Passive Options-Based Investment Strategies: The Case of the CBOE S&P 500 BuyWrite Index." *The Journal of Investing.* (Summer 2005).

When adopting covered call writing for a stock portfolio, you have choices: You may write covered calls most of the time but refrain when you believe the market is poised to run significantly higher. Of course, one never knows when those strong bull markets are going to occur or when they may end. In fact, the majority of investors seem to get it wrong by jumping into the market near tops and unloading near bottoms. Unless you know you have good market-timing skills, it's better to adopt the more conservative method of writing covered calls on most, if not your entire, portfolio—and to continue with that strategy year after year.

If picking individual stocks is not your forte, then you can use the strategy with ETFs or index options (discussed in Part III). For the vast majority of investors who cannot successfully time the market on a consistent basis, the recommendation is to maintain a consistent long-term strategy. You may even decide to write calls on only a portion of your portfolio. Or you may decide to use the strategy in a conservative or aggressive manner.

But, of course, it's your money and you should invest it as you think best. My job is to provide additional tools to use when you deem it appropriate. CCW easily outperforms a buy and hold investment strategy most of the time: in down markets, in steady markets and in up markets—failing to outperform only during those strong upwards markets.

One further point: CCW is not recommended as the best available option strategy. Instead, I recommend it as an excellent learning tool. Once you understand how the three basic strategies work, you'll be able to move on to Part III and find strategies that provide even higher potential returns and with less risk. But, let's not get ahead of ourselves.

In 2004 Ibbotson Associates published a case study on the BXM buy-write options strategy which showed that BXM "has relatively good risk-adjusted returns. The compound annual return of the BXM Index over the almost 16-year history of this study is 12.39 percent, compared to 12.20 percent for the S&P 500. The BXM had about two-thirds the volatility of the S&P 500. The study provides credible evidence of the investment potential for the BXM Index."[9]

Because writing covered calls provides similar returns to owning a diversified stock portfolio, but with much lower volatility, it should be the preferred method for many investors. CCW is not the road to riches, but it represents an introduction into the world of options and is a perfect starting point, especially for investors who already own stocks or who like the idea of owning stocks.

Calculations required for covered call writing

Before we get started, there are a few basic calculations that are used repeatedly. It's important that we agree on definitions to avoid misunderstandings:

S = Stock price (for 100 shares). Use current price when option is sold, not original cost.[10]

P = Option premium, the price at which you buy or sell the option.

G = Gain (profit).

DP = Downside protection.

- ROI: The return on an investment is the profit divided by the amount invested.
- Amount invested: Cash required to purchase stock, but reduced by premium collected when writing call options.
- Use the current stock price rather than original purchase price because the current price represents the value of the investment *today* and allows you to determine the current return. If you prefer to track your results using original cost, then do so. The reason for carefully defining these terms is allow us to agree on the calculated results.
- ROI = $G/(S-P)$.

---

9. *Ibid.*
10. *This is how the calculations are made in this book. Keep your books in any manner that suits you.*

- Downside Protection: The amount the stock can decline from its present value before reaching the break-even point.[11] It's equal to the option premium divided by the amount invested. You lose no money on the trade if the stock remains above the break-even point at expiration (close of business on the third Friday of the month specified in the option contract).
- DP = P/(S-P).

In this book, when considering which option to choose for any given trade, I begin by examining each possibility from the point of view of an experienced, conservative trader. You must decide if this rationale works for you. If not, the discussion includes reasons why other choices are appropriate for investors with a different risk tolerance and different goals.

The purpose of this exercise is to help you quickly recognize the characteristics that represent an attractive choice when writing covered calls. As you gain experience, you learn to eliminate inappropriate choices quickly. The objective is to enable you to make decisions on your own, and in a reasonable amount of time. It's not fun to trade if it takes hours to reach a suitable decision. Our first example is thorough and takes time, but you will learn to do the same analysis much more quickly. As we examine examples, the decisions will come more readily as you recognize why a group of options can quickly be eliminated from consideration.

This learning method will help you develop a style of trading that suits your needs. My style is to write options with short expirations, i.e., options that expire in either of the two front months, but the option chosen must provide reasonable protection against loss, as well as a reasonable (a relative term) potential profit. Your goal is to find a style that suits your psyche, your pocketbook and your comfort zone.

Let's take an in-depth look at covered call writing with our first example.

---

11. *Assuming the position is held through expiration, the price below which your investment loses money.*

Chapter 11

Covered Call Writing: Making the Trade

Assume you own 500 shares of DOGS, the only publicly traded company that breeds animals for shows and state fairs. If you don't already own the shares, you simply buy them and proceed as if you owned them earlier. This $19 stock is reasonably volatile, and that means the option premium looks attractive to sell.[1] To complete the strategy, you must write (sell) five call options. The main focus of this discussion is helping you decide which calls to write. Assume the nearest expiration is 30 days from today and the stock does not pay a dividend.

As can be seen in Table 11.1, there are 16 different calls options from which to choose. Sometimes you find many more choices and sometimes fewer. Let's take a detailed look at the

---

1. Reminder: More volatile stocks have options with higher premiums than less volatile stocks.

options and discuss the pros and cons of writing each. Many times the most attractive opportunities can be found by writing the options that expire in the front month (next to expire). But that method requires that you take the time to find new trades every month. That's not a problem for many active traders, who can easily spend the required time preparing for and making the necessary trades. However, if you are an investor who wants to gain the benefits of using options but have neither the time nor inclination to trade frequently, choose options with longer lifetimes. Keep in mind that trading less often reduces expenses (commissions).

Remember, each option represents 100 shares of stock, and a $1 premium ($1.00 per share) equals $100 per contract. We'll progress through these options, beginning with the near-term, and proceeding with options with sequentially longer lifetimes.

TABLE 11.1: DOGS call options, stock at 19.00, IV 46

MONTH	TIME	STRIKE	BID	ASK	TIME PR	ROI UNCH	ROI ASSIGNED	ANN ROI ASSIGNED	DP
Aug	30	17.5	$1.90	$2.10	$0.40	2.34%	2.34%	28.07%	10.00%
Aug		20.0	$0.55	$0.70	$0.55	2.98%	8.40%	100.81%	2.89%
Aug		22.5	$0.10	$0.20	$0.10	0.53%	19.68%	236.17%	0.53%
Aug		25.0	$0.00	$0.10	$0.00	0.00%	31.58%	378.95%	0.00%
Sep	58	17.5	$2.25	$2.45	$0.75	4.48%	4.48%	27.79%	11.84%
Sep		20.0	$0.95	$1.15	$0.95	5.26%	10.80%	67.06%	5.00%
Sep		22.5	$0.35	$0.50	$0.35	1.88%	21.62%	134.20%	1.84%
Sep		25.0	$0.10	$0.20	$0.10	0.53%	32.28%	200.33%	0.53%
Nov	121	17.5	$2.90	$3.10	$1.40	8.70%	8.70%	25.87%	15.26%
Nov		20.0	$1.65	$1.85	$1.65	9.51%	15.27%	45.44%	8.68%
Nov		22.5	$0.85	$1.05	$0.85	4.68%	23.97%	71.31%	4.47%
Nov		25.0	$0.45	$0.60	$0.45	2.43%	34.77%	103.45%	2.37%
Feb	212	17.5	$3.50	$3.80	$2.00	12.90%	12.90%	21.91%	18.42%
Feb		20.0	$2.40	$2.60	$2.40	14.46%	20.48%	34.78%	12.63%
Feb		22.5	$1.55	$1.75	$1.55	8.88%	28.94%	49.14%	8.16%
Feb		25.0	$0.95	$1.15	$0.95	5.26%	38.50%	65.38%	5.00%

These are the 16 DOGS call options currently listed for trading. There are four different strike prices in each of the four expiration months. Each call is individually considered as a candidate to be sold when adopting the strategy of covered call writing.

Month = Month in which options expire (third Friday)
Time = days to expiration
Time PR = Time premium in option (total premium minus intrinsic value)
ROI Unch = Return on investment if DOGS is unchanged (i.e., $19 per share) at expiration
ROI Assigned = Return on investment, if assigned an exercise notice
Ann ROI Assigned = Return on investment assigned, annualized
DP = Downside protection. Amount stock can decline before break-even point is reached

Taking this logical path forces us to begin with the Aug 17½ calls, an in-the-money option whose bid price is $1.90. For many people first learning about options, it appears very strange to buy stock at $19 today and then immediately agree to sell that stock to someone else at a lower price ($17.50). That definitely seems to be a money-losing proposition. Please be assured that this is merely an illusion and that you can write this call option and earn a profit when doing so.

If it makes you uncomfortable to sell your stock at only $17.50, look at it this way: In reality, instead of buying 500 shares of DOGS at $19 per share, you are "renting" them for 30 days. You put up a deposit of $17.10 per share ($19.00 paid for the stock, less the $1.90 premium you collect when selling the call option) and agree to relinquish your shares at $17.50 per share when the "lease" expires in 30 days. However there is a catch—if the other party decides not to own the shares when the lease expires, the lessor has the right to abandon those shares, making you their rightful owner. This is analogous to the current sad situation in which a homeowner, who finds the mortgage is greater than the value of the home, walks away, abandoning the house to the mortgage company. Thus, if the stock is worth less than the strike price, the owner gives them to you. If the lessor elects that option, you are obligated to take ownership of the shares.[2]

The Aug 17½ call is $1.90 bid. This call option is in-the-money by $1.50 (the stock price exceeds the strike price by $1.50) and has a time premium of $0.40 per share.[3] The good news is that this option provides excellent protection against loss. If the stock price doesn't decline by more than the $1.90 premium when expiration day arrives, you'll earn a profit on this trade. It's highly unlikely that the stock drops that much (10 percent) in 30 days, but DOGS is a volatile stock, and it can happen. If you sell this call, you'll probably earn a profit equal to the time premium ($40 per contract), less commission. Of course, you'd give up any chance to make additional profits if the stock rallies. That's the constant tradeoff—selling an option that provides excellent protection means losing the ability to profit if the stock rallies.

The return on investment (ROI) for 30 days is better than 2 percent. Here's how to calculate ROI: The current stock value is $1,900. You collect an option premium of $190, reducing investment cost to $1,710. If you earn $40 on that investment, that's a return of 2.34 percent. That's a very nice return for only 30 days, especially when the risk of loss is so small. This option is definitely worth considering, especially for the conservative investor, because it offers excellent protection along with a nice profit potential. After all, if you earn 2.34 percent every 30 days, your money doubles in 2.5 years.[4]

This is an attractive choice, but, we've only considered one call option and it's too soon to decide. Before considering alternatives, it's important to mention (again) that commissions play a significant role in the profit picture—and this is especially true when you trade small quantities. There is no point in collecting $40 in premium and paying your broker $10 in commissions and another $10 (or more) when you are assigned an exercise notice. In that scenario, your broker earns half the profit. On the other hand, if you trade 500 shares, then the broker's share is still $20, but that represents only 10 percent of the profits. The point is that if you trade small quantities, it may be better to collect more premium per trade and to trade less often. You do that by writing options with longer lifetimes.

The August 20 call can be sold for $55 per contract. That's not a lot of money, but it's almost 3 percent of your $1,845 (stock value, less premium) investment. At 3 percent every month, your money doubles in two years.[5] The $55 premium doesn't

---

2. You are not forced to maintain ownership and can sell the shares, but you may not decline to own them.
3. Time premium is total premium ($1.90) less the intrinsic value ($1.50).
4. A $1,000 investment that compounds at 2.34 percent per month is worth $2,001.53 after 30 months.
5. A $1,000 investment that compounds at 3.00 percent per month is worth $2,032.79 after 24 months

provide much downside protection, but because the strike price is above the current stock price (that means the call is out-of-the-money, or OTM) there's a chance to make even more (up to $1 per share) if the stock price is above 19 when the option expires. If this stock performs well and you are eventually assigned an exercise notice, you'll sell the shares at $20 (strike price). That makes the potential ROI more than 8 percent (see Table 11.1). There are three factors to consider when deciding if this is an appropriate option to write.

- The ROI is almost 3 percent for 30 days—if the stock price is 19.00 in 30 days. That's a good return.
- Because the option is OTM, additional profit is possible if the stock moves higher—as much as $500 ($1 on each share). That's an annualized return of 100 percent. Excellent.
- Downside protection is very limited. Not so good.

The Aug 20 call is worth considering. A conservative investor probably prefers the additional downside protection (available by writing the Aug 17½ call) that reduces the chances of losing money, but there are advantages to writing this option, especially for investors who are bullish on DOGS (and if you are not bullish, why do you own this stock?), or who prefer to write OTM options—giving themselves the opportunity for additional capital gains.

{ NOTE: Most covered call writers prefer selling OTM options, hoping to earn extra capital gains. I believe more conservative investors should consider ITM options, as long as they provide an adequate return.

Let's consider more alternatives

August 22½ and 25 calls are totally unappealing. There's not much point in selling an option for only $10, as it provides neither protection nor an

acceptable cash premium. It's true that writing the Aug 22½ call makes it likely you'll pocket the $10, but why give up the possibility that something spectacular may happen for a measly $10? And even if nothing big happens, if the stock rises to 20 in the next few days, you can sell the Aug 22½ calls for a better premium at that time. This is an easy decision for me—I'd rather hold the stock without writing calls than write them for a very small premium. However, an investor who wants to be a long-term owner of these shares may be willing to sell these calls and consider the $10 premium as equivalent to a $10 cash dividend. (Don't forget to consider commissions when trading such low-priced options.)

August options offer two decent choices—one for the conservative investor (17½ calls), and another for the more bullish (20 calls) investor. Let's see if options that expire in other months have something better to offer.

Moving out a month, September expiration is 58 calendar days away. By definition, intrinsic value (if any) does not change when the number of days to expiration changes. But, these options may be more attractive to sell than August options because they have a higher time premium. That time premium is important. It represents the entire profit potential when writing an ITM option. It also represents an important part of the profit potential if you write an ATM (at-the-money) or OTM (out-of-the-money) call.

{ NOTE: When you write an ITM option, there's no opportunity to earn extra profit because you are committed to selling stock at the strike price. Thus, when writing ITM calls, the entire profit comes from the time premium.

The current bid price for the September 17½ call is $2.25. If you write this call, you'd collect $225 (unless you decide to try to sell the call at a slightly better price).[6] The intrinsic value is still $1.50 per

6. Remember, you don't have to sell your option at the bid price. If willing to take the chance that the stock moves lower and the bid for the calls you are trying to sell decreases, you can try to collect a higher premium when selling any option.

share, but the time value is $75 per contract, and that's $35 more than the Aug 17½ call. This is a fairly attractive proposition, especially for the less aggressive investor. First, you are protected against losing money if the stock drops by as much as $2.25 because that's the amount of cash received when writing the call. That's a decline of almost 12 percent (Table 11.1). As far as profits are concerned, the most you can earn by writing this call is the $75 time premium. You earn that much if eventually assigned an exercise notice—and that's the most likely result.[7] That's a return of 4.48 percent on an $1,675 investment ($1,900 stock value less the $225 option premium). On an annualized basis, that's more than 27 percent—a very nice return for an investment with a high probability of being successful. Sure, the stock could tumble below 17.5, but it's an unlikely occurrence over such a short period of time. Writing this call is a distinct possibility.

{ *NOTE: I mention that it's possible for the stock to drop below the strike price when expiration arrives, but dismiss that possibility as unlikely. You must remember this when investing in the stock market: Unlikely events do happen. Thus, it's crucial to your long-term survival as an investor to be certain you don't invest too much money in one situation, just because winning is highly likely. If you have the financial ability to buy 500 DOGS, don't buy 2,000 just because it looks like easy money. My trading mantra: It's easy to make money trading options, but you must be certain you don't incur large losses. That means risk management is important and you should never own a position that's too large, just because it looks easy to make money. Writing these Aug or Sep 17½ calls is likely to be profitable, but please don't put yourself in jeopardy. Some companies do issue surprise announcements containing bad news.*

You collect $95 for writing the Sep 20 call. If the stock is unchanged when expiration arrives, the ROI is 5.26 percent. That's a decent return. On an annualized

basis, the return is similar (33 vs. 36 percent) to that available from writing the Aug 20 call. The Sep 20 call doesn't provide much insurance against loss, but if insurance is the primary concern, writing this call is more attractive than writing the Aug 20 call. It also allows for the chance to make an additional $500 if the stock is above 20 when expiration arrives. This is a reasonable choice for the bullish or aggressive investor, and worth considering by the slightly conservative investor because it offers some downside protection, as well as the opportunity to earn a good annualized return. This call stays on the list of possibilities. In fact, many covered call writers choose to write this call because it offers something for everyone—opportunity for capital gains, some downside protection and a decent time premium.

The $35 premium you collect by writing the Sep 22½ call is unattractive to me, it but appeals to the long-term investor who prefers not to sell the stock and who likes the idea of collecting time premium by writing covered calls. There's almost no downside insurance and only a small chance of being assigned an exercise notice. It comes down to these questions:

- For the conservative investor: If you don't want to sell your shares, are you willing to accept a payment of $35 in return for possibly being forced to sell those shares at 22½? Each individual investor must make that choice, but for me, this option is not a good candidate for writing because the premium is simply too small and provides almost no protection. I don't want to depend on the stock going higher to earn a decent profit.
- For the long-term investor: The $35 "dividend" is attractive. If assigned an exercise notice, how disappointing can it be to earn $1,925 in 58 days?
- For the bullish investor: Are you that bullish that writing the Sep 22½ isn't good

---

7. *For that to not be the result, the stock must decrease to less than 17.5 in 58 days. Certainly a possibility, but not likely.*

enough? If the stock does rise above $22.50, how disappointing is it to sell at that price? Remember, when writing covered calls you cannot expect the best possible outcome from every trade. Even the aggressively bullish investor can find something to like about writing the Sep 22½ call. Just remember, these small premiums provide little protection.

The Sep 25 call can be sold for $10 and definitely is not worth the effort. If this is the call you prefer to sell, hold the stock, hoping DOGS rallies, and perhaps you'll have an opportunity to sell this call for an acceptable price later. It's better not to sell any call than to settle for a premium this small. When writing covered calls, there must be some benefit. Low premiums provide almost zero downside protection and little profit potential. The only investor to consider this option (and I strongly recommend against it) is someone who wants to own this stock for years and finds $10 (less commissions) to be a worthwhile dividend. But this is not an appropriate option for anyone, in my opinion—not at this price.

Moving out to November, the 17½ call carries a premium of $290 and expires in 121 days. The intrinsic value remains at $150 and the time value is $140. By writing this call, the investment cost is reduced from $1,900 to $1,610. If you earn the time premium ($140) at expiration, it represents an 8.70 percent return (26 percent annualized). Writing this option provides a good return that comes with excellent insurance against loss. The stock must dip under 16.10, a decline of 15 percent, before reaching the break-even point. As is typical when dealing with longer-term options, the annualized returns are less than those available from writing shorter-term options. Writing this call does not appeal to me because the numbers do not compare

favorably with those of the Sep 17½ call. If I decided to write a 17½ strike call option, I'd choose Aug or Sep because they afford a significantly higher annualized ROI. However, writing this option should appeal to a conservative investor who does not have time to devote to making frequent trading decisions.[8] Choosing longer-term options reduces the annualized profit potential, but it does require less work, reduces commission expenses and provides excellent downside protection. This option is worth considering for investors who prefer to trade less often.

The November 20 call is $1.65 bid. The time premium (the DOGS 20 calls are OTM and have zero intrinsic value—thus, the entire premium is time premium) provides a return of 9.5 percent ($165 on an investment of $1,735). If you write this call, you are protected if the stock dips to $17.35. These are attractive numbers. But, the annualized return does not compare favorably with the earnings potential for writing shorter-term options. This is an attractive call for the aggressive investor and moderately conservative investor who don't want to be bothered writing options every month or two.

The November 22½ call can be sold for $85, an attractive premium for an option that is fairly far out-of-the-money. Before writing this option, you must be convinced you want your capital tied up in this position for four months. Obviously, this is a good situation for long-term investors who want to own DOGS, collect an option premium and not be concerned with carefully monitoring their covered call portfolios. If the stock rallies beyond the strike price, and if eventually assigned an exercise notice, the profit ($435 or 24 percent ROI) ought to be acceptable. I'm not interested in writing this call; but because covered call writing is a very flexible strategy, and because there is no "best" call option to write, the Nov 22½ call is appealing to investors

---

8. *Even when you cannot take the time to trade often, it's important to analyze your holdings periodically. There may have been a good reason to purchase stocks you own, but is there a good reason to continue to own them? The answer is not always yes.*

who are more interested in the opportunity to earn additional profits from an increase in the stock price than in protecting their capital.

The November 25 call presents a situation similar to writing the Nov 22½ call. However, the premium ($45) is so low that I do not recommend tying up your money for four months.[9] Yet there are long-term investors who may find writing this call acceptable.

February calls don't expire for seven months. Too far in the future for me, but certainly this is a reasonable choice for investors who want to benefit from writing covered calls but want to spend as little time as possible on the process. The $350 available from writing Feb 17½ calls represents $200 in time premium (and $150 in intrinsic value). If the stock is above the strike price seven months from now, that $200 time premium becomes profit. That's a return of 12.9 percent, or 22 percent annualized (see Table 11.1). As is customary when dealing with longer-term options, the annualized return is less than that available from writing shorter-term options, but the higher premium provides greater downside protection. And there's nothing wrong with earning almost 13 percent every seven months. These numbers are fairly attractive for some conservative investors, but I wouldn't lock myself into this position for seven months.

{ *NOTE: Don't get the impression that covered call writers always earn huge returns. Bear markets wreak havoc on investors whose portfolios are laden with covered call positions. The potential 21 percent annualized profit available when writing the Feb 17½ call is outstanding. The discussion may seem to discard this potential profit as too small to bother, but nothing is further from the truth. I'm not saying you can't do better, but this is a pretty impressive return for most investors.*

The February 20 calls have an attractive premium ($240), especially for an out-of-the-money option. Writing this call offers a good combination of protection (more than 12 percent) and profit potential (14.5 percent if the stock is unchanged and 22 percent if assigned an exercise notice) for anyone willing to hold this position until February.

The premium available in the further OTM Feb calls is sufficient that the idea of selling them cannot be dismissed. You collect $155 by selling the Feb 22½ call. That's enough premium to provide some decent protection against loss. The only problem for me is the annualized ROI. It's less than I want to earn, considering that simply owning this volatile stock already carries some risk of loss. This option is an OK choice for the long-term investor who wants to adopt a buy and hold strategy with this stock.

The Feb 25 call can be sold for $95. This call may be attractive to the long-term investor who is quite bullish and who doesn't like the idea of making frequent trading decisions. But, it's not suitable for my investment philosophy. But remember: the idea is for you to write call options that suit your investment philosophy, not mine.

Style

As mentioned above, as you gain experience selecting which option to write, you eventually adopt a style of trading. You may prefer selling out-of-the-money options, hoping to make large profits as your stock increases in value. You may prefer the additional safety that comes with writing in-the-money options. Don't be surprised if you alternate between these strategies depending on market conditions. Similarly, you may decide that writing short-term options suits you best. Or perhaps mid- or even longer-term options may be more attractive. My current

---

9. *When you write the covered call option, it means you cannot sell your stock unless you repurchase the call. Many brokers don't allow you to hold a naked call position. As discussed earlier naked calls are very risky because of the possibility of unlimited losses.*

personal style involves writing short-term, in-the-money options. But that was not always my style. Not too many years ago I preferred writing options that expired in six to eight months. When you adopt a style, don't feel you have made a permanent commitment. It's OK to alter your style when you encounter different market conditions or as your investing philosophy changes over the years.

Finding your investing style involves locating your comfort zone. Many people find it psychologically satisfying to adopt CCW because of fewer (and smaller) losses and more frequent profits. If preservation of capital is important to you, then adopting one (or more) of the three basic conservative strategies will allow you to invest and remain within that comfort zone. If you are conservative with your investments, don't be tempted by the higher potential profits available from adopting the most aggressive strategies. If you can achieve your goals by adopting a conservative style, why take the risk of being more aggressive and perhaps failing to meet your goals? When you find yourself comfortable with the risks you take and with the profits you earn, you have successfully found your comfort zone.

If you prefer to be more aggressive, options can be used to seek significantly larger profits. And you can still reap the benefits of using options to hedge or reduce the risk of owning your investment positions. Being aggressive doesn't mean seeking unrealistic returns, but it does mean you must take more risk than the conservative investor. One adage in the investing world is that greater returns on your investment are not given away. To earn those greater rewards you must either have extraordinary skills or you must accept greater risk.

By working with the basic strategies, you gain the hands-on experience necessary for success with other strategies. Learning to use options

TABLE 11.2: How time to expiration affects ROI and insurance

TIME	STRIKE	ROI	ANN ROI	INSURANCE
30	17.5	2.34%	28.07%	10.00%
58	17.5	4.48%	27.79%	11.84%
121	17.5	8.70%	25.87%	15.26%
212	17.5	12.90%	21.91%	18.42%
30	20.0	8.40%	100.81%	2.89%
58	20.0	10.80%	67.06%	5.00%
121	20.0	15.27%	45.44%	8.68%
212	20.0	20.48%	34.78%	12.63%
30	22.5	19.68%	236.17%	0.53%
58	22.5	21.62%	134.20%	1.84%
121	22.5	23.97%	71.31%	4.47%
212	22.5	28.94%	49.14%	8.16%
30	25.0	31.58%	378.95%	0.00%
58	25.0	32.28%	200.33%	0.53%
121	25.0	34.77%	103.45%	2.37%
212	25.0	38.50%	65.38%	5.00%

Options are grouped by strike price. As time to expiration increases, annualized ROI decreases, but protection against loss increases. ROI increases, but when comparing trade possibilities, annualized returns are more meaningful.

successfully is a process—and the more you learn, the easier it becomes to use options.

As you gain experience deciding which specific option series[10] to write, you begin to develop an option writing style. After the DOGS example, readers who are already familiar with option trading may recognize whether they prefer the greater profit potential available when writing near-term (or OTM) options, or the additional downside protection available from longer-term (or ITM) options.

It may be too soon to recognize which covered call positions provide the secure feeling that's necessary to trade within your comfort zone. That will come later, after you trade with real money and find your own trading style. And don't expect to know right

---

10. "Series" is the term used to describe a specific option. For example, IBM Nov 105 put is a specific option series.

TABLE 11.3: Time premium vs. strike price

MONTH	STRIKE	TIME PR		MONTH	STRIKE	TIME PR	
Aug	17.5	$0.40		Nov	17.5	$1.40	
Aug	20.0	$0.55	ATM	Nov	20.0	$1.65	ATM
Aug	22.5	$0.10		Nov	22.5	$0.85	
Aug	25.0	$0.00		Nov	25.0	$0.45	
Sep	17.5	$0.75		Feb	17.5	$2.00	
Sep	20.0	$0.95	ATM	Feb	20.0	$2.40	ATM
Sep	22.5	$0.35		Feb	22.5	$1.55	
Sep	25.0	$0.10		Feb	25.0	$0.95	

ATM options have the highest time premiums.

away. It may take a bunch of trades before you recognize which style suits you best.

{ *NOTE: Just because one style proves to be more (or sadly, less) profitable than you hoped should not be the only basis for choosing a style. Comfort is just as important as profits. If you were nervous about positions that ultimately made you good money, remember that nervous feeling and decide if it's what you want to feel going forward. Comfort has its own rewards.*

Looking at the data from a different perspective

Let's summarize the discussion above by rearranging the data, making it easier to reach a final decision on which call to write. This helps you compare the relative merits of each option, and this is important, especially the first few times you adopt covered call writing. As you gain experience, some choices jump right off the page, making the selection process much more efficient. Taking the time to carefully consider each choice now hastens the day when that occurs. Let's consider the data in Tables 11.2 and 11.3.

ROI vs. time to expiration

As seen in Table 11.2, for any given strike price, the annualized ROI is greatest for the front-month option and steadily decreases as the lifetime of the option increases. That should come as no surprise. Earlier we discussed that an option's time premium erodes every day and that the rate of this time decay accelerates as expiration approaches. Thus, shorter-term options lose more time premium per day than longer-term options. When ROI is annualized, we prorate that rapid time decay, and it should not be surprising that short-term options provide the potential[11] for the highest annualized returns.

When it comes to providing downside protection, the opposite is true—short-term options provide the least protection against loss. That's understandable because the more cash you collect when writing a call, the greater the protection. And longer-term options trade at higher prices, and thus, have more time premium.

When interested in higher annualized returns, choose shorter-term options. When interested in greater protection, choose longer-term options. Don't ignore downside protection in your search for higher returns. These higher returns are accompanied by greater risk (because protection is less). As long as you are satisfied with that protection, then writing shorter-term options may be appropriate for you.

ROI vs. strike price

Look again at Table 11.1. When the ROI calculation is based on the assumption that the stock rises above the strike price and you are assigned an exercise notice, ROI increases as the strike price increases. This data is provided to enable you to see the maximum possible return on an investment. Because we never know (at least I never know—more power to you if you do)

---

11. The word "potential" has been used many times in this book. That's all it is: potential. You don't earn this profit every time. In fact, sometimes you incur a loss.

whether the stock is going to move higher or lower over the lifetime of the option, we also consider the ROI assuming the stock price is unchanged when expiration day arrives. Finishing unchanged is also an unlikely occurrence, but it provides a useful basis for generating information you can use to select the option to write.

Don't jump to the conclusion that writing the highest possible strike price is a good idea just because it gives you the chance for a very profitable trade. First, the further OTM the strike, the less likely it is that the stock rises to that level before the option expires. Second, the higher the strike price, the less premium you receive when selling the call. We not only write options to make money, but we also write call options to provide income (the greater the time premium, the better) and to obtain insurance against loss (the higher the option premium, the better). Thus, it seldom pays to write call options that are significantly out-of-the-money.

Time premium vs. strike price

The data in Table 11.3 show that a call option's time premium rises then falls as the strike price changes. The option with the most time premium for each expiration month is always exactly at-the-money (ATM). If it turns out that your option-writing style involves writing options with maximum time premium, then you can save time by concentrating on only those options with strike prices that are near the stock price.

Summary of personal preferences

Writing ATM options appeals to some investors because it offers an attractive combination of time premium and insurance against loss. The more conservative investor is likely to be more comfortable when the option is slightly in-the-money (ITM), while the majority of investors tend to be optimistic and choose to write slightly out-of-the-money (OTM) options. It's worth repeating that there's no best choice when it comes to selecting options to trade.

Timing your trades

Let's assume you've been writing covered calls for a while and have discovered that your preferred style is to write calls that are in-the-money by 1 to 2 percent and whose expiration date is 13 weeks from your trade date. If your stock is currently trading at $40 per share, it might occur to you that your preference dictates selling the covered calls when stock is priced a bit higher (between 40.40 and 40.80), enabling you to write calls with a strike price of 40 when those calls are in-the-money by 1 to 2 percent. Or when ready to sell calls, there may be no expiration 13 weeks in the future, and your choice is limited to either four, eight or 17 weeks. What should you do?

The answer to these questions depends on the reason you adopt a covered call writing strategy. If your goal is to increase your income stream by collecting time premium or if your goal is to generate income while obtaining downside protection, then waiting is counterproductive. My recommendation is to write those covered calls without waiting for conditions to be perfect After all, it may be your preference to write calls that are in-the-money by a small amount (or expire in 13 weeks), but sometimes market conditions require a bit of flexibility. Once you discover your style it will be easier to select an appropriate call to sell and choose positions that fit your comfort zone. By knowing that you prefer 13 weeks, it's an easy decision to eliminate the four-week options and choose between the eight-week and 17-week expirations.

On the other hand, if you are an investor who believes you are skilled at timing the market and that you just know the stock is going higher, you are in position to wait for the stock to rally. But, that's not going to be a successful plan for the vast majority of individual investors. From the options that are available to you now, it's probably best to write an option that best suits your current needs and takes advantage of the ticking clock. You collect time decay when selling options because options are a wasting asset. When possible, you want to gain the advantages of time working for you—and the sooner the better.

As our example with DOGS shows, writers who prefer ITM calls can use any call with a 17½ strike price to obtain both time premium and downside protection. Writers who prefer OTM calls have the potential for higher profits, but in return, they have less protection. If your preferred choice is to write calls that are very close-to-the-money,[12] you prefer the stock be nearer one of the available strike prices. But as seen with the DOGS example, you are forced to choose between writing the 17½ call, writing the 20 call, waiting for the stock price to change or finding a different stock to trade. If you don't own shares of DOGS, it's easy to find another place to invest your money. But if you already own these shares and if you want to write covered calls for the advantages we've discussed, waiting is usually not your best option.

Choosing the call to write

One of the purposes of this (lengthy) discussion is to allow you the opportunity to consider the advantages and disadvantages of choosing each call option as a CCW candidate. If you think about the various possibilities from the point of view that makes the most sense to you, your risk tolerance and your financial objectives, and not from my point of view, then you can discover how to make covered call writing a worthwhile strategy. CCW is a strategy that enhances your earnings (most of the time), but it's also a strategy you are likely to find viable for many years.

Which option to write?

We have covered a lot of territory but have not made any trades nor earned any money. Rest assured that other examples in this book are not as lengthy. It's time to make some trading decisions.

We considered writing each of the DOGS options on its own merits. Tables 11.2 and 11.3 allow you to compare the relative merits of writing options that expire in the same month or have the same strike price as each other. You can see how the time premium in an option varies with strike price and time to expiration. There's a lot of data and it may feel difficult to reach a decision when you begin using this strategy.

Because there is no single "best" call to write, several options make suitable choices to help you meet your investment objectives.

The decision, at last

For me, a fairly conservative investor, but one who is willing to accept risk to make money, there is no clear-cut decision. Three choices are very attractive, but I'm writing the Aug 17½ calls, with Sep 17½ call as a close second choice.[13] The profit potential is only $40 per option, but that provides the chance to earn an acceptable rate of return—especially when considering how much protection this call provides. It's the combination of excellent protection and a fair profit potential that appeals to me. Sure, I'd like to earn a higher rate of return, but this time I'll settle for less because of the high probability of success. If the protection were a bit less, I'd be inclined to be more aggressive and write the Aug 20 call. Thus, I'm going to enter an order to sell (to open) five DOGS Aug 17½ calls at a limit price of $1.90, or better.

When writing covered calls, compromise is the order of the day. You give up something to gain something else. What you are trying to do is adopt an investment strategy that helps you achieve your investment objectives. Thus, the covered call position should:

- Provide enough profit potential to be worthwhile. If you are too concerned with limiting losses, you may not earn enough

---

12. "Close-to-the-money" means almost at-the-money.
13. If the Aug call were 0.05 less, I'd definitely choose Sep. The decision is that close for me.

money from the trade to make it worth your time and effort.

- Provide enough insurance (some investors require very little protection) to make you comfortable with the risk and reward of the position.

In this scenario, I chose Aug 17½ call because the ROI is just too attractive, especially when bundled with such excellent downside protection. This choice is based on my conservative nature when writing covered calls. This is a prudent course to follow for those readers who are gaining their first experience with an option strategy. It's a good idea to begin using options slowly and to undertake a trade that's likely to be a winner. Once you gain more experience, if it fits your trading style and personality, you may decide to accept a little more risk in an attempt to earn a larger profit. My bottom line is: don't get greedy. You can earn good profits by adopting strategies that are less risky than simple stock ownership. Gordon Gekko may have said that "Greed is good,"[14] but earning money with reduced risk is better.

{ *NOTE: The conservative Aug 17½ is not appropriate for everyone. In this example using DOGS options, there is truly something for everyone. Unfortunately, in the real world, there are usually fewer good choices, and occasionally the choices are so poor, that it's best to find a different stock to trade.*

---

14. *In the movie, "Wall Street."*

Chapter 12

Covered Call Writing: After the Trade

It took a while to get here, but we've gone through the decision-making process and made our first trade together. Now it's time to consider what to do next. Here's a summary of the initial transaction:

- You own 500 DOGS. You continue to own those 500 shares, but cannot sell them unless you buy back the calls. (If you sell your stock, your position becomes a naked call.) If the stock pays a dividend (DOGS does not), you, the stockholder, receive it.[1]
- You received $950 from the option sale, (five DOGS Aug 17½ calls at $190 each), less commission. (Commissions vary, so be certain you know what your broker charges.) The cash goes into your account the next business day and begins to earn interest.

---

1. *The risk of not receiving the dividend is discussed later in this chapter.*

What happens next?

Once in a while you may be assigned an exercise notice prior to expiration. But don't expect it to happen because it's a rare occurrence. Let's assume time passes, nothing out of the ordinary happens (always a good situation for covered call writers), no adjustments are required and expiration arrives. There are three possibilities. This discussion is from the point of view of someone who chooses to write Aug 17½ calls.

- If you wrote options that expire later, then you still own your covered call position and you can ignore the fact that August options are expiring. But, if you substitute another appropriate month for August then this discussion applies to you.
- If you choose to write an option with a different strike price, the discussion also applies to you. Simply change the strike price from 17½ to the appropriate number.

Scenario one

DOGS has not done well, has declined below the 17.50 strike price and your options finished[2] out-of-the-money. Whoever owns the options allows them to expire worthless. The call owner has no need to exercise options to buy stock at $17.50 when it's available at a lower price. The main point for you, the call writer, is that the options expire and you are no longer under any obligation to sell stock at the strike price. You still own 500 shares of DOGS and also have the $950 premium. If the stock is above the $17.10 break-even price, you have a small profit. Next Monday when the market opens (or any time thereafter), you sell another five options against your 500 shares. If you decided not to wait for expiration and already

sold new calls before the Aug calls officially expired, I hope you repurchased the Aug calls before doing so. That prevents you from being naked short calls.

This is not the result you expected, but it's a (relatively) satisfactory result. Other investors who own DOGS lost $1.90 per share more than you did. Thus, as a covered call writer you benefited. You may not have a profit, but you are definitely better off having adopted this strategy.

Scenario two

DOGS stock closes at 17.50, and the option is at-the-money. You don't know whether the option owner takes your stock. You must wait until Monday morning to find out, although many brokers make this information available Sunday via the Internet. Please verify whether you still own your stock—preferably before the market next opens for trading.[3]

- If you have not been assigned an exercise notice, you are free to write covered calls against your stock and collect another premium.
- If you have been assigned, you no longer own this stock, but you have the proceeds from the sale and you earned the maximum possible profit for the position. Your next decision is how and when to reinvest that money.
- Occasionally you are assigned on some calls, but not all. That's OK. Proceed as above, writing the appropriate number of call options.

This is a satisfactory result. You earned the entire time premium in the option, which is the maximum profit available from this trade. If you still own the shares, you can expect to receive a good premium when writing the Sep (or Oct) 17½

---

2. "Finished" refers to the closing stock price on expiration Friday.
3. It's your broker's responsibility to notify you before the market opens, but don't stand on ceremony. If you don't know if you were assigned an exercise notice, please call your broker (before the market opens) and firmly request that information. If not assigned, you may want to write five new call options and you cannot sell those calls unless you know you own the shares. If you can look at your account online, the information you need should be readily available.

calls, because at-the-money options provide the most time premium. You may choose to write Sep or Oct 15 calls (when they are listed next Monday), if they contain sufficient time premium.

Scenario three

DOGS finishes above the strike price (as expected). You are assigned an exercise notice, thereby selling your stock and earning the maximum profit this strategy affords. You no longer own any DOGS shares. This is a satisfactory result.

All scenarios appear to afford a good result. If true, why doesn't everyone write covered calls? Why haven't brokers told all their clients about this magic bullet? Why hasn't the press raved about covered call writing? What can go wrong? What are the risks? These questions are considered below.

What do you have to gain by adopting CCW?

What do you have to gain by writing covered call options? The short answer is, to make money more consistently and with less risk, when compared with simply owning stock. The vast majority of the time that an investor adopts CCW, the goal is to earn additional profits by collecting time premium, but, as you will learn, this versatile strategy can be used to accomplish other investment objectives.

When writing a covered call, you must accept a maximum price you can receive for your shares. If that's acceptable to you (and it's not acceptable to every investor) then you are paid a cash premium that is yours to keep no matter what else happens. That cash helps you meet important investment objectives:

- Earn more frequent profits. When holding stock, the only time you earn money is when the stock price increases. When you write a covered call, you also earn money when the stock price rises—even though that amount is limited. But, you also make money when the stock price remains essentially unchanged or decreases in value—if that decrease is less than the option

premium collected. It's a comforting feeling to own stock, see it decline over the lifetime of the option, and still earn a profit!

- Insure a modest portion of the value of your investment. When you own stock, if the price drops (for example) $2 per share, your loss is $2. When writing covered calls, that loss is reduced by the option premium. Thus, if you write a call option with a premium of $0.90, your loss is only $1.10 per share—not a triumph, but a better result than achieved by the traditional investor who owns stock and who does not write covered call options.

{ NOTE: *If the idea of having extra insurance to prevent a large loss is important to you, then pay special attention to the collar strategy, thoroughly discussed in the next chapter.*

What do you have to lose? What can go wrong?

Although covered call writing is a conservative strategy, it's not without risk:

- If your stock undergoes a severe downward move, you incur a loss. The premium you receive from the call sale may only offset a portion of the loss.

- If your main objective in writing the covered call is to sell stock at the strike price, it's possible to miss the sale. For example, if the stock price climbs above your target sale price (the strike price) during the lifetime of the option, and subsequently declines and is below the strike price at expiration, the call owner does not exercise the option and you do not sell your shares. If you had entered a good 'til cancelled sell order instead of writing the covered call, the stock would have been sold when it reached your price. If the price decline (after reaching your target) is sufficiently large, you not only miss the sale but may incur a significant loss. The proceeds from the call sale reduce the loss, but that's not much of a consolation.

{ *NOTE: Some beginners are under the mistaken impression that when they write covered calls and the stock subsequently rises beyond the strike price (i.e., the call is now in-the-money) the option owner immediately exercises the option. I have no idea from whence that misconception arises, but be certain you understand that it's not true. The call owner determines if and when to exercise, and it is almost always a mistake to exercise a call option before expiration.[4] Thus, it's possible to miss selling your stock at the target price when you write a covered call.*

- If your stock rises through the strike price and makes a major advance, you cannot earn any extra money. Because you sold the call option, your maximum selling price is established (it's the strike price). You still have a good profit (some investors mistakenly believe they lose money in this situation), but this profit is less than you could have earned without the option sale.
- If you own a dividend-paying stock, it's possible to fail to collect the dividend. The call owner has the right to exercise the call any time before it expires. When the dividend is large enough, the option owner exercises (ITM options only) the day before the stock goes ex-dividend. That means you may be assigned an exercise notice and must sell your stock the day before the dividend. If the stock pays significant dividends, and if you are counting on collecting that dividend, this can be a problem. It's important to understand that not all options that are in-the-money are exercised for the dividend (see sidebar). If you do fail to receive the dividend because of an early exercise, it's not all bad news because you sell the stock at the strike price, locking in a profit. Because the stock sale occurs before expiration, you are in position to reinvest the proceeds and put the money back to work sooner than you had planned.

Exercising an Option for the Dividend

"Exercising for the dividend" means exactly what it sounds like: to exercise an option to collect the dividend. These examples discuss each situation from the point of view of the call owner, not the writer. Nevertheless, whether you're the owner or the writer, it's important to understand the decision that must be made by the call owner.

1. High-dividend stocks. HIGH pays a quarterly dividend of $0.40. The stock is trading near $22 per share and goes ex-dividend on Thursday, one day before Oct expiration. Any investor who owns the Oct 20 calls (or any lower strike) must either sell the call or exercise it for the dividend. If not, money is lost. Why? Because there's so little time remaining before expiration, there's no time premium remaining in the option (this is especially true for calls that are deeper in-the-money). The call is trading very near its intrinsic value, or $2.00. Thursday morning, the stock goes ex-dividend, and all things being equal, opens at $21.60 (closing price minus the dividend). The Oct 20 call trades near $1.60.[5] When the option is not exercised (or sold) money is lost because the option price drops from $2.00 to about $1.60 (the premium decrease equals the dividend) with the stock price unchanged (and down $0.40 is considered unchanged when the stock goes ex-dividend by $0.40). If the option owner does not want to own stock, the call can be sold. But holding it overnight is a big mistake.

---

4. *The exception is to collect a dividend.*
5. *If this is a high-volatility stock, then the option trades at a higher price. But stocks that pay such high dividends are almost never volatile.*

{ NOTE: You may ask: What's the big deal about exercising? If I buy stock by paying the strike price, doesn't the stock price drop by $40 and thus, don't I lose $40? Answer: Yes, you do "lose" the $40. But you receive the $40 dividend to make up the difference. The call owner does not receive that dividend.

2. Low-dividend stock. LOWD is a stock that pays a small quarterly dividend of two cents per share. As far as option traders are concerned, this dividend can almost be ignored. The only time it may be of concern occurs when the stock goes ex-dividend very near expiration Friday. There's no point exercising LOWD options for a dividend at other times. Why? There are three reasons: First, the cost to carry (own) the stock from the date the call is exercised through expiration must be considered and compared with the size of the dividend. Even a $20 stock costs $1.92 per week (at 5 percent interest) to own 100 shares. Thus, to own the stock for one week to collect a $2 dividend earns you only eight cents per option. Second, when you exercise an option you sacrifice any remaining time premium. Thus, collecting a small dividend is almost always a losing proposition because the volatility and interest factors that make up the time value of an option (discussed in Chapter 6) are almost always greater than the small dividend. Third and most important is risk. When you own an option, all you can lose is the value of the option, but if you exercise the call and take ownership of the stock, it's possible to lose a great deal more money if something bad happens to the stock price.

3. Front-month options are not the only options exercised for a dividend. Consider HIGH in the example above. With the stock trading at $22 per share and paying a 40-cent dividend, some Nov calls should also be exercised. The cost to carry stock for four weeks at 5 percent interest is $5.77 for the Nov 15 and $7.69 for the Nov 20.[6] Those are very low costs for collecting a $40 dividend. If the stock is sufficiently volatile (not likely for a stock that pays an 8 percent dividend), it's possible (but not likely) that the time premium in the Nov calls is too high to exercise the option.

A good question is: If you own this option, how do you know whether to exercise? When an option is an "exercise for the dividend" then there should be zero time premium in the bid price. That means the bid is equal to, or less than, the intrinsic value of the option. When you see that, if the stock is going ex-dividend the following morning, it's almost always right to exercise the option to collect that dividend. When the dividend is large enough and the option is deep in-the-money, sometimes options expiring later than the front two months are exercised for a dividend.

For those of you who use option calculators to determine the fair value of an option, if an option is an exercise for the dividend then the theoretical value of the option equals its intrinsic value and there is zero time premium.[7]

---

6. The cost of carry depends on the purchase price—and that's the strike price multiplied by 100.
7. Also, the delta is 100. Delta is discussed in Chapter 16.

Keep in mind that you limit your maximum profit when writing covered calls. You do get excellent benefits in return, but there's another risk associated with writing covered call options. It's impossible to quantify, because it's a psychological risk. If you are an investor who hates to accept anything less than the best possible result, this strategy won't work for you. Most of the time this method produces excellent results, but on occasion, not writing calls achieves a better result. That's the tradeoff, and each investor must make the decision as to whether CCW is a viable strategy.

Those are the major risks associated with selling covered calls. I believe these risks are small when compared with the benefits and that most investors should at least consider using options in this manner—especially as an excellent learning tool when first getting started with options.

When you compare the buy and hold strategy with the covered call strategy:

- Writing the call allows you to you make **more** (or lose less) money if your stock price declines.
- Writing the call allows you to you make **more** money if your stock is unchanged.
- Writing the call allows you to make **more** money if your stock goes up by a small amount.
- Writing the call makes you **less** money if your stock rises above your break-even price.[8] You still make good money, but not as much as you could have made.

There's a saying on Wall Street: "Sometimes the bulls win, sometimes the bears win, but the pigs always lose." Don't be greedy. Invest wisely, take good profits, take them often and allow the earnings to compound over time. You do very well by making good returns on many trades, even if you occasionally fail to collect a bonanza. Over the past 18-plus years, as demonstrated by BXM data (Chapter 10) buy and

hold performs on a par with covered call writing. But CCW give you a more comfortable ride—i.e., less portfolio volatility and something else that's very psychologically rewarding—the possibility of earning decent profits in years when the market declines.

Most of the time, when expiration rolls around (sometimes it seems like forever before it arrives), you are pleased with the results of CCW. Once in awhile, you do better without the call sale. Over the long run, there are many more profitable outcomes, and your portfolio undergoes fewer extreme moves.

The versatile covered call

Let's consider writing covered call options to achieve different investment objectives. CCW is a versatile strategy that helps you meet a variety of investment objectives. Most of the time when you adopt this strategy, your goal is obvious: to make money. But CCW can help you achieve different investment objectives.

Turning a non-performing stock into a profitable investment vehicle

When choosing which call option to write you must consider the reason you own the stock. For example, suppose you own shares of DULL, a company whose stock has traded in a narrow range for the past several years and has contributed no profits to your portfolio. You don't want to sell the shares at the current price because you still have confidence in the ability of the company to increase its earning power in the coming years. But you are tired of not having DULL contribute to the growth of your investment portfolio. CCW is an excellent strategy for generating income while waiting for good things to happen.

If you find yourself in this unpleasant situation, then writing out-of-the money calls is an appropriate strategy. If the stock continues to trade in its recent narrow range, the cash you collect when writing covered calls becomes your compensation for

---

8. *Just as we calculated a break-even price when the stock declines, there is also an upside break-even price and it's equal to the strike price plus the option premium. Above that price, you earn more money by not writing the covered call option.*

continuing to hold the stock. Keep in mind that this non-volatile stock is not going to have attractive premiums. In fact, you may find yourself writing calls for only 15 or 20 cents. I usually suggest ignoring such low-priced options, but in this situation, you can look at that option premium as if it's a dividend (although it's not taxed that way). If assigned an exercise notice, you'd be delighted to finally earn a profit for being a loyal shareholder because you'd only be obligated to sell your stock if DULL awakes from its lethargy and soars above the strike price. Either way you make money from this under-performing stock—you collect the "dividends" and sometimes you also earn your profit.

Selling your shares above the current market price

You can use covered call writing when you want to increase your chances of selling stock at a price higher than its current market price. This aspect of writing covered calls is seldom discussed, but it's an important tool to have in your investing arsenal and should be used much more often by investors and traders.

Let's look at an example to see how this works. Assume you own 200 shares of KIT, a retailer of kitchen appliances. You've owned this stock too long and are interested in selling—at the right price. This is an ideal scenario for writing covered calls.

EXAMPLE

Assume KIT is trading at 38 and you decide to sell your shares if it trades as high as 40. The traditional method for selling those shares is to enter a good 'til cancelled (GTC) order with your broker to sell 200 shares at $40. If the stock rises to that level you sell your shares. If not, then you continue to own the shares. Once you enter the order, there's nothing more to do (except remember that the order is outstanding). If your sell order is executed, your broker notifies you. If the stock doesn't reach your price, nothing happens.

Covered call writing offers a superior alternative. Instead of placing the GTC order, you can write a covered call option that gives someone else the right to buy your stock. As you know, when you write that call option, you receive an immediate cash payment. Let's look at options you can write that increase your chances of selling stock at $40.

Consider the options listed in Table 12.1. Notice that there are no strike prices above 40. It's not that those options aren't available to trade, it's because you have no reason to consider writing them. Remember, your goal is to sell stock at $40, and you are trying to use covered call

TABLE 12.1: KIT call options, stock 38.00, implied volatility 31, 25 days before February expiration

MONTH	TIME	STRIKE	BID	ASK	TIME PR	ROI	ANN ROI	INSURANCE
Feb	25	35.0	$3.30	$3.50	$0.30	0.86%	12.45%	8.68%
Feb		40.0	$0.50	$0.60	$0.50	4.00%	57.60%	1.32%
Mar	53	35.0	$3.70	$3.90	$0.70	2.04%	13.86%	9.74%
Mar		40.0	$1.00	$1.20	$1.00	5.41%	36.72%	2.63%
Apr	81	35.0	$4.10	$4.30	$1.10	3.24%	14.42%	10.79%
Apr		40.0	$1.45	$1.65	$1.45	6.70%	29.79%	3.82%
Jul	172	35.0	$5.20	$5.40	$2.20	6.71%	14.04%	13.68%
Jul		40.0	$2.70	$2.90	$2.70	10.48%	21.94%	7.11%

Finding the best option to write when goal is selling stock at $40 per share.

writing to increase your chances of achieving that result. If you sell calls with a strike price of 40, and if you are assigned an exercise notice, you not only achieve your goal, but, as an added bonus, you keep the option premium. There is no need to consider options with a higher strike price.

When choosing the option to write in this scenario, I look for a trade that gives me the *best chance* to unload my 200 shares of KIT and collect at least $40 per share. If I enter a GTC order to sell stock at $40, although there's always the chance of being lucky, the order probably goes unfilled because KIT has not been doing well and I see no reason for it to suddenly come to life. I can improve my chances by writing covered calls, and here's how I consider my options:

If I choose a call with a $40 strike price, and if I am lucky enough to be assigned an exercise notice, then I'll obviously accomplish my objectives. But, I don't really believe this stock has a good chance to move above 40 any time soon. (I hope I am wrong about this.) If I write the March 40 calls, collecting $100 for each option, and if they expire worthless, I can meet my target by selling the shares at $39.[9] If the stock is lower than 39, I can repeat the process by writing Apr or May 40 calls (May options are listed for trading after the March expiration). If I repeatedly collect a $1 premium when selling calls, sooner or later I'll collect enough premium to achieve my $40 target by simply unloading the stock.[10] But, it's not quite that simple. If the stock moves lower, the $40 strike price moves further out-of-the-money and the premium for writing calls also declines. There's also the risk of the stock moving substantially lower, eliminating all possibility of selling near $40. Writing covered call options again and again (as each expires worthless), looks like a great method, but in the

real world stocks sometimes decline, making the plan unworkable.

To provide some protection against a decline in the stock price, I can sell the Jul 40 call and collect $270. I'd have an additional $1.70 per share of downside protection, but I don't like the idea that Jul is so far in the future. But there's a tradeoff. If those calls eventually expire worthless, I meet my objective by selling my 200 shares at $37.30 or higher ($2.70 now and $37.30 later is still $40.)[11]

Writing the Jul 40 call is a compromise—a higher premium, but a longer time before expiration day arrives. I must decide which gives me the better chance to meet my goal. If I choose the Mar 40 call, I'd have to hope the stock is $39 or higher 53 days from today. And if it's not that high, I'd still be OK if the premium for the May 40 makes it attractive to write. If I choose the Jul 40 call, the stock must be $37.30 or higher. That's more protection to the downside, but I'd have to wait 18 additional weeks. Who knows where the stock will be trading at that time? I certainly have no idea. It's a difficult choice. But, before I reach a final decision, I must consider alternatives. Can I achieve my objective by writing any of the 35 calls?

Yes I can. The Jul 35 call can be sold for a premium of $5.20 per share. I know July is still months in the future, but if the stock remains above 35 when July expiration arrives (and that's a reasonable hope), I achieve my goal because I collect $520 now, and another $3,500 when assigned an exercise notice in July. I'm not thrilled with the prospect of holding KIT that long, but there's an excellent chance the stock is above $35 at that time. And I'd rather collect more cash right now just in case something bad happens to KIT shares.

---

9. *$1 for writing the call now plus $39 for selling the stock later gives me my $40 selling price.*
10. *If I write calls four times, collecting $1 for each, I can sell stock as low as $36.*
11. *I'm ignoring the additional cost of carrying the stock for such a long time because if I own stock and enter a GTC order to sell my shares at $40, I still pay the cost to carry stock.*

I don't have to consider the return on my investment because my only reason for writing this call is to find a way to unload my shares at $40, and I'm looking for the best way to accomplish that. Selling the Jul 35 call gives me the highest probability of collecting at least $40 for my shares. As with all option trades, this choice is not without some risk. If the stock trades at 40 soon, I'd quickly sell the shares with a GTC order. But if I write the call, my cash is tied up in this position until Jul expiration arrives—or until I am assigned an exercise notice.[12] There's very little chance of being assigned an exercise notice before expiration, so the decision is: Do I lock myself in this position for six months with an excellent chance of meeting my investment objective, do I enter a GTC sell order and hope for the best or should I write one of the calls with a 40 strike price? Once again, there's no "best" answer for every investor, but I'm writing those Jul 35 calls. It's tempting to write the March 40 calls, but I'd rather make the trade that gives me the best overall chance of selling KIT at $40.

As mentioned earlier, this is a great way to use an option strategy—and most investors are not aware that this method is available to them. It also presents an opportunity for you to demonstrate some stock market savvy the next time someone you know is discussing plans to sell stock if and when it reaches a target price. Just ask, "Have you considered writing covered calls to give yourself a much better chance to sell your stock?"

Covered call writing is a good option strategy to get you started in your option trading career. By reducing risk, it helps you own a less volatile portfolio. It also gives you a real world opportunity to see how options work when they are part of your portfolio. By writing (covered) options as your initial strategy, instead of buying options, you begin with a method that has a high probability of earning money.

Before moving on to the second of our three basic conservative strategies, let's pause for a very

important discussion that helps you trade more effectively and efficiently. And that means more money in your pocket.

Risk management

Many investors who choose to adopt covered call writing as an options strategy have experience owning individual stocks. For those investors, there's not much to say about risk management. We all know that stocks have a tendency to rise over time, but there are periods in which stocks go nowhere, as well as times when stock prices collapse.

I assume that those investors have some risk management plan in place—some point at which they reach a logical decision. Perhaps their plan is to judiciously sell a small portion of holdings, or maybe their plan is to slowly add new positions to their portfolio. The point is to have a plan so that you do not get caught in a panic situation in which you dump all, or a significant portion of, your investment portfolio right near the market bottom (when the pressure of mounting losses becomes unbearable).

When you adopt CCW as an investment strategy, the good times take care of themselves. However, some attention must be paid to the possibility of a severe market correction. It usually comes when least expected and can be quite punishing. When you write covered calls, you have a modicum of protection against loss. More conservative investors have more safety, but the protection is limited and large downturns produce losses, even when writing covered calls. In the following chapter, you'll learn about the collar strategy, which goes one step further than writing covered calls and offers (for a price) some assurance that your portfolio isn't hurt in a market downturn. For now, let's look at risk management from the point of view of a covered call writer.

If you already have a risk management plan from your days as a stockholder, reexamine those

---

12. Reminder: while the option is still outstanding I have a potential obligation to deliver the shares. Thus, I cannot sell my shares unless I also buy back the call option to eliminate that obligation.

plans to determine if you believe the plan is still appropriate now that you are planning to expand your investment horizons.

The major risk when writing covered calls is a severe decline in the shares of the asset underlying your calls. The simplest method to cut risk is to unload the position. I'm not recommending you do that, merely mentioning that it's the simplest path. If you do decide to sell some of your stock, it's necessary to repurchase one call option for each 100 shares of stock sold.

Because you are venturing into the world of options, it's comforting to know there are option strategies available to help minimize your losses and reduce (but not eliminate) the possibility of further losses—if the stock continues to decline. I'd like to provide one piece of advice: It's OK to lose money on some positions. Don't hold onto a position just because you cannot tolerate taking a loss. If you do lose money on a position and decide to take that loss, you can reinvest that same cash into a position with better prospects. Isn't that what matters most? Don't you want your money invested where you believe you can earn profits? It shouldn't matter to you which stocks provide those profits. Your goal is to grow your portfolio. Too many investors get married to a position, vowing to stay with it until it becomes profitable. Many successful traders know to cut losses. The fact that options allow you to mitigate some of those losses and adjust the position to give you a good chance to turn that loss into a profit does not mean you must make that attempt. If your reason for owning the stock has changed, if this stock is no longer attractive to you, there is no reason to continue to own it. I reiterate—it doesn't matter where you earn your profits, just as long as you earn them.

When you want to continue to own a stock that has moved against you, there are steps you can take. The most frequently used (and abused) method is known as rolling the position. When you roll, you repurchase the options sold previously, and simultaneously (or very shortly thereafter) sell a different option. In the case of a covered call gone bad the roll is "down and out," which means that the call is rolled down to a lower strike price and out to a more distant expiration. The purpose of such a roll is to take in more cash, and that cash provides additional protection against a further decline. Let's look at an example to see how this works.

EXAMPLE

You bought 1,000 shares of FIXT, a local business that provides handyman, plumbing and electrician services. You hope this chain grows into a nationwide business. You paid $32.50 for your shares and sold 10 Dec 30 calls that expire in two months. You received $4.00 for each call, establishing your break-even price as $28.50.[13] You felt reasonably secure with this position, but two weeks later the company pre-announces that earnings are lower than expected. The morning after the news is released, the stock opens at $28 and quickly drifts to $27.50. This is not a total disaster, but it's certainly unpleasant. In only two weeks the stock is lower than your break-even point. You decide that this stock is worth holding, but you are not going to sit still and take a further beating without protecting your position. You decide to buy back your Dec 30 call, paying $1 (which is more than you'd like to pay, but you are getting a nice price on the option you are selling) and sell the Jan 25 call for $5.20. You collect a net credit[14] of $420 for each of 10 spreads. A spread is a simultaneous transaction in which you trade two or more different options. In this case, you bought Dec 30 calls (to close) and sold Jan 25 calls (to open). There is further discussion on spreads in Part III.

---

13. You paid $32.50 and collected $4. Your net cost is $28.50 and you lose no money if FIXT is above that price when expiration arrives in December.

14. The cash collected for the combination trade. If it costs cash, you pay a debit.

Because you collected cash, your break-even price has been reduced by $4.20 and is now $24.30, excluding commission expenses. You are now obligated to sell your shares at $25, and thus, your profit potential is small. To earn that profit, the stock must be above 25 when January expiration arrives in seven weeks. The profit potential may be fairly small ($700 total), but the good news is that you have *any* profit potential considering that you just bought a stock that tumbled more than 15 percent only two weeks after you bought it. But your immediate concern is not whether you have a profit when this position is closed, but how you can best preserve your assets by not taking another beating on this position.

You have now rolled your position and you own the FIXT Jan 25 covered call position. This is not a perfect position, and the stock could easily head lower, but you have made the decision (for now) to continue to own your investment in the company. Your FIXT investment is safer than it was this morning before you rolled. But this is not a position that's guaranteed to become profitable. You intend to keep an eye on the stock and decide if this investment fits into your comfort zone, or if further action must be taken.

Rolling the position is not the only method available to mitigate risk. Another method used by some gamblers—the martingale betting system[15]—is too risky to consider here. Let's just say that the idea is to double the position at the lower price, hoping the stock recovers—and then double once again if it continues to move against you. This approach is far too risky to be worth your time.

We'll go no further at this point, except to mention that one way to be certain that further losses are small is to purchase put options for protection. One reason many investors prefer not to do that is because those options are not cheap—especially after the stock (or the entire market) undergoes a sharp decline. If you do buy those puts to protect your covered call, you convert the position into a collar, and that brings us to the next basic strategy.

---

15. *The strategy has the gambler double the bet after each loss, so that the first win recovers all previous losses plus the original stake. Such a gambler requires infinite wealth and thus, the method does not work in the real world.*

1. Writing covered calls is a strategy with unlimited profit potential.

○ **TRUE**   ○ **FALSE**

2. When compared with a buy and hold strategy, writing covered calls increases your chances of making money.

○ **TRUE**   ○ **FALSE**

3. Covered call writing is an ideal strategy for the investor who wants to quickly double the value of an investment portfolio.

○ **TRUE**   ○ **FALSE**

4. When you start a new position by buying 300 shares of stock and writing three call options, you are:

A. Selling three calls to open
B. Selling three calls to close
C. Buying three calls to open
D. Buying three calls to close

5. As the writer of covered calls, you:

A. Have no control over the exercise decision
B. Decide if and when the call option is to be exercised

6. The option with the largest time premium is:

A. ITM (in-the-money)
B. ATM (at-the-money)
C. OTM (out-of-the-money)

7. From these choices (all are on the same underlying asset and expire in the same month), the call option with the highest premium (price) is:

A. ITM (in-the-money)
B. ATM (at-the-money)
C. OTM (out-of-the-money)

8. From these choices (all the same strike price and underlying stock), the call option that has the highest premium (price) expires in:

A. The front month
B. Three months
C. Six months

9. Rolling a position is a risk-reducing technique used when your covered call position is not working as expected. Why does it reduce the risk of losing additional money?

10. CCW is a method you can use to increase your chances of selling stock at your target price.

○ **TRUE**   ○ **FALSE**

Chapter 13

Collars: The Ultimate Portfolio Insurance Policy

If the idea of writing covered calls appeals to you, but you are uneasy about the possibility of losing substantial sums in the event of a sudden decline in the stock market, then the strategy of using options to "collar" the value of your investment is right up your alley. When you collar an investment, you establish a maximum value that your investment can achieve (identical to the covered call writing process), but you also lock in a minimum value by buying an insurance policy. Buy and hold investors have neither the disadvantage of limited profits nor the advantages of limited losses.

Those minimum and maximum values are set when you establish the collar position, and you can set those values wherever you prefer. As you might expect, the more profit potential you allow or the more insurance you demand, the more the collar costs. When using collars, my goal is to pay no cash out of pocket for the collar. It's possible to choose strike prices so you collect cash when opening the collar, with the opportunity to earn satisfactory profits. Keep in mind that because you are protected against a significant loss when you own a collar, and because that protection is not free, the profit potential is even more limited than when you write covered calls. This strategy is not appropriate for investors who seek substantial capital gains, but is better suited for conservative investors for whom preservation of capital is their primary investment objective.

One other advantage of owning collars is that these positions significantly reduce your portfolio volatility. If you prefer not to see large swings in the market value of your holdings, then owning collars limits those swings. Traditional stockholders always see their stocks rise and fall in value. If you have the skills to select stocks that continue to rise as time passes, or if you have the ability to sell some of your holdings near market tops and reinvest your cash near market bottoms, then there's little need for you to use collars. However, if your stocks regularly rise and fall and if you prefer to limit the peaks and valleys in your net worth, then collars may represent what you need. Although the primary purpose in learning to use options is to generate additional income, the very important secondary purpose is to help you reduce risk and protect your portfolio holdings. The collar strategy places emphasis on the protective properties of options.

The collar strategy is underutilized because it appears to be so conservative. But those who adopt the collar strategy to secure the value of an investment portfolio also have the opportunity to earn significant profits. And that possibility is often overlooked by today's investors. Learning how collars work is an important part of an options education because it provides an opportunity to see how put options can be used as an insurance policy.

Another reason relatively few people adopt collars is that most investors simply are unaware that this strategy exists. This unfortunate situation is one of the results when brokers, doing their clients a great disservice, fail to educate investors about the benefits of using options.

Collars represent an ideal investing method for obtaining an insurance policy to protect your portfolio against a large loss. People buy insurance for their homes, cars and other valuable assets, but few understand that collars can be used as insurance protection for their life savings. And the best part is that the collar can be structured so that this insurance policy costs nothing (but it does limit profit potential). If this sounds too good to be true, it's not. But there's a tradeoff. Any investor willing to accept a cap on his or her potential profits can gain the benefits of using collars.

The collar defined

A collar is a position consisting of three parts, or legs:

- Long stock
- Short call
- Long put

The term, "collar," is derived from the fact that a collar, or limit, is placed on the maximum profit or loss that can be attained from the position. What makes owning a collar so different from a traditional investment is that you have insurance against the possibility of incurring large losses. When you own stock, it's unlikely, but possible, that something bad can happen and the stock's value could be cut in half (or even worse). When you own a collar, you are protected against that possibility. Because of this insurance feature, collars are an attractive investment choice for the conservative investor.

If you are not a conservative investor, it still pays to understand how collars work because in Part III you will learn how to adopt a strategy that provides the same safety features as the collar, but which can be used by very aggressive investors trying to earn much higher returns from their investments.

Dissecting the collar

Let's look at the three legs that constitute a collar more closely. The first two legs, long stock plus a short call should be familiar. It's a covered call position, the first of our three basic conservative option strategies. As you already know, when you use the covered call, your upside profit potential is limited, but the strategy is attractive because it allows you to make money as the value of the call option erodes over time.

The third leg, or the purchase of a put option, converts a covered call into a collar. Owning the put protects the value of your investment against a catastrophe because that put grants you the right to sell your stock at the strike price, no matter how low the stock may go. On the other hand, the put must be purchased, and most of the time it loses value as time passes,[1] and thus reduces profits earned when the stock price increases. Is it worth reducing your profit potential to have an insurance policy? That's the decision you must make for yourself. But for many, it's the insurance policy that makes this investment method so attractive.

When establishing a collar position, both the put you purchase and the call you sell are out-of-the-money options (most of the time).

First, the bad news:

The put option is not free. By buying the put, you reduce your profit potential.

Next, the (very) good news:

When you establish the collar, you limit your losses. No matter how far the stock market, or your individual stock, tumbles, you always have the right to sell that stock at a predetermined price—the put's strike price. This provides peace of mind and real security.

As an aside, it amazes me that this investment methodology is not taught to every novice investor by the brokerage houses. Some brokers provide seminars on the basic use of options, but teaching options rookies how to insure the value of a portfolio ought to be something that brokers want to do for their customers. It's an especially valuable concept for beginners who lack the experience to recognize that bear markets can wipe out a substantial portion of every investor's net worth.

Collars can be structured so that the profit potential is substantial. By choosing appropriate strike prices for the put and call, you can always generate cash when establishing your collar. And that cash represents an important part of your profit potential.

What do you want to happen when you own a collar?

When opening the position, it's usually best to collect cash by selling the call at a higher premium than you pay for the put, although you may not always choose to do so. If the underlying stock remains essentially unchanged over the lifetime of the options, then both options expire worthless and the initial cash you collected becomes your profit. This profit is not available to the stockholder who simply owns the shares without bothering to establish a collar position.

You also earn a profit whenever the stock trends higher or declines by a small amount. The only time you lose money (a limited amount) when you own a collar occurs if the cash collected from the options is insufficient to offset a loss resulting from a small decline in the stock price. We are referring to those situations in which the decline is relatively small and the stock remains above the put's strike price. The value of the collar becomes apparent when the stock plunges below the put's strike and you cut your losses by exercising your put option.

---

1. It loses value most of the time because it only gains value when the stock price drops sufficiently.

The collar strategy is profitable most of the time, yet few investors find it attractive because profits tend to be small. But, the insurance aspect should encourage more and more conservative investors to adopt collars. Are you one of them?

To get a better idea of how all this works, let's consider some examples.

EXAMPLE

A basic collar

You own 500 shares of DECK, a company that manufactures playing cards and accessories. DECK last traded at $33 per share. You decide to establish a collar for your 500 shares by selling five call options and buying five put options. Assuming the third Friday of October (expiration) is six weeks from today, you decide to:

- *Sell five DECK Oct 35 calls*
- *Buy five DECK Oct 30 puts*

If the implied volatility (IV) of DECK October options is 35, (assuming interest rates are 5 percent and the stock pays no dividend), you can expect to receive approximately $60 for each call and be required to pay $30 for each put.[2] If you require a refresher about how options are priced, refer to Chapter 6. Thus, the net credit (cash collected) for each combination (buy put, sell call) is $30 and you collect a total of $150 for your 5-lot.

What happens next?

Let's assume you hold this position through expiration.

Scenario one. DECK closes between the strike prices (30 and 35). Both options expire worthless.

You collected $150 in option premium, and you keep that cash with no further obligations. This is a good result for you. Compared with an investor who owns 500 shares but doesn't establish a collar, you earn an additional $150.

Scenario two. DECK is above the higher (call) strike price. Your puts are out-of-the-money and you allow them to expire worthless.

The calls you sold are in-the-money and you are assigned an exercise notice. You sell your DECK shares at the strike price, or $35 per share.

This is a good result for you. You not only keep the $150 in option premium, but you also sell your shares at $35. Over the six-week lifetime of the options, you earned $2 per share on $500 shares (that's $1,000) plus the $150 in option premium. Your net profit is $1,150, less commission. This represents the maximum profit available from this collar position.

It's possible that this is not the optimum result. If DECK shares last traded above $35.30 (the price at which you earn a profit of $1,150 without having a collar position), then those investors who own stock without a collar earn more money by simply holding the shares. That's OK. First, you cannot expect to make the maximum possible profit on every trade. Second, without the collar you wouldn't own an insurance policy, and owning that policy is worth something to you.

You opened the collar position for two reasons. First, to prevent a big loss. Mission accomplished. Second, to allow yourself the opportunity to make a decent profit. Mission accomplished once again. To give yourself these benefits, you must sacrifice something. That sacrifice is accepting a limited profit. This time, the collar did limit your gain. If you find that upsetting, if you feel that you must always make the maximum on any trade, then you are going to have a difficult time accepting any strategies recommended in this book. Options are used to for hedging purposes—and although that reduces potential losses, you must accept the fact that it also reduces potential profits.

The objective of this book is to help you adopt methods that allow your portfolio to grow

---

2. You are not expected to determine these prices in your head. I used an online calculator.

consistently year after year and to reduce the chances of large losses. If your goal is to ignore risk in an attempt to maximize your profits, none of the basic conservative strategies is going to suit your investment style. Be patient, because your needs are addressed in Part III.[3]

This is the opportune time to reiterate a point made earlier. Some brokers charge a high fee for an exercise or assignment, while others charge nothing. Some brokers charge much higher commissions to buy or sell stocks and options than others. If you are not using a deep discount broker for these collar positions, then your profits are less than they should be. If you believe it's in your best interests to use a full service broker, please be certain that your broker provides services that warrant those higher fees. If not, it's OK to maintain an account with that broker, but you can also open another account with a deep discount broker for your option-related trading.

Scenario three. DECK is below the lower (put) strike price. (Bummer!) The calls are OTM and expire worthless. Your puts are ITM and you exercise them, thereby selling your shares at the strike price ($30).

This is not the result you wanted. Yet, by establishing a collar, you saved yourself some cash. First you keep the $150 in option premium, reducing your loss by $150. Second, by selling shares at $30, you prevent an even larger loss because DECK is currently trading lower than $30 (how much lower is not an important part of this discussion, but if it's significantly lower, your collar saved a bundle).

You opened the collar position to protect yourself against a big loss. This time the collar served its purpose. It's unfortunate that you suffered a loss, but as is true whenever you collect on an insurance policy, the loss is limited to the deductible.[4]

Instead of the relatively small loss incurred, would you have preferred a much smaller loss?

You can meet that objective that by buying a put with a higher strike price. When you do that, it's much more difficult to earn a profit because the cost of the put is so high. As we consider additional examples, you learn to choose the strike prices to change the risk/reward parameters of the collar. When you play with the numbers, you see that it costs money to reduce possible losses. You make a decision that gives you the best compromise for your situation. You cannot insure the entire value of your portfolio and still give yourself the chance to earn huge profits. It's always a tradeoff.

In-depth analysis when initiating the position

Let's take a look at another example. This time we'll carefully examine each decision made by the investor.

EXAMPLE

A hot stock

You decide that biotechnology represents the wave of the future, and after careful research, you decide to buy 400 shares of WDRG (WonderDrug Inc.), paying $31 per share. You buy these shares with the expectation of making a good-sized profit, but because you recognize that this stock has a history of being extremely volatile, you come to the conclusion that it pays to give up some upside profitability for downside protection. You plan to insure the value of your investment by initiating the position as a collar.

Let's look at the available call and put options and decide which are best suited for your purposes. In this case, you are willing to lose some (but not too much) money if your hunch on this company doesn't prove to be successful, but you insist on giving yourself the chance to make a good-sized profit. After all, you are buying the shares for its upside potential.

---

3. *Gains are still limited but can be substantial.*
4. *The lower the strike price of the put you buy, the larger the "deductible."*

The option data is presented in Tables 13.1 through 13.4. Note that option premiums are much higher for WDRG options than they were for DECK—and that's because WDRG is much more volatile than DECK. Investors pay higher prices for options when the underlying stock is volatile. The current implied volatility of WDRG is 50.

TABLE 13.1: WDRG Jul call options, stock at 31.00, 35 days before expiration, IV 50

EXP	STRIKE	BID	ASK	TIME PR	MAX GAIN
Jul	17.5	$13.50	$13.80	$0.00	$0.00
Jul	20.0	$11.00	$11.30	$0.00	$0.00
Jul	22.5	$8.50	$8.80	$0.00	$0.00
Jul	25.0	$6.20	$6.50	$0.20	$0.20
Jul	27.5	$4.00	$4.30	$0.50	$0.50
Jul	30.0	$2.40	$2.60	$1.40	$1.40
Jul	35.0	$0.55	$0.75	$0.55	$4.55
Jul	40.0	$0.10	$0.20	$0.10	$9.10

July calls for WonderDrug, Inc.

TABLE 13.2: WDRG Aug call options, stock at 31.00, 63 days before expiration, IV 50

EXP	STRIKE	BID	ASK	TIME PR	MAX GAIN
Aug	17.5	$13.50	$13.80	$0.00	$0.00
Aug	20.0	$11.10	$11.40	$0.10	$0.10
Aug	22.5	$8.60	$8.90	$0.10	$0.10
Aug	25.0	$6.50	$6.80	$0.50	$0.50
Aug	27.5	$4.60	$4.90	$1.10	$1.10
Aug	30.0	$3.10	$3.40	$2.10	$2.10
Aug	35.0	$1.20	$1.40	$1.20	$5.20
Aug	40.0	$0.35	$0.55	$0.35	$9.35

August calls for WonderDrug, Inc.
Time Pr = time premium (option price less intrinsic value)
Max Gain = profit per share, if assigned an exercise notice

Call option (Tables 13.1 and 13.2)

I'd like to collect a large premium for the call I sell, but I also believe in the future of this company. There's a distinct possibility that WDRG has an edge when it comes to finding the next big drug in the fight against cancer. Thus, there's no reason to write in-the-money calls. I'm planning to write OTM options—either the 35 or 40 strike price (the stock is currently $31). But before I make the final decision, I'll consider the other options just in case one of them offers an excellent combination of time premium and downside protection.

Deep in-the-money call options are bid no higher than parity (the option's intrinsic value) for July and barely above parity for August. When selling an ITM call, the time premium represents the profit potential, and these options have none. Thus, selling in-the-money options is inappropriate.

What about selling an at-the-money call, such as the Jul 30 or Aug 30? The Jul 30 call can be sold for approximately $2.40. That's $1 in intrinsic value (the stock is $31) and $1.40 in time value. The $1.40 is attractive, but I'm too bullish on this stock to accept this premium. The Aug 30 call doesn't do it for me either, as an additional $70 in time premium is not good enough to make me change my mind. I'll stick with my original plan and look at the OTM calls. With a more neutral outlook on this stock, these ATM calls would be more appealing.

I can sell calls that expire in either five or nine weeks. The Jul 40 only pays a dime (i.e., 10 cents per share or $10 per contract) and for that price, I'm not going to sell calls. I can get $35 for the Aug 40 call, and I can probably get $40 or $45 if there's trading volume in these options. I note that the open interest is over 500 contracts, so there's a chance I can split the market[5] and sell my calls above the bid price. If the stock zooms above 40, I have a nice profit, but I don't expect to be that

---

5. Enter an offer (or a bid) that is between the current bid and ask. In other words, I can try to receive a higher price by offering my calls below the current ask price.

lucky, especially before expiration (although I have high hopes that it happens later).

Perhaps it's wiser to write the 35 call. It has a much higher premium, and if the stock rallies that far, I'll earn $4 per share profit, in addition to the option premium. That's pretty good for just a few weeks. I prefer selling the near-term option, as it usually generates the highest annualized bang for the buck. But this time, I can get $55 or $60 for the five-week option (Table 13.1), and I can get at least double that for the nine-week option (Table 13.2). Thus, in this situation, the nine-weeker offers a higher annualized return.[6]

That feels right. I'll try to sell Aug 35 calls. But I'll offer four calls at $1.30, trying to collect a few extra dollars. But, I won't be stubborn. I already own the stock and I'd like to get the calls sold as quickly as possible. If I can't get a fill within a half-hour, I'll reconsider my price.

Put option (Tables 13.3 and 13.4)

There aren't many good choices where the puts are concerned. I don't want to buy a deep in-the-money put option because I'm too bullish on this stock and these puts cost far more than I'm willing to spend. I'd only do that if I wanted to be certain to sell my shares when expiration arrives. So I'll consider other choices. Because I'm selling Aug calls, I'm buying Aug puts. If I buy a put that expires in July, after July expiration I would own long stock and be short Aug calls (a covered call position). I would be forced to buy Aug puts to maintain the collar on my investment. It's almost always better to establish the collar by having a position in which both options expire at the same time.

The 17.5s, 20s, 22.5s and 25s are all inexpensive options, but I'd hate to sell my stock at 25 (or lower). That potential loss represents a greater risk than I want accept. If I buy the Aug 25 puts at $50

and sell the Aug 35 calls at my price of $130, I'll net $80 cash. That means in the worst-case scenario, I'll be forced to sell my shares at 25, losing $6 per share (I'm buying stock at 31). The $320 ($80 for each collar) reduces the loss to $2,080, but that's not much consolation. Those puts don't feel right. I want better protection.

Let's see what happens if I buy the 27.5 puts. I'll have to pay $1.10, or perhaps $1.05.

That results in a small credit because I'm selling calls at approximately 1.30. If forced to sell my shares at 27.5, I'd lose $3.50 per share. That's a loss of $1,400, minus the $100 or so that I net for the options—a good-sized loss, but acceptable under these conditions. I really like the prospects of this company. If I were a more conservative investor, I wouldn't settle for these numbers. Of course, a much more conservative investor would never buy WDRG, so there's no reason to dwell on that.

TABLE 13.3: WDRG put options, stock at 31.00, 35 days before expiration, IV 50

EXP	STRIKE	BID	ASK
Jul	17.5	0.00	0.10
Jul	20.0	0.00	0.10
Jul	22.5	0.00	0.20
Jul	25.0	0.10	0.25
Jul	27.5	0.45	0.65
Jul	30.0	1.35	1.55
Jul	35.0	4.40	4.70
Jul	40.0	8.90	9.20

July puts for WonderDrug, Inc.

TABLE 13.4: WDRG put options, stock at 31.00, 63 days before expiration, IV 50

EXP	STRIKE	BID	ASK
Aug	17.5	0.00	0.20
Aug	20.0	0.00	0.20
Aug	22.5	0.10	0.30
Aug	25.0	0.30	0.50
Aug	27.5	0.90	1.10
Aug	30.0	1.90	2.10
Aug	35.0	4.90	5.20
Aug	40.0	9.00	9.30

August puts for WonderDrug, Inc.

---

6. Earning $60 in five weeks is clearly less, when annualized, than earning twice as much ($120) in less than twice as much time (nine weeks vs. five weeks).

My mind is made up. I'll bid $1.05 for the puts and try to sell the calls at $1.30. If I am unable to trade these options at my prices within in a few (10 to 30) minutes, I'll change my order and hope I can get filled at the current price of $1.10 and $1.20.

BOTTOM LINE: The collar is established by buying stock at $31, selling Aug 35 calls at 1.30 (my price) and buying Aug 27.5 puts at $1.10 (a nickel higher than I had hoped to pay). I collected a total of $80 for the option trades. My net cost for the stock is $30.80 per share.

- Maximum possible profit occurs if I sell stock at 35 (a profit of $1,680).
- Maximum possible loss occurs if forced to sell stock at 27.5 (a loss of $1,320).

Post-expiration decisions

As expiration day approaches, it's important to have a basic plan. If it appears that you have no remaining position because either the calls or puts are in-the-money (you exercise puts, or are assigned an exercise notice on the calls—either of which results in no residual position), it's a good idea to know if you want to reestablish a new position in the same stock.

Once expiration has come and gone, if you no longer own the shares, your choices are to:

- Reinvest the proceeds of the sale in shares of the same stock. You may feel the stock is bargain priced and want to reinvest, or perhaps you feel the stock has risen rapidly and you are sorry you sold the shares and want to reestablish a position.
- Remain in cash.
- Invest the proceeds in a different stock.

It's a good idea to keep an updated list of new investment ideas for times when you have cash to invest.

If the stock has undergone a steep decline and you chose to exercise your puts, you have two ways to look at the situation. The stock has performed badly and some investors, seeing how badly the stock has performed, are thankful they owned puts and have no further interest in the stock. Other investors feel that the stock has dropped to such a low level that they want to repurchase the shares. These investors cannot resist the temptation to own the shares again—because the price is so low. This is one of those decisions each investor must make on his or her own.

The most likely outcome: The options expire worthless

Depending on your style and the strike prices you choose, much of the time the calls and puts expire worthless. As a result, you continue to own the shares. You will probably want to establish a new collar. The usual procedure is to place that order Monday morning following expiration. If you adopt that policy, you are taking a very small, but real, risk that bad news might come to light over the weekend. If that happens, the stock could open significantly lower Monday morning and all the effort you made to maintain a collar position would be for naught. Of course, there's also an equal chance that good news is released, resulting in a higher stock price. If you want to take this risk, and it really is a small risk, that's up to you. To eliminate that risk, you can roll the position Thursday or Friday of expiration week (refer to Chapter 12). When you own a collar, rolling involves both puts and calls.

Let's assume that WDRG performed well and closed last Friday at 33.50 per share. The puts and calls expired. It's now Monday, following August expiration and you want to set up a new collar.

EXAMPLE

Shifting strike prices

You still own 400 shares of WDRG, but the company has issued a news release that may play a significant role in the company's future. WonderDrug has been testing a promising, new medicine and is announcing the results of phase I trials within two or three weeks.

Because news is pending and there is a strong probability that the news will have a major impact on the stock price, there has been a great deal of interest in the options. Option volume has quadrupled, and the demand for both puts and calls has driven the price of all options higher. As is typical in such situations, the near-term options—the ones you want to trade—are in greatest demand. Some players, expecting good news, have bid the calls significantly higher, which means the implied volatility (IV) is above is normal range. The out-of-the-money call options are trading with an IV over 80. That's good news for you because those are the calls you prefer to write.

Similarly, put buyers abound. It's common for the stock price of biotech companies to tumble by more than 50 percent when bad news is released. WDRG has a promising future, but only if they make money before consuming all their cash on hand. If this company is forced to abandon its new drug because of unsatisfactory phase I results, it's bad news for shareholders. The puts are trading with an even higher implied volatility (90), and that means there are no cheap puts to buy.

September expiration is 32 days in the future. The markets for the Sep options are listed in Table 13.5.

How to make the decision

I still refuse to sell ITM calls because the news might be excellent. On the other hand, I must buy puts that are not too far OTM because the news might be dreadful.

This time the Sep 40 calls are worth considering. That's especially true because I can buy the Sep 27.5 puts for approximately the same premium. I'm really hopeful that the news is good, but recognize that I'm taking a significant risk with

TABLE 13.5: WDRG options, stock at 33.50, 32 days before expiration, IV 80 (C), 90 (P)

EXP	STRIKE	C BID	C ASK	TIME PR	MAX GAIN	P BID	P ASK
Sep	20.0	$13.50	$13.80	$0.00	$0.00	0.05	0.20
Sep	22.5	$11.10	$11.40	$0.10	$0.10	0.15	0.35
Sep	25.0	$8.90	$9.20	$0.40	$0.40	0.45	0.65
Sep	27.5	$6.80	$7.10	$0.80	$0.80	0.95	1.20
Sep	30.0	$5.10	$5.40	$1.60	$0.17	1.80	2.05
Sep	35.0	$2.50	$2.80	$2.50	$4.00	4.30	4.60
Sep	40.0	$1.10	$1.30	$1.10	$7.60	7.80	8.10
Sep	45.0	$0.50	$0.70	$0.50	$12.00	12.00	12.30

September puts and calls for WonderDrug, Inc.

Time Pr = time premium (option price less intrinsic value)
Max Gain = profit per share, if assigned an exercise notice

that position. To makes the trades, I'll enter a spread order[7] to buy the Sep 27.5 puts and sell the Sep 40 calls for even money (meaning the call premium equals the put premium). I'm not concerned about not collecting a cash premium to own this collar for another month because all I want is protection against a disaster. Normally it's important to generate cash from the option trades, but with a big news event in the works, that importance is dwarfed by the likelihood of a huge price change for the stock. I don't expect both options to expire worthless this time and I want the chance to make money if the news is good while not losing too much (a relative term) if the news is bad.

{ NOTE: If you are not familiar with the concept of entering a spread order, here's how it works: The broker (electronic or live) is instructed to buy one option and to sell another. But there are conditions. First, both parts of the order must be filled. It's not acceptable for the broker to fill one part (leg) but not the other. Although the

---

7. An order to fill two different trades simultaneously or neither. In other words, there is no danger of selling calls without buying puts and vice versa.

transactions can occur at any price within the current bid/ask range, the order is not filled at any price that suits the market makers (unless you are foolish enough to enter a market order). Instead it must conform to the limits indicated when the order is placed. In this case, the order tells the broker to buy the puts with the proviso that the calls are sold at that same, or higher, price. If both options are priced at $1.15, or $1.10, or any other price, I'd be satisfied with the fill.

Results

This time, the outcome of the investment is expected to be known before the options expire. When the news is released, the stock will probably undergo a large price change. The problem is, no one knows just how large, or in which direction. For example, if I knew that the stock is gapping up to 50 or down to 15, I'd be buying calls and puts, not holding onto my collar.[8]

Let's make the assumption that something favorable happens (for a change). In the world of biotechnology, the news is often disappointing, but sometimes the bulls are rewarded. The company reports that the trial shows promising results and that phase II trials are already underway. The stock gaps to $42 per share and there are still three days remaining before Sep options expire.

Now that the news has been released, IV collapses (because *another* significant price change is very unlikely) and the options are trading with an IV (50), near its customary level. This is a good result for you. If the stock remains above 40, you allow your puts to expire worthless and you are assigned an exercise

notice on your calls, thereby selling your shares at $40. The stock was priced at 33.50 when you opened this month's collar, earning the tidy profit of $6.50 per share, or $2,600. And that's just the profit for the past month. You also earned a profit in August.

A word of caution: This outstanding result is possible when you adopt the collar strategy, but it's very unusual. Most investors who use collars play the position more conservatively and earn less money than illustrated in the example.

Rolling the position

Let's assume you are thrilled with your success and want to own WDRG through one more expiration cycle. Because you are expecting to be assigned an exercise notice on your Sep 40 calls, to maintain ownership of the stock, you must buy back those calls (to prevent being assigned an exercise notice). Doing so cancels your obligation to deliver the shares to the call owner. But your puts are going to expire in three days, and your plan has been to own these shares only with an insurance policy in place. Thus, at the same time that you repurchase those Sep 40 calls, you plan to sell new call options and buy new put options. Selling the Sep 27.5 puts is probably out of the question because they are so far out-of-the-money there are not likely to be any bids for them.

First you must decide which options (Oct or Nov) to trade. Then you must construct a spread order that eliminates your September position at the same time that it establishes your new position. Let's see how this works.

---

8. *Because I don't know, I'm not going to gamble by buying options. But, for the purposes of discussion, if I did want to bet that the stock is trading at 15 or 50 after news is released, I'd be buying a combination of puts and calls (known as a strangle). If I bought the Sep 27.5 put and the Sep 40 call, I'd be investing about $250 for each strangle. If the stock drops to $15, then the put is in-the-money by 12.50 points, allowing me to (at least) quintuple my investment. If the stock moves to $50, then the call is worth at least $1,000 (its intrinsic value) and my investment quadruples. Those are the possibilities that make investors want to buy options. If the idea of buying options sounds attractive, refer to the discussion in Chapter 9.*

EXAMPLE

Keeping the profit train moving

It's Wednesday, three days before Sep expiration, and four weeks, or 31 days, before the October options expire. The data are in Tables 13.6 and 13.7.

Thought process

I don't like the idea of paying $2.30, or 30 cents over parity to repurchase my Sep 40 calls, but if I enter a spread order, I may be able to pay a little less.[9] Looking at the October option prices, I don't like what I see.

TABLE 13.6: WDRG options, stock at 42, 3 days before expiration, IV 50

EXP	STRIKE	CALLS	BID	ASK	PUTS	STRIKE	BID	ASK
Sep	40.0		$2.10	$2.30		27.5	0.00	0.05

Covering the short Sep 40 call.

TABLE 13.7: WDRG options, stock at 42, 31 days before expiration, IV 50

EXP	STRIKE	CALLS	BID	ASK	PUTS	BID	ASK
Oct	30.0		$12.00	$12.30		0.00	0.20
Oct	35.0		$7.30	$7.60		0.15	0.35
Oct	40.0		$3.50	$3.80		1.35	1.60
Oct	45.0		$1.25	$1.50		4.10	4.40
Oct	50.0		$0.30	$0.50		8.10	8.40

October puts and calls for WonderDrug, Inc.

There's too little premium in the Oct 50 calls, so that's out of the question. Similarly, the deep in-the-money Oct 30 and 35s also have too little time premium to sell (The 30s are $12.00 bid and every penny of that represents intrinsic value (zero time value).

The 35s are not much better, with $7 in intrinsic value and only 30 cents in time value. It looks like my choice is between the 40s and 45s. I can sell the Oct 40 calls and collect a premium of $3.50. That's $2 in intrinsic value and $1.50 in time value. I've already made a bundle on this stock, so if I can eke out another $1.50 (less the cost of the put I buy), that's good enough. After all, this stock cannot rise forever. (Yes, I know it may rise significantly from here, but I don't want to be too greedy.)

If I sell the Oct 45 calls. I'd collect $1.25 in time premium. Not bad. But, I must take into consideration that it's going to cost me more than $2 to buy the Sep 40 calls and I'd like to collect net cash when I roll the position. That means I'm going to sell the Oct 40 call.

The put is a much easier choice. The 30s are too far out-of-the-money and the others are too costly. The 35 put is all I need.

I'm now ready to roll this position. I'll enter two separate orders—one for the call spread and one for the put. Because the call side is clearly the important part of what I'm trying to accomplish this time, I'll enter that order first. Thus, I'll enter the following spread order:

- Buy to close four WDRG Sep 40 calls
- Sell to open four WDGD Oct 40 calls
- Net credit $1.30 ($3.50 minus $2.20)

By entering the spread, I'll either get both legs filled or neither. And if I do get a fill, then I'd be buying the Sep 40 calls at $2.20 and selling the Oct 40 calls at $3.50 (or equivalent prices). As soon as I get that fill, I'll place an order to buy to open 4-lots of WDRG Oct 35 puts at 30 cents. I doubt that I'd be forced to pay 35 cents, but I will if I must. There's no reason to take any chances here, especially for only $20 ($5 x 4 puts). I want to own those puts.

If I get my prices on both orders, I roll the position and collect another $1 in credit per collar,

---

9. *$0.30 over parity seems like a lot of money with only three days to go, but this stock was recently much lower and who knows—profit takers may appear out of the blue and drive the stock price below 40. I have a very nice profit to protect. It's worthwhile to pay that 30 cents as insurance. Besides, I need this trade because my puts are essentially worthless.*

or $400 total. If the stock remains above 40 when October expiration arrives, that $400 is additional profit for holding the position one extra month. The worst-case scenario occurs if the stock drops below 35 and I am forced to exercise my puts. If that happens, holding for the extra month costs $4 per share. How did I get that number? My position is currently worth $40 (if I don't roll, I'll be assigned an exercise notice and will sell the position, collecting $40 per share). If I sell at $35 later, I'll lose $5 per share. But, I am taking in another $1.00 in cash by rolling the position. Thus, I'd be worse off by $4 per share if forced to sell my shares at $35. That's $1,600. Generally, it's not a great idea to risk $1,600 to make $400, but this stock has behaved well and the company has no announcements expected over the next month. I think it's a reasonable investment.

Managing the collar

Collars require less management than almost any other option position. Assuming you established the collar with profit and loss parameters that were acceptable to you, there's probably no need to adjust the position. If the stock is declining, you may choose to find a way to reduce the potential loss, but if you have a put that provides all the protection you require, you may also choose to sit tight, hoping the stock rebounds. I don't recommend trading on hope. But, when you own the put and your maximum loss is not much larger than the current loss, it may pay for you to simply hold the position. It's an individual choice and one that each investor must make, if and when necessary.

Your major decisions are:

* Once the options expire worthless, should I reestablish the collar?

* If yes, which options do I buy and sell?
* If no, should I own the stock without the protection of a collar?
* If one of the options is in-the-money, should I allow the position to go away,[10] or should I roll it?

These examples illustrate how to initiate a collar position and some of the choices you have as expiration nears. We discussed two different ways to change the option strike prices. First you can open a new collar (after expiration) with different strike prices. Next you roll the position prior to expiration when preferring not to be assigned an exercise notice on ITM calls.

Sometimes you may want to roll a position before expiration when it's advantageous to do so, and it's not necessary for the calls to be in-the-money. A discussion of how and why you may want to roll the position was covered in Chapter 12.

Collars represent an excellent strategy for the conservative investor. Limiting the potential loss, coupled with the opportunity to earn a decent profit, makes this an ideal strategy. Later, in Part III, we'll examine how more aggressive traders use collars.

BOTTOM LINE: As you progress through this book, you will notice that as new strategies are added to your trading arsenal, one of the top priorities is being certain that you protect yourself by owning positions in which all losses are limited. One of the strongest arguments for option trading is that it's an easy way to make money. But, the crucial factor in determining your long-term success is being certain that your losses are limited. You never want to be in a position to suffer through a huge loss that wipes out months or years of profits. That cannot happen when you collar a position.

---

10. Whether I am assigned on the calls or exercise the puts, there is no residual position.

1. How does a collar differ from a covered call?

2. Collars are risky positions, suitable for very aggressive investors.

○ **TRUE**   ○ **FALSE**

3. Collars must be closely monitored to protect against the possibility of a significant price change that places you in jeopardy of a significant loss.

○ **TRUE**   ○ **FALSE**

4. Collars can be used to insure the value of a stock portfolio in a manner similar to insuring the value of your home or other valuable possessions.

○ **TRUE**   ○ **FALSE**

5. When you own a collar position, most of the time the put option you bought expires worthless. Does that suggest that buying the put is a bad idea and that it's a bad decision to own a collar position?

○ **TRUE**   ○ **FALSE**

6. When you own a collar, the put limits your losses, but you have unlimited potential profits.

○ **TRUE**   ○ **FALSE**

Chapter 14

Writing Cash-Secured Puts

Writing cash-secured, or naked, puts is the last of our three basic conservative option strategies. Some professional advisors steer their clients away from writing naked puts because they claim it's too risky. Those professionals do their customers a major disservice. Many individual investors never bother to learn about options once they hear those negative statements from the "pros."

Except for extremely bearish prognosticators, no one suggests that owning stock is anything but the most prudent of investment strategies. It's touted far and wide as sage advice that investors must invest in the stock market to maintain spending power and keep up with long-term inflation. Yet, writing naked put options is more conservative and less risky than buying stock and deserves consideration as an investment alternative by many investors. Many buy and hold investors would fare better if they incorporated put writing into their investing arsenals.

Why is selling naked puts less risky than owning stock? When you buy stock, you pay for the shares now. When you sell puts, you receive a cash payment in return for accepting an obligation that may require you to buy stock later. It's the same stock, and the only difference between buying it now and buying it later is that it costs more[1] to buy it now. When you sell puts, the premium effectively reduces the price you pay for stock (assuming you eventually are assigned an exercise notice). If the price declines and stockholders lose money, the put writer loses less. Part of the time that a stock declines, the put writer earns a profit.[2] When writing puts, profits are limited, and that's the tradeoff. If the stock soars, the stockholder fares better than the put seller.

Options are inherently neither risky nor dangerous. What is dangerous is investors trading options before understanding what they are trying to accomplish. It's OK to occasionally use options to speculate, but options were invented as risk-reducing investment tools—and I hope to convince you to use options primarily as a hedging tool that reduces risk.

Definitions

Assume you find a stock in which you want to take a bullish position. If you sell puts instead of buying shares, you are naked short those puts. Selling naked puts is not risk free, but it's not the same as selling naked calls (because potential losses are limited with puts). If you sell puts instead of buying stock, you have less risk than the investor who buys stock.

When selling puts, your broker requires that you have sufficient assets in your account to meet the margin requirement.[3] If you have enough cash in your account to pay for the shares (if eventually assigned an exercise notice), then you are selling cash-secured puts.

EXAMPLE *If you sell five XYZ Jan 50 puts, there's the possibility that you become obligated to purchase 500 shares of XYZ at $50 each. Thus, if you have $25,000 cash in your account, the put sale is "cash secured." Although you are not allowed to sell naked call options in a retirement account, you are allowed to sell cash-secured puts in an IRA, or other retirement account.*

A simple strategy to execute

Covered call writing involves two transactions—buying stock and selling calls. The collar strategy involves three transactions—buying stock, selling calls, buying puts. Naked put writing is the simplest of all, involving only the sale of put options, and requires paying the fewest commission dollars.

For each put sold you collect the premium and accept an obligation to buy 100 shares of stock at the strike price. That obligation is in effect until the option expires (or until you repurchase the same option in a closing transaction).

When adopting covered call writing, you have a bullish position: long stock and short calls. You benefit as time passes and the option decays. If the stock goes higher, you always earn a profit. If the underlying declines, you can earn a profit or loss, depending on how far the stock declines.

Each of those characteristics is present when you sell naked (or cash-secured) puts. Selling puts is a bullish position and you benefit as time passes. If the stock rises, you always make money—either by allowing the put to expire worthless, or by buying it back at a lower price than you sold it. If the underlying asset declines, you may have either a profit or a loss.

---

1. *When you buy stock, you use cash—cash that could be sitting in your account earning interest. When you buy stock later, you not only earn interest while waiting to buy the stock, you also collect the option premium.*
2. *When the decline is less than the premium collected.*
3. *Details of that requirement are discussed later in this chapter. When you buy stock you are required to deposit at least 50 percent of the cost. The margin requirement for writing puts is much less.*

These two strategies appear to be very similar, and we will discuss just how similar they are in the next chapter.

EXAMPLE

You recently visited a new retail store that opened in your neighborhood and noticed that it's always crowded. You decide to investigate and like what you see. The merchandise is neatly displayed, the employees are polite and knowledgeable and there are enough cashiers to keep the lines moving. After completing additional research on the company that owns the stores (RETS), you decide to establish a bullish position by selling put options. The stock is currently trading at 21. It's Monday morning (December options expired last Friday). RETS options currently trade with an implied volatility of 36. Let's consider which option (if any) to sell. All data refer to Table 14.1.

RETS has 12 puts listed for trading. We'll consider each in turn. For the purposes of this discussion, assume you are willing to own 500 shares. Thus, you plan to write five put options.[4]

{ NOTE: It's important not to fall into a trap—and it's a treacherous trap. When an investor decides to buy 500 shares of a $21 stock, such as RETS, it's understood that he or she is investing about $10,000. If $10,000 is the right amount to invest in this stock at this time, there's seldom any temptation to buy more than 500 shares. But, when the put writer sells five puts at a low price—perhaps $50 to $200 per option—unless that investor truly recognizes that each put includes an obligation to purchase 100 shares of stock at a later date, it's easy to look at the relatively small amount of cash involved in the transaction and decide that five puts is a tiny trade. Surely (thinks our misguided investor) it's OK to sell 10 or 20 of these puts—after all 20 puts at $50 each is only $1,000 and if buying stock, I'd be investing $10,000. Please, do not allow this

TABLE 14.1: RETS puts, stock 21, IV 36

MONTH	TIME	STRIKE	BID	ASK	TIME PR	ROI	ANN ROI	DP
Jan	25	17.5	$0.00	$0.10	$0.00	0.00%	0.00%	16.67%
Jan		20.0	$0.35	$0.45	$0.35	1.69%	24.41%	6.43%
Jan		22.5	$1.65	$1.90	$0.15	8.53%	122.79%	0.71%
Feb	53	17.5	$0.05	$0.15	$0.05	0.24%	1.62%	16.90%
Feb		20.0	$0.60	$0.75	$0.60	2.94%	19.98%	7.62%
Feb		22.5	$1.90	$2.15	$0.40	9.95%	67.57%	1.90%
May	116	17.5	$0.30	$0.40	$0.30	1.45%	4.50%	18.10%
May		20.0	$1.00	$1.20	$1.00	5.00%	15.52%	9.52%
May		22.5	$2.35	$2.60	$0.85	12.60%	39.11%	4.05%
Aug	144	17.5	$0.40	$0.50	$0.40	1.94%	4.85%	18.57%
Aug		20.0	$1.15	$1.35	$1.15	5.79%	14.48%	10.24%
Aug		22.5	$2.50	$2.75	$1.00	13.51%	33.78%	4.76%

Data for all RETS options
ROI = Based on the assumption that the put is secured with cash
DP = Downside protection

4. Reminder: If you are assigned an exercise notice, you are obligated to purchase 500 shares at the strike price.

to happen to you. It may be tempting to try to earn $1,000 by selling 20 puts at $50 each rather than $250 by selling "only" five puts. But you must understand that the market does not always behave as you want it to behave. If the stock suddenly drops below the strike price you may be assigned an exercise notice earlier than expected.[5] If that misguided investor suddenly finds 2,000 shares in the account, $40,000 is required to buy those shares. That's four times as much as the investor wanted to invest in this company—an inefficient way to trade. Imagine how much worse it becomes if a margin call[6] is created because of that involuntary $40,000 stock purchase. If you want to buy 500 shares, then five puts is the appropriate number of puts to write.

Selecting the put

The Jan 17½ put is not a consideration. First, there's no bid. Second, even if you were able to sell this put for $0.05 it's not a good idea to write options for such a low price. It's not worthwhile to tie up your assets[7] with so little to gain.

I can sell the Jan 20 put and collect $0.35 per share. If the option expires worthless, the $35 profit represents a 1.78 percent (24.4 percent annualized) ROI.[8] This is nothing spectacular, but it's a reasonable return for a four-week investment.

The Jan 22½ put is in-the-money by 1.50 points. Thus the $1.65 option premium represents $1.50 in intrinsic value and only $0.15 in time value. The time value in an option represents the profit potential, if the stock price is unchanged when

expiration arrives. If I sell this option, there's little downside protection. My break-even point is only $0.15 lower than the current stock price, or $20.85. If the stock goes lower, I lose money. That's not an attractive proposition. In fact, it's not much better than buying stock. But it's enough better (I collect $15 time premium per option and avoid paying interest to carry the stock) to consider as an alternative to buying stock. But if not interested in buying stock, this is the wrong put to write. I prefer scenarios that allow me to earn a profit if the stock rallies, holds steady or declines by a small amount. Writing ITM puts is a one-way bullish play. And that's OK, if that's the objective. Just be aware—writers of ITM puts with little time premium must be right to make money, and the general idea behind selling option premium is to earn a profit most of the time without predicting market direction.

When writing covered calls, we considered the maximum possible potential profit, even when it's an unlikely occurrence. We'll do the same here. If the stock rises above the strike price and the option expires worthless, I keep the entire $165 per option, or 7.91 percent ROI, as profit. And that's an attractive prospect for the aggressively bullish investor.

BOTTOM LINE: Selling in-the-money (ITM) puts with little time premium is seldom attractive to the naked put seller. Just because you are bullish on the stock, doesn't mean it's going to move

---

5. *When a put becomes deep in-the-money (stock significantly below the strike price) there's an incentive for the put owner to exercise (this is very different from calls, where there's no incentive to exercise early). Why? Many times a put owner also owns stock. By exercising, the put owner releases the cash tied up in the position (long stock + long put) and interest can be earned on that cash. When the put is deep ITM, there's little to be gained from owning the put and stock. The put served its purpose in preventing a huge loss, and is no longer needed.*

6. *If you receive a margin call, you must make a rapid deposit of funds into your account. Some brokers give you 10 minutes; others give you a full week. If unable to meet the margin call, your broker closes positions until your margin requirement is small enough that you can meet it. Avoid margin calls.*

7. *If you sell cash-secured puts, your cash is tied up in the position. Even if you use margin, there's too little to gain for this trade to make sense. Don't sell options for nickels and dimes ($0.05 or $0.10).*

8. *For each option sold, $2,000 cash is required. But, the $35 premium can be used, making the net investment $1,965.*

higher. To increase the probability of making money from a position, it's far better to write options that are at- or out-of-the-money. Do you prefer the higher probability of a winning trade, or the higher profit potential of correctly predicting the stock moves higher? That's the choice you make every time you choose which put to write. I believe in making money steadily over time and always choose to write OTM puts rather than ITM puts. But, the purpose of this discussion is to demonstrate the pros and cons of each potential candidate and to enable you to think logically through the process so you can choose an option that's appropriate for your investment style. It's your decision.

The Feb 17½ put has far too little premium to consider selling. The Feb 20 put can be sold for $0.60. If I find this put to be an attractive candidate, I'd try to sell the put at $0.65. Those extra nickels add up over time— when you can get them. If this put expires worthless, ROI is almost 3 percent (20 percent annualized). When compared with writing the January put, the February put provides a bit more downside protection, and a bit less of an annualized ROI.

Writing the Feb 22½ put provides more time premium per contract ($40 vs. $15, compared with Jan), but it's still an ITM put option, which does not fit my investment objective requiring a higher probability of earning a profit. For an investor who loves this stock and is willing to take the chance of having limited insurance, this option is a reasonable choice.

May and Aug options expire in four and seven months, respectively. As is always the case, the more time remaining in the option, the greater the time premium you receive when writing the option. That higher time premium affords additional downside protection, a reduced

annualized return, and the ability to spend less time with your option-writing program.[9]

Take a look at the May 17½ put. That's a very safe put to sell. By that I mean there's very little chance the stock will fall below the break-even point (17.20). The probability of keeping the $150 ($30 for each of five puts) is very high. So is this a good put to sell? No. If you look at the annualized return, it's only 4.5 percent— less than you can earn from Treasury bills, certificates of deposit and even many savings accounts. This may be a safe investment, but there's a chance of losing money and the return is far too low to even think twice about selling this put. The same is true for the Aug 17½ put. The only way this put becomes a satisfactory trade occurs when the put can be repurchased for a quick profit. If you hold through expiration, the less-than-Treasury-bill profit is simply not worth the risk. If you repurchase quickly,[10] then the annualized return becomes acceptable.

In this scenario, most put writers opt for a put with a 20 strike. My choice is to sell the Jan or Feb. Others may prefer to trade less frequently and opt for the May or Aug 20 put. Those who are more bullish and less concerned with downside protection may choose a put with a 22½ strike.

BOTTOM LINE: None of these puts makes an outstanding choice, but for an investor interested in this stock, there are acceptable puts to write.

Why write naked puts?

Writing puts is a bullish strategy for both long-term investors and short-term traders. It can

---

9. Trading less often saves time and commission dollars. But that doesn't mean you should allow yourself to get lazy. Don't ignore your positions. They should be monitored at least weekly to be certain that no adjustments are necessary—and that includes the possibility of closing the position before expiration to lock in a nice profit, or adjusting (or closing) a losing position.

10. There's no way to know if you will be able to do that. This trade is not recommended.

be used to achieve either of two very different investment objectives:

- Profit. You have a bullish outlook for a stock or index and expect the price of put options to decline as the stock rises (or time passes). Your plan is to buy back the put option at a much lower price or perhaps allow it to expire worthless. If your plan is successful, you earn a nice profit. Traders, or investors who hold positions for short periods, can benefit by adopting this strategy.
- Buy stock at a discount. If the put option is in-the-money when expiration arrives, you are assigned an exercise notice and become obligated to buy a stock you want to own[11] at a discount to today's price. This is an intelligent method by which an investor gradually adds positions to a long-term portfolio. Of course, you don't always buy stock. That's just fine. If the option expires worthless, you keep the option premium as a consolation prize.

EXAMPLE

WXY is trading at 30 and you want to pay no more than $27 per share to own this stock. If you write a put option with a strike price of 30 when the premium is $3 or more, you have the chance to achieve your goal. If you are eventually assigned an exercise notice, you buy stock at $30. But, because you collected $3 per share in option premium, your total cost is $27. If you are not assigned an exercise notice, then you keep the $300 premium as your profit.

If you want to buy shares at $27 after expenses, then try to collect an extra 5 or 10 cents when selling the put. Be sure you understand that if you try to get that small,

extra premium, you may miss the trade— and a profitable opportunity.

Knowing you require a premium of $3 or more, you must decide which expiration months are acceptable. Obviously, it's best to sell the near term put for $3, but when the put premium is too low, you have two choices: 1) wait for the stock to decline and the put to reach your price; or 2) choose a longer-term put. That's a trading decision you make for yourself. Some investors are willing to write a put with a six-month (or longer) lifetime if it allows them the opportunity to purchase stock at their price, while others patiently wait for the stock to come in (trade lower). Do the math and decide if any puts are appropriate to write.

If willing to buy stock but prefer to take a trading profit, write a put that meets your requirements for profit potential both in dollars and ROI, and hope you are not assigned an exercise notice. The point of being willing to buy stock is to allow for the possibility of being assigned.

BOTTOM LINE: When you sell a put option, you receive cash that is yours to keep, no matter what else happens. In return for that cash, you accept obligations; specifically you give someone else the right to force you to buy 100 shares of a specific stock at a specific price for a limited period of time. As is the case when you sell call options, you have no say as to whether you are eventually assigned an exercise notice—that decision, and the timing of that decision, rests entirely with the option owner.

When you write (sell) naked put options and hold the position through the option's expiration date, there are only two possible outcomes, depending on the price of the underlying stock.

---

11. If you are a long-term investor and not willing to own this stock at the strike price, don't sell puts. Writing puts is used for stocks you want to accumulate over time.

Each of those outcomes accomplishes one of your original goals (you earn a profit or you own stock at a discount).

> NOTE: If you buy stock at the strike price, you own the shares at a price that looked attractive at the time you sold the puts. However, if assigned an exercise notice, the stock is obviously priced below the strike price. Thus, the premium you earned when selling puts determines whether the position is currently profitable.

Making trading decisions

Before trading, certain decisions must be made—first and foremost is choosing the underlying asset. Remember, put writing is a bullish strategy. A decision to sell naked puts should be based on these criteria:

- A stock (or index) on which you are bullish. If you are investor, it must also be a stock you are willing (or eager) to own. It's not smart to write puts on some random stock just because you find the option premium attractive.

> NOTE: Traditional buy and hold investors make money when their stocks increase in value. You, the uncovered put writer, also make money any time the stock goes higher. However, you earn a profit when the stock remains relatively unchanged or decreases by a small amount—and the buy and hold investor cannot do that. It's far easier to find a stock that doesn't decline than it is to find a stock that must go higher. But don't choose stocks randomly.

- The price you want to pay for stock, if assigned.

Next step: deciding which put option to write

- Choosing the put strike price
  - How much profit potential do you want? The higher the premium, the greater your profit potential.
  - How much risk are you willing to take? The further out-of-the-money the option, the more likely the put expires worthless.
  - How badly do you want to buy the stock? The higher the strike price, the more likely you are to be assigned an exercise notice.

- Choosing the expiration date
  - How long do you want to own the position?
  - Options with shorter expirations give the seller less potential profit *per trade*, a greater annualized potential profit and less protection against a loss.

BOTTOM LINE : There is no "best" put to write because each investor has a different investment objective, risk tolerance and comfort zone. Choose a put that provides the opportunity to earn a return that meets or exceeds your minimum. When writing naked puts (or covered calls), I suggest that the average investor consider 2 percent per month as a reasonable target—when writing ITM calls or OTM puts. For those who are more conservative, 1.5 percent per month may be more appropriate. Aggressive investors can aim higher, but if you try to earn more than 4 to 5 percent per month,[12] you must trade volatile stocks and thus, take on additional risk. When you write OTM covered calls or ITM puts, you can also have capital gains if your stocks increase in price. The 2 percent referred to in this discussion applies to time premium when the call is ITM or the put is OTM.

---

12. Keep this in mind. While a 2 percent monthly return is fine when markets are calm, when the markets are volatile and option premiums are higher, you may find yourself aiming for higher returns. That's OK. The warning is not to trade high-volatility stocks just because they are high-volatility stocks. Do your research and only adopt bullish positions in stocks for which you have good reason to be bullish.

Calculations

Your maximum profit occurs when the put expires worthless because you keep 100 percent of the premium. When discussing covered call writing, the profit calculation is straightforward. You have a profit (or loss) and you know how much is invested (cost of stock less option premium). When you write uncovered puts, you don't buy anything and may wonder how to determine how much money is invested in the position. Because I recommend writing cash-secured puts rather than writing puts on margin, I consider the cash put aside to purchase stock (if assigned an exercise notice) as "the investment." As with other option strategies, you can reduce that cash requirement by the option premium.

EXAMPLE

WXY is trading at $31 and you sell four WXY Dec 30 puts described above and collect $320 for each, making your break-even point $26.80. To be cash-secured, you must set aside $12,000 to pay for 400 shares of WXY at $30 per share. But you can use the premium ($320 x 4) and thus, your investment is the $10,720 cash you set aside. And there's a small bonus: When selling puts, cash is deposited into your account and your broker pays a reasonable rate of interest on that cash.

Assume expiration day arrives, the option is out-of-the-money and expires worthless. Your profit is $1,280 (plus earned interest, less commissions) divided by the investment ($10,720). If commissions and interest cancel each other, then the profit is 11.9 percent. In this example, there is no annualized ROI to calculate because the time to expiration was not relevant.

If you decide to be more aggressive and write puts on margin, then you use leverage and have the potential to earn (or lose) a much higher return on your investment.

Assume the margin requirement for the above trade is $3,280, and your profit is $1,280. Your investment is the $3,280 you put up to meet the margin requirement, and the ROI is 39 percent. This is an outstanding rate of return. But keep in mind that using leverage is a two-way street and it's possible to lose more than your original margin requirement of $3,280. Trading with leverage increases both risk and reward and it's not for everyone. That's why I recommend selling puts only when secured with cash.

Margin

Although I recommend that newcomers to the options world avoid using margin, once you gain experience and have confidence that options can be used conservatively to generate profits, you may decide to use margin. And more experienced traders may already use margin. It's relatively simple to calculate the current margin requirements (though some brokers have different requirements and margin requirements change over time).

When writing naked puts, if you choose *not* to be cash backed, your broker requires a deposit as collateral for the position. The *initial* margin requirement is determined in the folllowing manner (with a minimum of $250):

- 20 percent of the price of the underlying stock[13] plus
- The premium collected from the option sale minus
- The amount the put option is out-of-the-money.

---

13. *The requirement is less (15 instead of 20 percent) for certain broad-based indexes.*

EXAMPLE

Stock price is 28. You sell 10 Nov 25 puts at $1.00. Note that the options are out of the money by 3 points.

The margin requirement for selling each put is:

20% of stock price = $2,800 x 0.2 ($560)
Premium collected = $100
Out-of-the-money amount = $300
Margin requirement = 560 + 100 – 300 =
$360 per put, or $3,600 total.
To be cash secured, $24,000 cash is required.[14]

Tips for investors (people with a long-term approach to investing)

- Maintain an updated list of stocks you want to own and your target buying price.
- Know which strike prices are possible candidates for selling.
- Determine the minimum premium you must receive to buy stock at your target price, if assigned. For example, if you collect $2 for a put with a strike price of 25, your potential purchase price for the stock is $23.
- If you are a proponent of technical analysis (and even if you aren't) be aware of support and resistance levels for stocks on your list. Consider writing a put option when the stock price is just above support.[15]
- Monitor the market prices of put options under consideration. If you don't want to miss an opportunity, and especially if you don't have time to constantly monitor the market, enter an order[16] to sell specific puts at a limit price.

{ *NOTE: Don't enter too many such orders at one time because a severe market sell-off may make you short too many puts.*[17]

Tips for traders (people who hold positions for a relatively short time)

- Maintain a list of stocks on which you are considering making a bullish trade.
- When the timing is right, sell an appropriate put (strike price and premium suit your needs).
- Pay attention to support levels and be prepared to write put options when the stock is priced just above support. If the stock breaks support, be ready to close the position.
- Monitor put prices. When profit potential and risk/reward profile look attractive, enter an order to sell puts.

Other considerations when entering a trade

EXAMPLE

YXW, a reasonably volatile stock, is currently trading near $30 per share. Accept the following four statements as a given:

1) Either you are an investor interested in buying YXW at 27 or you are a trader who is bullish on YXW and interested in opening a long position near current levels.

---

14. $25,000 to buy 1,000 shares at 25, less $1,000 collected in option premium.

15. If the stock breaks support you may decide to take a quick loss and close the position with a small loss. Better yet, if support holds, the stock doesn't decline and you earn your profit.

16. An order good for just one day is best, but if you lack the time, then make the order good for the week and you can reevaluate the situation over the weekend. GTC (good 'til cancelled) orders are inappropriate for options (opening orders) because the market price of options changes significantly as time passes. (Also, you don't want to have to worry about remembering your outstanding orders.)

17. In a declining market, if you decide to continue selling puts, by not entering all your orders at one time you receive better and better prices as the decline continues.

2) It's Monday immediately following March expiration. April expiration is four weeks away and May expiration is an additional five weeks in the future.
3) Apr 30 put is $1.25 bid. Apr 27½ put is $0.55 bid
4) May 30 put is $2.00 bid. May 27½ put is $0.95 bid

Investors

Sell the Apr 27½ put at $55 per contract.

If the stock is above the strike price when expiration day arrives, you earn a profit of $55, or approximately 2 percent (of the $2,695 investment[18] when the put is cash backed).

If the stock is below the strike price when the market closes on expiration day, you are assigned an exercise notice, obligating you to buy the stock at $26.95 per share—just below your target price.

Either result is acceptable.

Traders

Sell either the Apr 30 put or the Apr 27½ put.

Choose the Apr 30 put if confident the stock is moving higher. You earn $125 (4.34 percent ROI)[19] if the stock remains above the strike price.

Choose the safer Apr 27½ put when mildly bullish. The maximum profit potential is not exciting ($55), but there is an excellent chance to earn that profit.

May puts are also reasonable to write if additional insurance is your objective. Most traders reject this choice.

Selling either April put provides the opportunity to earn a quick profit if the stock performs as predicted.[20]

Disadvantages to put writing

From a trader's point of view, profit potential is limited. If you buy stock, it's possible to have a substantial gain.

Advantages to put writing

You can earn a profit when the stock price does not increase. If you write a put option, time becomes your ally, especially when the stock remains near its current price level. When you choose a lower strike price (an out-of-the-money put) you may earn money even when the stock drops below the strike price. That's a new experience for a bullish trader and should more than compensate you for limiting your profit potential—unless you are a gifted stock picker.

{ NOTE: As a trader looking to earn a profit as quickly as possible, there's no reason to hold a position until expiration. You may decide to buy back the put any time you are satisfied with the profit or are no longer bullish on the stock. Investors also take advantage of the early buy back, but it's for a different reason. The two main reasons for repurchase are a) when the price is so low that there's little to be gained by holding, or b) the option that you plan to sell next (after expiration) is currently attractively priced, so it makes sense to pay a small price to close out the option you previously sold, freeing yourself to sell the new option (This combination of trades is rolling the position, previously discussed in Chapter 12). Of course, you can always sell the new, attractively priced put option first,[21] but that involves extra risk.

---

18. Strike price ($2,750) less the $55 premium.
19. $125 profit, $2,875 investment.
20. Most traders go long and short based on their market expectations, and options can support a trader's needs. Long-term investors make fewer predictions, although everyone likes to buy stock (or sell puts) when they believe the stock is going higher.
21. This is NOT the same situation as with a covered call in which selling the new option leaves you with a naked call position, which is unwise. When you sell the new put without buying back the old put, you double your position, and that's often a poor decision. Not covering those inexpensive, soon-to-expire options is a losing strategy over the long term.

Exiting the trade

Knowing when to exit a trade is often as crucial as knowing when to enter a trade, but it deserves less emphasis when adopting the strategy of writing naked put options.

Investors seldom close a position before expiration, because being assigned an exercise notice is a viable alternative for them. I recommend that investors consider closing a position that has worked well and the put can be bought at a low price. Of course, "low price" is a relative term. For me, it means paying $0.05 whenever there are at least three weeks remaining in the option's life, but this is another decision that each trader must make. There's not much to be gained by waiting for that last five cents. I often pay $0.10, but that depends on time remaining, overall market volatility and whether there is a different put I am yearning to sell.[22] Take your profits. Don't take extra risk for little reward. Don't be greedy.

Traders close their profitable positions more often. The decision is based on a trader's outlook for the stock in the immediate future.

When considering whether a specific set of conditions is suitable for writing naked put options, each individual must make the final trade or don't trade decision. The following discussion is designed to give investors from different backgrounds a better feel for how he or she can approach writing naked put options.

Because each reader enters the options world from a different place with different levels of experience and various trading backgrounds, it's worthwhile to consider how to approach a trade from a variety of experience levels. Let's consider how investors and traders of different experience levels may approach writing naked put options and how adopting that strategy fits into their individual investment styles.

Stock UVW is trading at $41. It's shortly after the July expiration and the Aug 40 put can be sold for $1.00

Thoughts of the experienced put-selling investor

I've been watching UVW and it's been approaching my target price of $39. I'm going to write the front month puts for a buck ($1.00). In any event, I'm a winner. I'll either own 400 shares at $39, or I'll keep the premium and walk away with $400.

Thoughts of the first-time seller of a naked put options

I'd like to own 400 shares of UVW stock. I'm a bit nervous about selling put options because my broker doesn't think it's a good idea. But I've been reading an excellent options book and I'm convinced the strategy is much more conservative (and profitable) than my broker realizes. If I proceed with my plan to sell four of these puts, it's going to be a nervous four weeks as I wait for expiration. But, I must remember that only two things can happen. In four weeks I'll either own the 400 shares at $39 per share, or I'll have a profit of $400. Both of these alternatives appeal to me.

Of course, I could simply bid $39 for the stock, and there's a chance I'll buy it. But if the stock rallies, as I believe it will, I won't be able to get the stock at my price. If I sell the put option, at least I'll have $400 as a consolation prize if I'm right about the stock.

I'm going to make this trade tomorrow morning!

Thoughts of the experienced trader who is a first time seller of naked put options

UVW is $41 and approaching support at 40.50. I'm convinced that taking a long position in the stock is the right move. I believe the stock moves higher within several months. Of course, I can simply buy the stock, but if I understand correctly, there

---

22. It's prudent and good risk management, to cover (repurchase) your short puts when selling new puts.

are advantages to selling put options. I know my profit is limited to $100 (the premium) for each put. But in return for limiting my profit, my break-even point drops from the current price of $41 to $39. I like the idea of having that extra cushion.

Because I'm not sure the stock will run higher immediately, by selling the puts, the passage of time becomes my friend. If I buy stock, I'll have to use cash. If UVW remains locked in a narrow range near its support level, I'll gain nothing. But, if I sell the put option, I not only collect time premium, but I can keep my cash and earn interest on that.

Yes, put selling seems like a good idea in this scenario and I'm going to jump into this strategy first thing tomorrow morning. I may even try to make a bit extra and try to sell those puts at $1.05.

Thoughts of the trader with experience as a put-writer

The UVW chart looks good here, but the stock may stay in a trading range before breaking out to the upside. I've seen this happen too many times. Instead of buying stock, I'll write these August 40 puts for $1. Sure, it limits my profit potential, but I want to make money if the stock trades in a narrow range.

If the stock hasn't moved much in a month, I'll decide whether to sell the September 40 puts, or buy the stock. But for now, I'm writing the August puts. I'll sacrifice the chance to make a large profit in return for a better chance to make some profit.

What can go wrong when you sell naked puts?

Like any stock market investment, if you have a long position you run the risk the stock declines in price. Writing puts gives you a long position. Thus, a significant decline usually results in a loss.

What can you do to minimize losses if the stock moves against you (lower)? You can sell

put spreads instead of naked puts (described in Chapter 18). Let's consider repairing the position.

Repair strategies (risk management)

In the example above, assume you decided to write the YXW Apr 27½ put at $0.55.

YXW rapidly declines to $24 per share.
You have several choices, depending on your priorities:

- If you are content to own the stock at $26.95, risking a further decline, do nothing because no repair is necessary.
- Most traders believe it is good money management to minimize losses and not hold losing positions hoping to recover the loss. If you want to cut your losses now, you can buy back the put. That means accepting a loss on this trade and acknowledging that every trade cannot be a winner.
- If you still want to own a long position in YXW, but want to do something to decrease the risk of further losses, then roll the position by buying back the Apr 27½ put and simultaneously[23] (or immediately thereafter) selling a new put with a lower strike price and a more distant expiration.

EXAMPLE

Let's say you decide to buy four Apr 27½ puts (to close) and sell four Jul 25 puts—or perhaps Oct 25 or Oct 22½ puts—to open. Now that you own a position in YXW, there are two paths to consider. Decide which is more important for you:

(a) Gain protection against further loss. Bring in as much cash as possible by selling an option with a higher premium.
(b) Give yourself the best chance to turn the position profitable over time. This entails

---

23. By entering a spread order.

greater downside risk, but may be a suitable choice if you still have a bullish outlook on YXW. Unfortunately, too many investors automatically make this choice. It is not a good idea to try to convert every losing trade into a profitable trade. Pick your spots carefully and decide if this stock is one you still want to own. Sometimes it's best to salvage what you can and find a better place to invest your money.

Two weeks have passed since the day you sold the puts and the YXW is at $24.

Apr 27½ put is offered at $4
Jul 25 put is $2.25 bid
Oct 22½ put is $2.00 bid
Oct 25 put is $3.10 bid

What should you do? There is no "right" choice when rolling. It's reasonable to buy the April put to close and to sell to open any of the three puts listed (or others that expire in January).

Choose the option that fits your comfort zone. Be certain you want to own the new position and don't force the trade just to do something. If you don't know which position you prefer, then it's probably best to close the position and take the loss.

If you are more concerned with limiting losses when the stock continues to decline, then writing the Oct 22½ put makes sense. On the negative side, you own a position with more than five months remaining before expiration day. On the other hand, the Oct 22½ put is out-of-the-money (currently) with a chance to expire worthless. This allows for the *possibility* of recovering some of your loss.

Let's look at the numbers when October expiration arrives:

- If YXW is higher than 22.50, the put expires worthless. You collected $55 for the initial sale, paid $400 to repurchase the put and collected $200 for selling the Oct put. All in all, you paid $145 to establish the position. You have no remaining position (your puts expired), and your loss is $580 ($145 x 4). That's not too bad, considering you went long YXW when it was near 30 and watched it drop to 24. You cut your losses by rolling and holding the position.
- If YXW is below 22.50, you are assigned an exercise notice. You buy shares at 22.50 (strike). Subtract from that the amount you collected for selling the put (negative $1.45),[24] and your shares cost $23.95 each. This is considerably better than the $26.95 the shares would have cost if you simply held and did not roll the position. You own the shares. What should you do next? You have three choices. You can sell stock and eliminate this loser from your portfolio, or you can hold stock and hope it recovers. The third choice is recommended, but only if you are willing to own stock: write covered calls. Covered calls writing is discussed at length in Chapters 10 through 12.

If you are still bullish but you also want to hedge your position and reduce further losses, consider selling the Oct 25 put at $3.10. It costs $90 to roll the position.[25] Because you collected $55 for the initial sale, you now have now incurred a debit of $35 cash (plus commissions).

When October expiration arrives:

- If YXW is above $25, the put expires worthless and your loss is only $35 per 100 shares. That's an excellent result, considering that YXW declined so rapidly.

---

24. Collected $55, paid $200. Net cost, $145.
25. Pay $4 for the Apr put and sell the Oct put for $3.10. Cost $90.

- IF YXW is below $25 you are assigned an exercise notice and are obligated to pay $25 for stock, making your true cost $25.35 per share.
- Because the stock is trading at $24 at the time you rolled the position, it's reasonable to expect to be assigned when expiration day arrives. As mentioned above, if assigned, writing covered calls is the recommended course, but only when you want to own this stock.

What to do when expiration day arrives

If the puts are out-of-the-money (and you have not previously covered them by paying $0.05), do nothing. Allow them to expire worthless. This frees you from any further obligations and the next day the market is open for business (or any time thereafter) you can reinvest the cash kept in reserve.[26]

{ *NOTE: If the put you plan to sell is attractively priced today, consider buying your worthless puts, paying $0.05 or less,[27] in order to take advantage of the attractively priced put. If the puts you sold appear[28] to be worthless, it's not necessary to wait until expiration Friday. Any time your short put can be bought cheaply it's a good idea to close that position. It's not necessary to collect that final 5 or 10 cents on each option you write. You are then ready to sell another put, if an opportunity presents itself.*

If you maintain a current list of potential investment opportunities, the weekend after expiration is the ideal time to select your top candidates in preparation for trading next Monday morning.

If the puts are in-the-money, you have three reasonable alternatives:
a) Buy them back. You have a profit or a loss depending on the price you pay for the puts.
b) Allow yourself to be assigned an exercise notice. You own a long position in the underlying stock and are in position to write covered calls.
c) Roll the position. Buy back the put you sold earlier and write a put option expiring in a future month. In the repair strategy described above, you rolled a position in order to reduce risk. In this scenario, the position can be rolled to make additional profits.

{ *NOTE: Don't roll the position just to have something to do. If you are not satisfied with the premium available, close your position. Forcing a trade is not a good strategy. You want to roll a position only when the profit potential is satisfactory. It's not essential to own a position in this stock; you want a position only when profit potential and risk are favorable.*

Writing covered calls if assigned an exercise notice:

If the put is in-the-money at expiration, you can expect to be assigned an exercise notice. If an investor, you can simply keep the stock and hope for the best. But, there's a better strategy. You collect a cash premium by selling someone else the right to buy your stock. Writing covered calls is discussed in detail in Chapters 10 through 12.

In the examples above, October expiration arrived and 400 shares of YXW stock were put to you.[29] Your cost is $23.95 in the first scenario or $25.35 in the second. You can write YXW Nov 25 or Dec 25 call, collect a premium and give yourself a chance to turn this position profitable. But that requires that you hold a stock that has performed

---

26. *The cash you were going to use to buy stock if assigned an exercise notice.*
27. *Today, all options trade in penny increments.*
28. *Stocks do make unexpected moves and waiting for expiration to collect the last few pennies occasionally backfires.*
29. *You were assigned an exercise notice.*

poorly. If that makes you uncomfortable, there's no need to invest in this company. Sell your stock and move on. Not every position has to be profitable. Your primary consideration is to avoid large losses.

These methods increase the probability of having winning trades, but they are basically bullish strategies. If the market tumbles or if you find stock selection to be challenging (as I do), then you may do better trading a diversified portfolio. That can be accomplished by owning exchange traded funds (ETFs), rather than individual stocks. Or, you can trade options on indexes, such as the Standard & Poor's 500, the Dow Jones Industrial Average or the Russell 2000.

If you are eager to learn more, then the material in Part III will be of interest. Before moving on, the next chapter gives you a much clearer picture of options and how they work. The knowledge gained may prove to increase your profits only occasionally, but the material is important to your continuing options education.

Writing naked puts is a strategy suitable for most investors, even though many investment professionals consider it risky. It's more conservative than owning stocks—and almost all professionals consider that strategy to be prudent.

One of the great advantages of this investment strategy for bullish investors and traders is that you are much more likely to show a profit than when you buy stock. Even though your potential profit is limited, the fact that you have so many more winning trades more than compensates.

One word of caution: Naked put writing is a bullish strategy and does not do well in bear markets. Don't sell too many puts—remember, if assigned an exercise notice, you buy 100 shares of stock for each put sold.

Happy put writing!

1. When you write naked puts, the potential loss is unlimited.

○ **TRUE** ○ **FALSE**

2. What makes a put sale "cash-secured"?

3. It's much easier to close (hopefully for a nice profit) a naked put position than a covered call position.

○ **TRUE** ○ **FALSE**

4. You are considering buying 400 shares of stock at $50 per share, investing $20,000. If you sell 10 puts instead of buying those 400 shares, and if you collect $100 for each put, you have far less risk because the investment is worth only $1,000.

○ **TRUE** ○ **FALSE**

5. When it comes to selling naked puts, it doesn't matter which stock you choose. If the market rises, you do well; if it sinks, you fare poorly.

○ **TRUE** ○ **FALSE**

Chapter 15

Equivalent Positions

This chapter provides tools you can use to gain a trading edge. There's nothing here that's absolutely essential when learning to trade options, but it's important for a better understanding of their versatility. There are two very practical reasons why this topic should be of interest:

- Trading equivalent positions occasionally provides an opportunity to make trades that are more profitable.
- Understanding this material allows you to trade more efficiently and reduce your trading expenses by lowering commissions. That alone makes it worthwhile.

When trading equity options, you always have choices. You can trade calls, puts and/or the underlying asset. When building a specific position for your portfolio, most of the time, the best method for constructing that position is to use straightforward means. If you want a specific option position (such as a covered call), then go ahead and buy stock and write the specific calls you have in mind. There's nothing complicated about that. But sometimes it's possible—and advantageous—to construct an equivalent position that uses different options. In the case of covered calls, if you sell a put option with the same strike price and expiration date as the call, there's no need to buy or sell stock because the naked put is a position that is equivalent to the covered call.

For our purposes, when two positions are equivalent, it means that each position makes or loses the same dollar amount at every possible price for the underlying.

If you take the time to understand the ideas described below, you discover that any position involving options can be transformed into a different, equivalent position. Such positions are called synthetic equivalents, or synthetics, for short. You may not trade synthetics often, but some of the more popular option strategies (covered call writing and collars) have synthetic alternatives that are more efficient to trade. That means it's easier to adopt those strategies when you use synthetics. As a bonus, commission expenses are reduced when you trade synthetics, thereby allowing you to keep more of the profits.

Before you decide that learning about equivalent positions is too sophisticated or requires too much effort, please understand that there's nothing complicated about choosing to own a position that's essentially the same as your desired position, but *appears* to differ.

{ *NOTE: If you have difficulty with algebra, don't be intimidated. Beneath each equation is an explanation in easy-to-understand language of the argument behind the formula. Readers who prefer to understand why certain things are true can follow the logic and see proof that supports the conclusions.*

Abbreviations

S = the number of shares (in round lots, or multiples of 100 shares) of stock

C = the number of call options

P = the number of put options

P_{50} or C_{15} = a put with a 50 strike price or a call with a 15 strike price

P_H or P_L = a put with higher (H) or lower (L) strike price

R = collar position

B = box spread (described later in this chapter)

The basic equation: S = C - P

This single equation represents the foundation of options trading. Let's look at this equation from three perspectives:

When P and C represent the same underlying asset and have the same expiration date and strike price, then the three basic synthetic equivalents are:

1) S = C – P

Buying 100 shares of stock is equivalent to buying one call and selling one put. For example, if you buy five ABCD Jun 40 calls and sell five ABCD Jun 40 puts, your position behaves exactly as if you own 500 shares of ABCD stock.

Proof

Assume you buy one XYX Apr 60 call and sell one XYZ Apr 60 put and hold this position until the options expire. When the market closes for trading on expiration day, if XYX last trades above 60, the put expires worthless and you exercise your call. Thus, your position is long 100 shares of stock. If the stock last trades below 60, the call expires worthless and when assigned an exercise notice, your position is long 100 shares of stock.

Thus, at any stock price, the position is equivalent to owning 100 shares of stock. But, there is a risk (see sidebar on next page on pin risk).

Pin Risk

The astute reader may ask what happens if the stock closes exactly at the strike price. That possibility represents a risk of owning synthetic stock instead of owning real shares. This risk, known as "pin risk," refers to the risk that results when the stock last trades at the strike price. When that occurs the stock is said to have been "pinned" to the strike price at expiration.

If the stock closes exactly at (and sometimes within a few pennies of) the strike price on expiration day, you never know whether you will be assigned an exercise notice or if the options expire worthless. The decision to exercise an option rests with the option owner. Thus, when you own synthetic stock, you don't know whether to exercise your long calls. You want to exercise calls if you are not assigned an exercise notice on the puts, but you don't want to exercise if those puts are assigned.[1] This can be a real quandary.

Most of the time when the stock is pinned to the strike price, the person who owns the option chooses not to exercise and the option expires worthless. But, if you choose to own an equivalent stock position instead of the "real" position, then you probably want to own stock at all times. Most investors prefer not to take the risk of finding a surprise in their account on Monday morning following expiration. It's not an enjoyable experience to discover that you are assigned an exercise notice on a call or put option that you thought expired worthless. Sometimes it's fun to find that you were not assigned on an option that was in-the-money by one or two cents, but not when you were counting on receiving that exercise notice. When you own synthetic stock, you may occasionally find that you have no position when you thought you owned stock.

There is a solution. The simplest path to eliminating pin risk is to exercise your call option and to buy back the put option, paying as little as possible (hopefully only $0.05, or $5 per contract). Being forced to spend that $5 plus commissions is not the ideal situation, but it does avoid an unpleasant surprise. Another way to avoid pin risk is to roll the synthetic stock position. That means closing your position in the front month and reestablishing the position with options that expire in another month.

You can always take the chance that if the stock last trades exactly at the strike price you can exercise your calls and hope you are not assigned an exercise notice on the puts. Obviously, taking this risk is not prudent. If you find yourself without your desired position, you can reestablish the position (real or synthetic) Monday morning. But be aware that sometimes the stock opens at a price that significantly differs from its previous closing price. When you have no stock position, if the stock price opens lower, you come out ahead. When it gaps higher, you have lost a profitable opportunity. Why take the chance? One reason for using options is to reduce risk and it's best not to take the risk of waiting until Monday to learn your fate.

---

1. If you fail to exercise calls and the puts expire worthless, you have no stock position, but if you exercise calls to get long stock and if you are also assigned on the puts, you find yourself owning twice as many shares as planned.

2) C = S + P

Buying one call option is equivalent to buying 100 shares of stock and buying one put. Some investors who own stock choose to purchase a put option as insurance against a catastrophic decline in the price of the shares. These investors can accomplish the same investment objectives by owning the equivalent position. That means there's no need to own the stock *and* the put. Instead, owning the call option with the same expiration and strike price as the put is the equivalent position.

That position (long put, long stock) is a synthetic call and is often called a "married put."

Proof

Assume you own one ABC Nov 40 call. When expiration arrives, if the shares last trade above 40, you exercise your call and own 100 shares of stock. If the stock last trades below 40, you allow your call to expire worthless and have no position.

If instead, you own 100 shares of stock and one Nov 40 put, consider what happens when expiration arrives. If the stock last trades above 40, you allow the put option to expire worthless and you own 100 shares. If the stock last trades below 40, you exercise your long Nov 40 put, thereby selling your 100 shares. That leaves you with no remaining position.

Thus, at any stock price you have the same position. There is no pin risk when you *own* the options and have control over the exercise decision.

3) P = C − S

Buying one put option is equivalent to buying one call and selling 100 shares.[2]

Because +P = C − S, then −P = S − C.

A covered call is S − C (long stock, short call) and is also called a "synthetic put." Therefore, a covered call is the same as −P. Instead of owning a covered call, you can have the equivalent position by selling one put with the same strike and expiration as the call.

These are equivalent strategies, but the minor advantages of selling naked puts (reduced commissions, ease of closing the position)[3] makes that method the better choice, most of the time.

Proof

Assume you own one JKL Feb 20 put. When expiration arrives, you are short 100 shares of stock below 20 (because you exercise your put) and no position above 20 (put expires worthless).

If you are short 100 shares of stock and own one Feb 20 call, when expiration arrives you exercise your call if the stock is above 20, leaving you with no position. Below 20, your call expires worthless and your position is short 100 shares of stock. Again, at any stock price the positions are the same, and because you own either the put or call, there is no pin risk.

BOTTOM LINE: A covered call position is equivalent to a short put position when the put and call have the same strike price and expiration date. It's important to be familiar with this equivalent position, in particular, because writing covered calls and naked puts are popular strategies frequently used by individual investors.

The astute reader may recognize that

- Owning stock allows you to collect a dividend (if the stock pays one), whereas the investor who sells puts receives no dividends.

---

2. *If you don't own the shares, that's OK. You can sell the stock short.*
3. *Buying the put is one simple transaction. To close a covered call, you must buy the call and sell the stock and be certain the prices are acceptable. That's much more difficult.*

- It requires cash to own stocks, requiring the payment of interest. The put seller pays no interest.

When the markets are working efficiently, these problems are automatically fixed. The pricing of options in the marketplace takes these factors into consideration. For example, we discussed that buying 100 shares of stock is equivalent to buying one call and selling one put. When you buy stock, you must pay interest. Thus, when you buy the call and sell the put, the cost of that interest is factored into the price of the options. If it weren't, everyone would save the cost of carrying (paying interest to own) stock and purchase the synthetic position instead—and the only people owning stock would be those who don't understand options. But, options are priced so that there's (usually) no advantage to buying the call and selling the put. Here is an example of how this works:

EXAMPLE

Let's assume you want to buy 100 shares of XYZ at $80 per share. To pay for the purchase, you use cash that's currently earning 5 percent interest. If you hold this stock for six months, then you lose the opportunity to earn $200 in interest on that $8,000. XYZ does not pay a dividend.

Now consider buying the synthetic stock instead. You buy one XYZ Nov 80 call (Nov options expire exactly six months from today) and sell one XYZ Nov 80 put. How much should you expect to pay for this position, assuming six months to expiration, 5 percent interest rates and stock priced at $80?

If you buy the call and sell the put at the same price, then you own a position that's equivalent to owning 100 shares and you save the $200 in interest that the investor who buys stock has to pay. That's not possible. Instead, if you attempt to buy synthetic stock you find that it costs roughly $200 more to buy the call than you can collect when selling the put. That's the same $200 in interest that it costs to carry the shares for six months. Thus, when options are priced correctly, there's no monetary advantage to owning real shares vs. owning the synthetic equivalent.[4]

{ NOTE: *Obviously $200 worth of interest used in this example is a variable and is constantly changing as the stock price, interest rates and time to expiration change. If the stock is above $80, or if interest rates are higher, or if more time remains before the options expire, then the position costs more.*

Using equivalent positions

When you recognize that one position is equivalent to another, it allows you to trade more efficiently. In the discussion above, we concluded that there's no cost advantage to owning synthetic stock instead of real shares. But there are situations in which synthetic stock presents an advantage. Let's look at a simple collar to see an example when a synthetic position is worthwhile.

If we let R = collar position (collars are discussed in detail in Chapter 13), then:

$$R = S - C_H + P_L$$

Collar = long stock, short call (with a higher strike price, H), long put (with a lower strike price, L). Assume all options have the same expiration date.

---

4. *But options are not always priced correctly and on occasion you may be able to buy the call and sell the put at a better price than it costs to own stock.*

Because we know that S - C_H (the covered call portion of the collar) is equivalent to a short put position (same strike price and expiration date), we can rewrite the equation:

$$R = (S - C_H) + P_L \text{ becomes } R = -P_H + P_L$$

In other words, the collar is equivalent to a position in which you sell one put with a higher strike price and buy one put with a lower strike price. This is a spread position.

Here's a bit of option jargon

- When long one put and short another, the position is called a "put spread."
- When long one call and short another, the position is called a "call spread."
- By definition, when you own the more expensive option and sell the less expensive option, you "buy the spread."
- When you buy the put spread and both options have the same expiration date, it's called a "bear spread" because you make money when the underlying asset declines.
- When you buy the call spread and both options have the same expiration date, it's called a "bull spread" because you make money when the underlying asset increases in value.
- When you sell the more expensive option, you "sell the spread."

Thus, instead of owning a collar position, you can choose to own the equivalent position. To accomplish that:

- Instead of initiating the covered call portion of the collar (long stock, short call), sell the put (same strike as the call).

- Buy the same put you buy when you own the collar.
- By doing that, you sell the put spread. Because you sell the bear spread the position is bullish.

Why bother with the collar equivalent?

Any time your stock doesn't pay a dividend (and many times even if it does) you may prefer to sell the equivalent put spread, rather than establish a collar position. When the options are priced correctly (as they are most of the time), there is no difference in profit potential or risk. Remember—when you own the collar, you collect dividends but must pay interest to carry stock. Unless the dividend is large enough to offset the cost to carry or you have a tax situation that favors collecting dividends, the put spread is a better choice for most investors.

Several reasons to choose the equivalent:

- There are two commissions (put and put) required to open a put spread. The collar requires three (put, call and stock).
- It's more efficient to trade the put spread. When you enter an order to sell a put spread, you find that market makers almost always quote spreads at a discount to the individual markets. By that I mean you seldom are required to pay the ask price on one leg and sell the bid price on the other. Remember, you are not forced to sell the spread at the price quoted by market makers. You may attempt to sell the spread at any price, knowing there's a chance your order is not executed. It's more difficult to get a good quote for a collar position—simply because it has three legs. You can readily trade the put spread in a single transaction, but may be forced to "leg"[5] into the collar trade.
- The same situation occurs if you decide to close the position. The advantages of trading

---

5. In this context, "leg" is a verb. It refers to trading one part of the desired position first, then the other(s). It's less risky to trade all parts of the position simultaneously.

two items, rather than three, remain. And that includes lower commissions.

- Depending on your broker, margin requirements may be lower for the put spread.

BOTTOM LINE: Selling the put spread, the synthetic equivalent of the collar, is easier to trade and requires paying fewer commission dollars. Investors who are unaware of equivalent positions never consider selling the put spread. And many investors who sell put spreads are unaware they are trading collars. If the conservative collar strategy (Chapter 13) suits you and your investment objectives, then you can make things easier for yourself by selling put spreads.

This is an important lesson. When you understand that a collar is a relatively conservative option strategy and that selling a put spread is its equivalent, you are better placed to recognize the advantages of selling put spreads. It's one of the least risky methods available to you, the individual investor, who wants to take a bullish stance on the stock market. Further discussion of this method is postponed until Chapter 18.

Let's look an example demonstrating that a collar is the synthetic equivalent to a put spread.

EXAMPLE

Collar
- *Buy 500 PQR at 50*
- *Sell 5 PQR Aug 55 call*
- *Buy 5 PQR Aug 50 put*

Equivalent put spread
- *Sell 5 PQR Aug 55 put*
- *Buy 5 PQR Aug 50 put*

These are equivalent positions because the first two legs of the collar (long stock, short call) are equivalent to selling the put (same strike price). Let's take a detailed look the expiration possibilities to see if these positions really are equivalent.

Position at expiration

Collar
- If stock is below 50, you exercise your Aug 50 puts. No remaining position.
- If stock is between 50 and 55, call and put expire worthless. Long 500 shares.
- If stock is above 55, you are assigned an exercise notice on the calls. No remaining position.

Put spread
- If stock is below 50, you exercise your Aug 50 puts. You are assigned an exercise notice on your Aug 55 puts. No remaining position.
- If stock is between 50 and 55, you are assigned on your Aug 55 puts. The Aug 50 puts expire worthless. Long 500 shares.
- If stock is above 55, both options expire worthless. No remaining position.

Thus, at any stock price, the positions are the same. Note that pin risk is present at the higher strike price with either position. At the lower strike, you own the puts and have no pin risk.

Profit and loss at expiration

Now let's consider the P/L for the trade. Both positions includes the purchase of Aug 50 puts. Thus, our task is to show that P/L for the covered call portion of the collar (long 500 shares and short five Aug 55 calls) is identical with that of the corresponding short put position (short five Aug 55 puts).

This proof is similar to that presented earlier in this chapter when we discussed buying XYZ Nov 80 calls and selling Nov 80 puts instead of buying stock:

1. When the options are priced correctly, the time premium you collect when writing the Aug 55 covered call is greater than the time premium you collect for writing the naked Aug 55 put. That appears to favor selling the call. However,

the difference in those time premiums is identical (when the markets are operating efficiently) with the cost of carrying the stock. In other words, the covered call writer collects extra time premium in the option, but pays that amount in interest. Thus, there's no monetary advantage to owning either position.

2. We showed that -P = S – C. That's the situation here: Selling the Aug 55P is equivalent to owning stock (S) and selling the Aug 55C.

Many times there is no advantage to trading the synthetic equivalent. That's not true for collars where the advantages are clear. Opening and closing spreads with two legs is far easier than positions with three legs.

It never hurts to consider alternatives when trading options.

Box spread

The box is another spread to help you gain a better understanding of equivalent positions and deserves a place in your arsenal of option knowledge.

The box is a riskless (and often rewardless also) position, but understanding the box is beneficial, even though you may never trade a box. The box spread consists of one call spread and one put spread, each with the same strike price. The options all expire in the same month and have the same underlying asset. If you buy both the call spread and the put spread, you are long the box. When you sell both spreads, you are short the box. The description of a box spread includes the underlying and both strike prices, e.g., ABC Apr 60/65 box.

$$B = (C_L - C_H) + (P_H - P_L), \text{ where } B = \text{box spread}$$

When expiration arrives, the box is worth exactly the difference between the strike prices. For example, if you own the FGH Jul 30/35 box, then you are

- Long the Jul 30 call
- Short the Jul 35 call
- Long the Jul 35 put
- Short the Jul 30 put

If the stock is above 35 (the higher strike) when expiration arrives, both puts expire worthless. You exercise your long Jul 30 call, paying $3,000 for 100 shares. You are assigned an exercise notice on the Jul 35 calls and sell your 100 shares for $3,500. Net to you: $500.

If the stock is below $30 per share (the lower strike), both calls expire worthless. You exercise your Jul 35 put, selling 100 shares and collecting $3,500. You are assigned an exercise notice on the Jul 30 put and pay $3,000 for 100 shares. Net to you: $500.

If the stock is priced between the strike prices, 30 and 35 in this example, then the options you are short (Jul 30 put and Jul 35 call) expire worthless. You exercise your Jul 30 call, paying $3,000 for 100 shares. You also exercise your Jul 35 put, selling your 100 shares and collecting $3,500. Net to you: $500.

Thus, at any stock price, the box spread is worth the difference between the strikes, or $500 in this example. In the strikes are 10 points apart, the box is worth $1,000 at expiration.[6]

You never want to buy or sell the box spread as an entity. However, knowing about this spread adds flexibility to your trading and sometimes allows you to trade more intelligently. Why not trade the box? First, it involves four commissions to open the position and then you must pay either four more commissions to close, or two exercise/assignment

---

6. *This basic fact is vital. I once heard of a new market maker who learned that a box is always worth $10. He went onto the trading floor and bought a boatload of boxes at $6 each. Unfortunately for that market maker, those were $5 boxes.*

fees. Second, there's no one to sell you this spread for less than $5.[7] And if you wanted to sell, you would never find anyone to pay as much as $5. (Yes, there are situations in which professionals trade box spreads, but you, as an individual investor, can ignore them as trading vehicles.) And boxes are subject to pin risk (if the stock is pinned to either strike price at expiration, you won't know if you are assigned an exercise notice on the option you are short).

Why care about box spreads?

Let's say you decide that BCD is a good, conservative investment and that you want to collar the position. Because you are aware of synthetics, you decide to sell a put spread, rather than bother with owning the shares outright. Thus, you plan to buy the Dec 45 put and sell the Dec 50 put. Let's say you can collect $150 when selling this spread. You can go right ahead and sell the spread, establishing the position you want to own. But, let's look a bit further into trade alternatives.

If you own one BCD Dec 45/50 box, your position is:

- Long Dec 45 call
- Short Dec 50 call
- Long Dec 50 put
- Short Dec 45 put

Because we know the box is a riskless spread, let's combine the box with the position you want to own, which is:

- Long Dec 45 put
- Short Dec 50 put

When we combine (add together) these positions, the puts cancel each other and we get:

- Long Dec 45 call
- Short Dec 50 call

It's definitely inefficient to make all these trades, but if you make them in your mind, sometimes you discover an equivalent position at a better price—and than means more money in your pocket. For example, one way to sell the put spread described above is to buy the corresponding (same strikes and expiration) call spread.

BOTTOM LINE: Buying a call spread is equivalent to selling a put spread with the same strike prices and expiration date. That put spread, in turn, is equivalent to owning the collar position. Thus, instead of owning a collar, you can sell a put spread or buy a call spread. Each position is equivalent to the others.

EXAMPLE

Above, we considered selling the BCD Dec 45/50 put spread for $150. Before you enter the order to sell that spread, take a look at the Dec 45/50 call spread. If you can buy it for less than $350, then buying the call spread may be a better deal for you. Here's some practical advice: Don't bother if the difference is only $5 because there's a small interest cost when you own the call spread. Buy the call spread when you can save $10 or more. This opportunity is not available often,[8] but unless you have an extreme urgency to complete your trade, it's worth your time to see if this opportunity is available.

---

7. *You can buy it for a bit less than $5, but it's not going to be a profitable trade. When you buy the box, you are using approximately $500 (or $1,000 if the strike prices are 10 points apart) in cash. The interest you fail to earn on that cash is always (when the markets operate efficiently) going to be greater than the discount you can receive on the box. In other words, if the cost to carry (own) the box from the time you buy it until expiration is $15, then buying the box for anything under $485 is not possible—and that ignores the extra expense of commissions.*

8. *The market makers never offer this opportunity. But sometimes, an individual investor like you offers to sell the call spread (in this example) at a better price than the market makers are offering to sell it. If no one buys that spread immediately, it's there for you to buy. When that happens, there is a decent chance that the spread is offered at a price that's advantageous to you.*

{ NOTE: *Comparing the price of the call spread with that of the put spread is a method that saves you money on occasion. If you feel it's not worth the effort, that's fine. But just knowing about these possibilities makes you a much smarter options trader than the vast majority who simply shoot from the hip and don't understand how options work.*

If the stock pays a dividend, the situation becomes more complicated because it's sometimes a good idea to exercise a call option before expiration—just to collect the dividend. To keep it simple, simply make the trade you prefer, and avoid the equivalent position when there is a dividend involved.

Let's consider how you can benefit from this information:

1. Determine the price at which you can sell the put spread.
2. Subtract that price from the expiration value of the box (the difference between the strike prices, multiplied by 100). In our example, you can sell the put spread for $150. Subtracting that from $500 yields $350. That's your target. The goal is to buy the spread for $340 or less. (Now that options trade in pennies, you can get more sophisticated and calculate the exact difference you require for additional profits.)
3. If the corresponding call spread can be purchased for less than the target, then it's more profitable to buy the call spread, than to sell the put spread.
4. When selling the put spread, your hope is that the stock rises above the higher strike and for the spread to be worth $0. In that scenario, the call spread is worth $500 (box is worth $500 and puts are worth zero). The profit potential from the put spread is $150 and from the call spread it's $160 (less cost to carry).

5. The most you can lose is the $340 cost of the call spread, or $350 when you sell the put spread. The spread can never be worth more than the difference between the strikes. (Chapter 18 contains greater details.)

Any time you can earn a larger profit by buying the call spread[9] it pays to buy it, rather than sell the put spread. When you're ready to sell the put spread, take a look at the corresponding call spread to determine if it's better to buy that spread instead. Most of the time you won't find a profitable opportunity, but any time you can make a few extra dollars—with no added risk—it's a good idea to do it.

Conclusion

- If the box is worth $500 (strikes five points apart), then the call spread and the put spread together are worth $500, less the cost to carry.
- If you can buy the call spread for less than it is worth, consider doing so.
- Remember, selling the put spread allows you to collect interest. Buying the call spread requires paying interest. Don't bother unless you can save enough to make it worthwhile—perhaps $10. Thus, go ahead with your original plan and sell the put spread if you cannot buy the call spread for at least $10 less than it's worth.

BOTTOM LINE:

- Selling a put spread is equivalent to buying the call spread with the same strike prices and expiration date.
- Selling a call spread is equivalent to buying the put spread with the same strike prices and expiration date.
- Selling the put spread or buying the call spread is equivalent to owning the corresponding collar (same strike prices and expiration).

---

9. *Be careful. It must be the spread with the same strike prices and expiration date as the put spread.*

By understanding that you can get the benefits of your desired position by making trades that give you an equivalent position, you occasionally earn extra dollars. But the real benefit derived from understanding the material in this chapter is that it gives you a significant advantage over the vast majority of individual investors who trade options without thoroughly understanding how options work.

As you trade and become more familiar with options, you can return to this chapter to reinforce what you already know and add to your knowledge base. This will become second nature as you gain more experience.

Quiz

1. If you buy three HHH Nov 40 puts and sell three Nov 40 calls, what is the equivalent position?

2. You are considering selling the YYY Feb 50/60 put spread and collecting $400. You can buy the YYY Feb 50/60 call spread for $620 instead. Should you do that?

3. How much is the GOOG Jun 500/560 box worth at expiration?

4. Trading box spreads is a money making strategy.
○ **TRUE**   ○ **FALSE**

5. You own the IBM Oct 110/120 call spread. On expiration day,

    A. IBM closes at 110. Do you have pin risk?
    B. IBM closes at 115. Do you have pin risk?
    C. IBM closes at 120. Do you have pin risk?

6. You want to sell the ABCD Jun 35/40 put spread for $1.25. You notice that the ABCD Sep 35/40 call spread is offered at $3.60. Should you buy it?

Part III

Beyond the Basics

Chapter 16

The Greeks

The importance of risk management has been mentioned repeatedly. When you use the strategies outlined in this book correctly, you earn profits on most of your trades. But losses are inevitable. It's crucial to your long-term success as an option trader to be certain those losses are not large enough to hurt. In other words, if you establish positions that earn $500 per trade, you cannot afford to occasionally lose $10,000. The best way to prevent large losses is to recognize the potential risk of each position. If that risk is too large compared with your average profit per trade, you have some alternatives: you can avoid the trade, reduce the size (number of contracts) of the position, or take out insurance.[1] But if you are unaware of the likelihood of losing money

---

1. We have not previously discussed the idea of buying separate insurance. All recommended trades in Part III have limited risk because the methodology includes buying one option for each option sold. But, sometimes it's a good idea to own additional insurance.

or the size of a potential loss, it's difficult to take appropriate action.

One way that option traders measure risk is by considering a set of mathematical parameters identified by Greek letters,[2] and known collectively as "the Greeks." When you quantify risk (exposure to loss), it's easier to decide if a specific position, or your entire portfolio, is within your comfort zone—or if steps should be taken to reduce (or eliminate) that risk. No one is suggesting you trade without risk. But your profit potential is limited when you adopt the recommended methods, and you must not allow losses to overpower those gains.

Once again, no mathematical skills (beyond simple arithmetic)[3] are required to use the Greeks. The term, "delta" was introduced earlier. In this chapter, delta and four other Greeks are described.

Each Greek measures the *sensitivity* of option prices (i.e., how much change to expect in the option price) when something in the marketplace changes. By understanding why option prices move higher and lower you learn how various market actions affect the value of individual options. By now you understand that calls increase in value as the underlying moves higher or as the implied volatility increases, but by using the Greeks you can make a good estimate of just how much the option price is expected to change. Estimating exposure to loss (as well as having a better understanding of potential gains) allows you to intelligently adjust (hedge) any risk factor that has increased beyond your comfort level.

You may even decide to pre-hedge, protecting against the unlikely possibility of losing money if some external event causes a significant market move. And sometimes that insurance policy not only prevents large losses, it turns what would have been a losing trade into a good-sized winner.

There are two sides to this insurance issue. If your portfolio places you within your comfort zone, then you probably don't have a need to pre-hedge. On the other hand, if your positions make you worry about losses, insurance is probably a good idea:

- If you pre-hedge a specific risk factor before being threatened, it's much less costly to buy that insurance. For example, you can buy a few calls and/or puts to protect your portfolio against a rare overnight market surge or collapse. This idea is discussed in Chapter 20.
- If you buy insurance only when it's needed, most of the time you never buy insurance. However, on those occasions when you require protection, it's expensive. For example, if you buy a few puts only after a substantial market decline, those puts have become substantially more costly because the market is lower (increasing the value of puts), and the higher implied volatility,[4] further increases prices.

Calculating the Greeks

The obvious question: How do you calculate the Greeks? Luckily it's not a problem. The calculator used in Chapter 6 to determine the theoretical value of an option does all the work for you. Such a calculator provides all Greeks discussed in this chapter and can be found at the CBOE website: www.cboe.com/LearnCenter/OptionCalculator.aspx.

---

2. With one exception: "Vega" is often used as one of the Greeks, even though vega is NOT a Greek letter.
3. The calculations themselves are not simple, but fortunately, you don't have to calculate your own Greeks. The data is readily obtainable.
4. IV increases substantially when the market declines because nervous investors buy puts for protection—just as you are attempting to do. This IV increase does not occur when the market rallies strongly, although it was not always this way. Through the 1970s and 80s, substantial rallies were accompanied by a large increase in the IV of call options.

Let's say you have a position and the underlying stock undergoes a significant move. You probably already know if the position is profitable, but if you determine the Greeks after such a move, it may help you decide whether to hold, adjust or close the position. Investors usually consider risk as something that measures potential loss, but it also helps you decide when to take profits. For example, there may be profit potential remaining, but if you already made 80 to 90 percent of the maximum profit and there's one month remaining before the options expire, it's often not worth risking that profit in an attempt to earn the last 10 to 20 percent. Why? Because there's very little likelihood of earning additional profits *quickly*. You can calculate how much the underlying must move, or how much time must pass, before you can expect your profit to increase by a specified amount. The longer you hold a position when there's little to gain, the greater the chance of losing your initial gains.

EXAMPLE

You sell 10 HUGS (a manufacturer of stuffed toy animals) Jul 40 puts at $0.60 each when the stock is trading near 44. Two weeks later, the stock rallies to 47.25 and Jul expiration does not arrive for another 50 days. The market in these puts is $0.10 to $0.15.

When you sold puts, the delta was -17[5] and you were long the equivalent of 170 shares. The current delta is -5 and you are long the equivalent of 50 shares. You have choices: If you pay $0.15 for the puts, you lock in 75 percent of the maximum profit ($45 out of a possible $60) for each option. You can try to buy the puts for less than $0.15 to lock in a higher profit. Or you can hold and try to earn the full $60 per option. How do you decide?

Each investor must choose the appropriate action for his or her comfort zone, and thus, as with most option decisions, there's no perfect action to take. Because the delta is currently -5, there's approximately a 5 percent chance that these options finish in-the-money[6] (stock lower than 40). It feels pretty good when the odds of making money are 19:1 in your favor, but when all you have to gain is that last 10 or 15 cents, and especially when there's still substantial time remaining, I recommend taking profits and finding another investment. This idea is not universally accepted and some prefer to hold out for every last penny and prefer to wait for the options to expire (hopefully worthless). Based on more than 30 years of option-trading experience, this is not recommended. First, there's too little to gain and you can do better investing your money in a new position. Second, unexpected, market-moving events do occur. It would be sad to turn this sure winner into a loser if something unexpected happened. This is not to suggest that you take quick profits as a general rule—do so only when there's little to be gained from continuing to hold a position.

In this scenario, you can enter a bid between $0.11 and $0.14 and hope to buy the puts at less than the current asking price (but there's nothing wrong with paying the offer, $0.15, if that feels right to you). The rationale is: You have most of the profit locked in quickly and there's not much profit potential remaining. If only seven days remained in the lifetime of the options, I wouldn't consider paying more than $0.05 (and for most traders, there's

---

5. *Use the CBOE calculator. Volatility = 30.*
6. *Remember, delta represents approximate probability of finishing in-the-money.*

nothing wrong with waiting for that last week to earn the last nickel).[7]

If you buy options, you profit from major moves and suffer if time passes and nothing good happens. You can use the calculator and the Greeks to estimate potential gains as well as the cost of waiting. Greeks help you get a handle on any option position and allow you to estimate how those positions perform under various market conditions.

{ *NOTE: You can get along without using Greeks. If you choose that route, you may fly blind part of the time and have difficulty estimating current risk. You'll probably survive, but you are at a disadvantage compared with investors who have a better understanding of potential losses. It's worth the effort to use the Greeks to help make intelligent trading decisions. Your broker should provide the Greeks for each position, which saves you the trouble of using the calculator. Many brokers provide the Greeks live online. If your broker doesn't, request it.[8]*

The Individual Greeks (delta, gamma, vega, theta, rho)
Delta

Delta measures how much change to expect in the price of an option (or position) as the price of the underlying asset changes by $1. Keep in mind that delta never gives the *exact* change in the price of an option because:

- Delta itself is not constant but changes as the stock price changes. The rate at which delta changes is measured by *gamma*.
- Delta represents the *theoretical* change in the option's price when the underlying stock (or

ETF or index) price changes. Most of the time the *real* change in the option price differs because other factors (including other Greeks) are in play.

- Delta is the theoretical percentage of the stock's move that appears in the option price. For example, an option with a 50 delta moves approximately 50 cents when the stock moves $1 (50 percent of the stock move). An option with a 20 delta moves approximately five cents when the stock moves 25 cents.
- When measuring the daily change in the stock price, one day passes, and that reduces the option's value. The Greek that describes this change is *theta*.
- Market factors may result in a change in the implied volatility (IV) of the options. A news event, or an influx of buy (or sell) orders may trigger such a change. "*Vega*" describes how an IV change affects the option price.

Delta is important. It may not predict the exact price at which an option trades when the stock price changes, but it provides a good estimate of your profit/loss. And that's the information needed to estimate the risk and reward for a specific position.

Although not part of the official definition of delta, it's a good estimate of the probability that the option finishes[9] in the money. In other words, when an option has a 36 delta (or -36), it finishes ITM 36 percent of the time. Obviously that means it finishes OTM (expires worthless) about 64 percent of the time.

---

7. *Waiting one week is not the same as waiting one month. It's extremely conservative to pay that $0.05, and there are good arguments against wasting nickels to buy in options that are obviously worthless. But, there is no such thing as "obviously" worthless. Markets can do very unexpected things once in a while. Holding out for the last nickel or dime is something I no longer do. Many years ago, I refused to buy in these "worthless" options. Of course, I won the bet most of the time, but every few years or so, it was a costly mistake. I no longer play the final nickel game and suggest you decide for yourselves whether it's worthwhile to play.*

8. *Some brokers refuse to provide the data. That is unacceptable to me.*

9. *Remember, "finish" refers to the stock's closing price on expiration Friday.*

NOTE: *An option with a 36 delta may expire worthless 64 percent of the time, but it does not mean the option remains OTM 64 percent of the time. Stocks move up and down—and occasionally the option expires worthless—but only after it goes ITM for an unspecified period of time. Thus, when you sell options (hoping they expire worthless), it may feel comfortable to sell options with a high probability of expiring worthless,[10] but the probability that the option remains OTM for its entire lifetime is not as high as the probability that it expires worthless. In practical terms this means you should not sell options, close your eyes, and hope for the best. Low probability events do occur and it's important not to let those events cause too much harm.*

Delta can be considered as "equivalent number of shares." Thus, if your position is long 87 delta, the position performs as if you own 87 shares of stock. That's why knowing your position delta helps measure risk.

Some additional details about delta:

- The delta of a call option is between 0 and 100. The value of a call option increases as the underlying asset increases. Thus, calls have *positive delta*. For example, if a call option has a 30 delta and the stock increases by $1, the price of the call is expected to increase by $.30.
- The delta of a put option is between 0 and -100. The value of a put option decreases as the underlying price increases, and puts have *negative delta*. For example, if a put option has a -60 delta and the stock increases by $1, the price of the put is expected to decrease by $0.60. If a put option has a delta of -45 and the

stock drops by $2, the price of the put option increases by approximately $0.90.
- The delta of the underlying asset is constant (100).

Each individual option has its own delta and deltas are additive. Thus, you determine the delta for a position by adding deltas for the individual options comprising the position.

EXAMPLE

If you own a collar, the position delta is:

- *100 (for the stock)*
- *Subtract the call delta (because you sold the call)*
- *Add the put delta (remember, the put delta is negative).[11]*

Using delta

You decide to take a bullish position in ARTS and, with the stock trading at $22.35, sell eight ARTS Nov 20 puts at $0.50.[12] ARTS owns a series of galleries specializing in works by early twentieth century artists. Using the calculator, you find the implied volatility is 50 and each put has a -22 delta. The delta of your position is +176 (-8 x -22).

Writing puts is a bullish strategy and +176 deltas confirms that. What can you do with this information? If ARTS moves higher by one point, you expect the position to earn $176. All by itself, this doesn't tell you much more than you already knew.

But, what happens if two days pass and you find the stock is trading at $20.25? How concerned should you be? Should you do anything with this position? The calculator tells you these options are worth $1.13 and the delta

---

10. *The probability that the underlying will touch the strike price during an option's lifetime can be calculated, but for the vast majority of traders, this can be ignored.*
11. *When you subtract a negative number you get a positive number. Thus, selling puts adds positive deltas to a position and buying puts adds negative deltas.*
12. *40 days before November options expire.*

is -43. Because you sold this put for 50 cents[13] and it's now worth $1.13, you have a loss of approximately $63 per contract.[14] Not much you can do about that, but by calculating the position delta, you find that you are now long 344 deltas.[15] If the stock continues to decline, your immediate exposure is $344 per point. It's appropriate for you to make a decision. Do you leave this position as it is?

If you are an investor willing to accumulate shares, the position is acceptable and there's nothing to do. When expiration arrives, you either own your shares or collect a profit when the option expires worthless.

For the trader who has no interest in owning stock, a decision must be made: Is it OK to hold this position knowing your current exposure? If the stock declines further, you lose about $344 for the first point (and an increasing amount after that). Does this position make you uncomfortable—are potential losses greater than you are willing to accept? I cannot answer for you, but by knowing the position delta, you can gauge your immediate risk and decide if this position remains within your comfort zone or if something should be done to reduce risk. Perhaps the Greeks of your entire portfolio may help you decide whether to hold or adjust. If you have a good balance of long and short deltas, then you may feel better about doing nothing with your ARTS position for the moment. On the other hand, if most of your positions are delta long, you may not be comfortable with the position. Bottom line: knowing the position delta helps you estimate the risk associated with holding a position and allows you to make informed decisions. Remember these are not always winning decisions, but don't let that concern you. Part of the time when you make

an adjustment the stock is going to reverse direction, making that adjustment unnecessary. That's simply the cost of doing business—and your business is protecting your assets.

We have not discussed specific adjustments to make, if you decide that a position's risk should be reduced, but the simplest path is to reduce your current position by buying back all or some of the puts sold earlier. You have other choices, some of which are discussed below and in greater detail in Chapter 18.

> NOTE: Some investors initiate positions and only consider expiration possibilities. They hope to make money over the long term are not concerned with risk, do not adjust positions and ignore Greeks. This is not the path to success. If you are aware of the risk and reward potential of any position you own, you are in control and are not forced to depend on luck. It's not necessary to make adjustments every time a position moves against you, but it's also not wise to always ignore these events. Understanding risk enables you to significantly reduce or eliminate the occurrence of large losses.

Gamma

Gamma measures the rate at which delta changes when the underlying asset moves $1. Because of gamma, delta is not constant and declines to zero when options are far out-of-the-money and increases to 100 (or -100 for puts) when options are deep in-the-money. Gamma is additive, meaning that for a given position, the total gamma is the sum of the individual gammas (add gamma for options you own and subtract gamma for options sold).

When investors buy options, gamma is their ally. This is especially true for OTM options. The lure of owning an option with a 20 (or -20) delta, watching the stock move in the right direction and seeing

---

13. That's 50 cents per share, or $50 per contract.
14. The actual loss is determined by the market price of the option, not its theoretical price.
15. (-8 x -43).

the option's delta increase (because of positive gamma) to 80 (or -80) is irresistible to some. These "exploding deltas" can produce large profits. For example, if you buy 10 puts with a -20 delta, your position is short 200 delta. If the stock moves quickly in your favor, you may find yourself with a large profit and a position that is short 800 delta.

When you sell options, gamma is the enemy and must be paid proper respect. It's because of gamma that it's best not to sell naked options.[16] When short put options, if the underlying moves lower, the value of those puts rises at an ever-increasing rate because of the effects of gamma.

Returning to our example, did you notice that delta was -22 when the ARTS puts were written and increased[17] to -43 after the stock declined? That's the effect of gamma. Thus, current delta gives you a good estimate of how the value of a single option (or an option position) changes as the price of the underlying moves one point, but gamma causes the effects to accelerate when the stock continues to move in the same direction. Gamma is the property of an option that makes it painful to be wrong when selling options or joyful to be correct when owning options. Gamma is the driving force behind the adoption of option strategies that limit losses.

> NOTE: Gamma is always a positive number. Because call options have positive gamma, call deltas increase as the stock price increases (but can never be more than 100). Because puts have positive gamma, put deltas increase (become more negative, but never exceed -100) as the stock price decreases. The gamma of at-the-money options is equal for both the put and call (same underlying asset, and same expiration). Once the stock price changes, those gammas are no longer equal.

Vega

Vega measures the sensitivity of the option price to a one point change in volatility. Vega is always positive because the value of both puts and calls increase as volatility increases. Vega is additive: add vega for options you own and subtract vega for options sold.

When you accumulate several positions, or a few large positions, you may not be aware that your portfolio has become subject to vega risk. In other words, a substantial change in implied volatility can add or subtract significantly to your account valuation. When your broker provides the Greeks, it's a simple matter to see your total vega and decide if you are long or short too much vega. It can become tedious to calculate vega for each position in your portfolio.[18] That's one more reason why it's important for your broker to provide the Greeks.

As you gain experience you learn which positions are associated with positive vega and which have negative vega. If you find that reducing (or increasing) vega is necessary to reduce the vega risk of your holdings, you add the correct type of position to help neutralize vega exposure.

As a quick guide:

- Options with more time to expiration have more vega than nearer-term options.
- OTM[19] options have the most vega, followed by ATM and then ITM.

Theta

Theta measures the sensitivity of an option's value to the passage of one day. When you own an option, you have negative theta because an option is a wasting asset and its value decreases every day. When you sell an option you have positive theta.

---

16. *Selling naked puts because you want to accumulate stock is an exception. The strategies discussed in Part III do not involve the sale of naked options. We always buy at least one option for every option sold.*
17. *Technically, when a number grows more negative, that number is decreasing. But, let's not nitpick. For our purposes, when the delta of a put option changes from -20 to -50, the delta is said to increase.*
18. *It's not difficult to use the calculator again and again, but it can become boring.*
19. *If too far OTM, all the Greeks become zero. Thus in this context OTM means not far out-of-the-money.*

The option strategies recommended in this book have positive theta and the passage of time is beneficial to your positions. Don't allow this short discussion to minimize that fact. These strategies all benefit from the passage of time.

Rho

Rho measures the sensitivity of an option's value to a change in interest rates. Because interest rates tend to change slowly (if at all), a change in interest rate is not that important to the value of an option (unless it's a very long-term option), and thus, rho is the least important of the Greeks.

Using the information

How does all this help? What are you supposed to do with the information? If you adopt the basic conservative strategies, then your portfolio is always bullish—and bullish is the traditional way that the vast majority of investors, who own stock and mutual funds, look at the stock market. Assuming you are comfortable with that, the Greeks don't provide a great deal of useful information for you. Yes, you can look at theta for your portfolio and get a handle on just how much you can expect to earn from time decay, but that information is probably not important to you, the investor. Short-term traders may be more interested in theta because they hold positions for less time.

EXAMPLE

Assume it's Jun 1, 20xx, interest rates are 5 percent, and ABCD pays no dividend. There are 50 days remaining to July expiration.

You own 1,000 ABCD (currently trading at 21.87) and wrote 10 Jul 20 calls (IV = 35). Stock has a delta of 100 (by definition) and you are long 1,000 shares. That's equivalent to 1,000 delta.[20] The Jul 20 call has a 79 delta. You sold 10 calls, and that contributes 790 short delta. Net: long 210 delta. Thus, your current profit/

loss expectation is approximately the same as if you own 210 shares of ABCD outright, instead of the covered call position. The calculator also shows that your position is short 85 gamma (10 x 8.5) and that your time decay for seven days is $.076 per share (or $7.60 per option contract).

If you are primarily an investor who plans to hold this position, the Greeks are less important. They provide a reasonable estimate of potential gains/losses over the near term, but because your intention is to hold and profit from theta, you have no plans to close this position. You expect to collect $76 from theta over the next week. That's not very much, but the position is working in your favor, as long as nothing bad happens to your ABCD shares. You are short gamma and understand that the delta of your short calls increases as the stock price increases. Thus, if the stock rises one point, the 8.5 gamma tells you that the delta increases from 79 to approximately 87.

Sample analysis

Assume you sold some puts on XYZ and that the stock quickly dropped from 53 to 48. You have negative gamma. As a result, this position is losing money and you are long delta. Assume you are long 500 delta and short 100 gamma. Your first decision must be whether you are comfortable with this position, knowing that if the stock declines another point you become long 600 delta.[21] If the decision is made to reduce risk, there are two issues to address. First you want some negative delta to make your position less long. You can sell stock, buy puts or sell calls. Second, your position can use some positive gamma. Of the adjustment choices, only put buying accomplishes both the need for negative delta and positive gamma.

You are not forced to buy puts—it's merely one of your choices. But, you are already short

---

20. *Delta is share equivalent. Thus, one share equals one delta.*
21. *Because your gamma is -100, if the stock moves one point lower, you gain 100 additional delta.*

puts and buying back some of those puts is the simplest type of adjustment. Alternatively, you can buy a different put and convert your current put position into a put spread (more on this topic in Chapter 18).

{ *NOTE: Be careful. When the stock is falling, it may seem that the best strategy is to sell call options to gain some negative delta. Please don't sell naked calls.[22] It's easy to fall into the trap of believing that the sale of OTM call options is safe. It does provide some positive delta and does add some more theta, but it adds very little downside protection (and that's what you need now) and introduces upside risk. While it's true that being short both puts and calls is a viable option strategy, it's far too risky for a less-experienced options trader. In fact, it's an unsuitable strategy for most investors and I suggest you never sell straddles (call and put with same strike price and expiration date) or strangles (different strike prices with same expiration date).* }

If you are 500 delta long, that's the equivalent of owning 500 shares. The question to ask is: Are you comfortable holding your position and its gamma in the current environment? If the potential loss from such a position is outside your comfort zone, then the answer is no and you should adjust the position by adding some short deltas.[23]

If you prefer to have a more market-neutral[24] portfolio, then it's mandatory to be aware of portfolio delta, and more importantly, gamma. Some professional traders are quite risk adverse and manage their portfolios by keeping delta, gamma, vega and theta as near zero as possible. There's no need for you to go that far, but unless you are always bullish, or want to place a bet on market direction, there's no reason to be long or short many deltas. One market-neutral strategy is covered in detail in Chapter 19.

Market exposure

Not all deltas are created equal. This becomes obvious if you consider this scenario: You are long 100 GOOG (Google) delta, a stock trading above $600 per share. If the stock moves 2 percent (12 points), your position makes or loses $1,200.

Compare that with being long 100 MSFT (Microsoft) delta. This stock trades near 35. If MSFT changes price by 2 percent your gain or loss is $70. Thus, if long 100 GOOG and short 100 MSFT, you are NOT market neutral. While it's correct to sum deltas for options of a specific underlying asset to determine a position delta, simply adding deltas of individual positions does not give you a true measure of market risk. Your portfolio may have zero delta, but if long 100 GOOG delta and short 100 MSFT delta, it's a bullish portfolio due to the nature of those deltas.

A better method for determining your exposure to a market move—in either direction—is to determine the "dollar delta." That means summing the delta for each individual underlying asset and then multiplying that delta by the share price. You then add together those dollar deltas to give you a clearer picture of where your portfolio stands. If you do that with the GOOG/MSFT portfolio, you get:

GOOG: $600 x 100 delta = 60,000 $delta
MSFT : $35 x (-100) delta = -3,500 $delta
Sum: + 56,500 $delta. Thus your portfolio is long, not neutral.

BOTTOM LINE: The Greeks help you manage risk of a specific position or your entire portfolio. It's not necessary to live or die by the numbers, but it is also not in your best interest to ignore this information.

---

22. It's OK to sell calls you own, as long as it does not leave short any naked calls.
23. You can add short delta by closing part of your position. You may also buy puts, sell calls or sell stock.
24. A market-neutral portfolio has neither a bullish nor bearish bias.

Delta and Time

The passage of time affects delta. When expiration arrives:

- If the option is in-the-money, it becomes equivalent to stock (delta = 100). This must be true because ITM options are exercised at expiration and turn into stock.
- If the option is out-of-the-money, it expires worthless and delta is 0.

As expiration approaches:

- The delta of an ITM option moves toward 100. The further ITM, or the less time remaining, the more rapidly delta becomes 100.
- The delta of an OTM option moves toward 0. The further OTM, or the less time remaining, the more rapidly delta becomes 0.

Monitoring risk and doing your best to minimize large losses is the path to success as an option trader. The practical importance of the Greeks becomes more apparent in Chapters 18 through 20.

If you are trading options for the first time, you may feel you are not yet ready to use Greeks. That's not a problem, if you make that a temporary situation. Get used to trading. That comes first. Gain experience opening and closing positions (hopefully for profits). Observe how options expire worthless. Roll positions (only if necessary). Return to this chapter later because this information is important for your long-term success. The Greeks

can help you decide if the position's risk is worth the potential reward. When wild things happen, profits or losses can exceed reasonable expectations. The Greeks are guidelines, not mathematical certainties, but they can be used to decide how much reward to attempt to earn—and the risk involved in seeking that reward. Use your judgment when opening positions and use the Greeks as instruments to help manage your portfolio.

Remember that Greeks help you quantify potential gains and losses. If you follow the advice in this book, all your trades have *limited* losses, and that's the best way to control ultimate risk.

1. You have a covered call position. You are long 200 shares and short two Oct 50 calls. Each call has a 65 delta. What is your position delta?

2. In the above example, if the stock moves from 51 to 52 today, do you expect to make or lose money? How much?

3. You own 10 put options. Are you long or short: gamma, vega, theta and delta?

4. A specific call option, whose vega is $0.040, is trading at $3. A sudden influx of buy orders drives the implied volatility from 35 to 40. What is the new price of this call option?

5. You sold 10 put options at $1.00 apiece. When the underlying stock declined by $1, you lost $200. If the stock declines another point tomorrow, do you expect to lose:

A. Less than $200
B. $200
C. More than $200

Chapter 17

European-Style Index Options

Trading European options differs from trading American options. Most of the high-volume index options traded in the U.S. are European-style. The strategies discussed in this last part of the book are especially appropriate for index options, and unless you have a strong preference for trading options on individual stocks, many of you will ultimately trade European-style options.

Thus far the discussion and trading examples have focused on American-style options because most investors own stocks and thus, when they begin to trade options, it's natural to continue to concentrate on the same stocks. But there are advantages to adopting option strategies when the underlying asset is a diversified stock portfolio,[1] rather than an individual stock. You may discover that you are more comfortable trading options on exchange-traded funds (ETFs) and indexes. Some index options are constantly at the top of the most actively traded list.

Your broker may provide helpful information, but he or she assumes you know what you are doing and is not likely to offer sufficient guidance unless you ask the right questions. Too many investors who use European-style options aren't aware of the fine print and take unnecessary losses.[2] Before you trade European-style options on a regular basis, be sure you understand the risks as well as the rewards.

We'll discuss the differences between European- and American-style options.

Difference one: settlement price

The first major difference between American- and European-style options is the manner in which the settlement price of the underlying index is determined. That settlement price is the official closing price for the index and is the basis for determining which options are in-the-money and the intrinsic value of those options. If you are considering trading index options, it's necessary to understand the process. Many a newcomer to index options has incurred a substantial loss because of his or her failure to understand this basic information:

When a stock closes for trading on the third Friday of the month, the last trade determines which options are in- and out-of-the-money. The last price is the final price. But, the rules are completely different with European-style index options.

- European options cease trading at the close of business on Thursday, one day prior to the third Friday of the expiration month. These options do not trade on expiration Friday, but their value is determined that day.

- The closing price of the underlying index on that Thursday is *irrelevant*. Difficult as it may be to believe, this is not the closing index price for the expiration month. In fact, the settlement price can be very different than Thursday's close.

- Many an investor thought that index options expired worthless only to find that the value of those options soared the next morning and that those "worthless" options were now in-the-money by many hundred (or even a couple thousand) dollars. Investors who owned those options were thrilled, while those who were short these options were filled with other emotions, including bewilderment and outrage.

- The closing price of the index (called the settlement price) is *calculated* based on the market opening on the third Friday. If you don't close your positions by the close of business on Thursday, then the final (settlement) value of your options is determined by how strong or weak the market opens on expiration Friday.

- Note the word "calculated." *The settlement price is not a real-world index price.* In fact, the settlement price is often significantly higher than the official daily high price or significantly lower than the official daily low price. Too many option traders have no idea how that's possible, but you are not going to be one of them.

- The settlement price is a *theoretical* price. It's calculated by determining the *opening price* of each component of the index (and that means all 500 stocks in the S&P 500 Index or all 2,000

---

1. *For readers who adopt strategies recommended in this book, it's best when the underlying asset does not undergo large moves. Because individual stocks are prone to surprise announcements, it's not unusual for individual stocks to gap higher or lower when news is announced. Although this occurs with diversified stock portfolios (when the entire market makes a big move), it happens far less often. For that reason, trading index options is often a wise choice.*
2. *Yes, some are fortunate enough to collect unexpected profits.*

stocks in the Russell 2000 Index, etc.). Then a theoretical price for the index is calculated *as if all components of the index were trading at their opening price at the same time.* It's important to understand that this settlement price is not a real-time price. It's likely that the index never trades at the official settlement price anytime during the trading day. Some stocks open at the opening bell, others shortly thereafter and some may not open until much later. In addition, stocks change price—some rise above the opening price and some fall below. The settlement price is based *only* on the opening price of each individual component of the index. Thus, traders who keep an eye on the actual price of the underlying index expecting the opening price to be the settlement price are often dismayed at how different those prices can be.

- The value of all outstanding options expiring in the current month depends on the settlement price.
- It may take several hours before the settlement price is published. For some indexes the settlement price is not published until the end of the trading day (Friday).
- The settlement price has its own ticker symbol. SPX is the symbol for the S&P 500 Index, but SET is the symbol for the settlement price for that index. Other sample settlement symbols are:
  RUT (Russell 2000): RLS
  NDX (Nasdaq 100): NDS
  DJX (Dow Jones Industrials): DJS

My two cents: If you adopt a strategy that involves the sale of European-style index options, give

serious consideration to closing the position no later than Thursday afternoon (of expiration week). It's seldom worth the risk to maintain that short position, hoping it expires worthless.[3] This risk is known as "settlement risk."

Difference two: cash-settled

European options are cash-settled. If an option is ITM when the settlement price is determined, the intrinsic value of the option, in cash, is removed from the account of the investor who is short the option and transferred to the option owner's account. When using American options, shares of the underlying asset (not cash) exchange hands via exercise and assignment.

EXAMPLE

#1

You paid $450 apiece for four NDX Jun 1950 calls (options on the Nasdaq 100 Index) one day when you felt bullish. At expiration, the settlement price of NDX is 1950.97. Your options are ITM, but this is not a victory for you. The intrinsic value of each call is $97, and $388 (4 x $97) is transferred into your account and the long call options are removed. It's as if you sold your calls and received $97 for each.

#2

You have a position in which you sold 10 SPX May 1500 calls (This is not a naked short, but the other parts of your position are not relevant to this discussion). At expiration, the index settlement price is 1508.73. That means the 1500 call is ITM

---

3. *This advice doesn't mean you must close all positions without thought. If you are short an option that's trading near $0.50 (for example), even if appears to be far out-of-the-money, it pays to buy it back. Every once in a while this option can become worth many hundreds of dollars because of a significant market move at the opening on expiration Friday. On the other hand, if you are short a spread that can never be worth more than $10 (discussed in Chapter 18), it's foolish to repurchase on Thursday afternoon for $9.80. The most you can lose by holding is the last $0.20. But, a significant market move can make this spread worthless, providing you with a gift of $980 per spread. If you own such a spread, rather than wait for that last $0.20, please consider selling and being satisfied with approximately 9.80.*

by 8.73 points and has an intrinsic value of $873. Because you are short 10 of these calls, $8,730 is removed from your account and the SPX May 1500 calls disappear. This result is exactly the same as if you repurchased those May 1500 calls at $8.73. Nothing bad appears to have happened.[4] You may have a profit or loss resulting from this position, but the bottom line is that expiration arrived, you bought back the calls sold earlier and you no longer have a position in these options.[5]

   This cash settlement feature of European-style options is efficient, but because of the method used to determine the final, or closing, price of the index, a new risk factor is introduced. Settlement risk is much greater than most investors anticipate, and I strongly recommend that you avoid being exposed to that risk. An index can easily move more than 2 percent on expiration morning.

EXAMPLE #3

SPX is trading near 1540 late in the afternoon, one day before expiration Friday.

a. You are long an SPX 1520 call option. The option is trading near $21. You decide to hold it overnight. Friday morning, the market opens substantially lower and the settlement price is only 1525.50. You receive $550 per option. True, the market could have opened higher, but why take that chance?

b. You are short five SPX 1530 puts. The market makers are asking $0.60 apiece for those puts. You are not going to let them take advantage of you. After all, the options expire tomorrow morning and they are 10 points out-of-the-money. So, you decide you'll teach them a lesson and refuse to pay that ridiculous price. The next morning there's bad news overseas and the nervous market opens lower. You note that the SPX opens near 1529. You are disappointed that your puts are in-the-money, but it's only $1 and that's not much worse than if you bought back those puts last night by paying $0.60 apiece. The rest of the day is better for the market. The opening price was the low for the day, and by day's end the market has recovered almost all of its losses.

You think no more about your expired puts, but in the afternoon you notice that SET, the official settlement price, is 1525.50. That means you are forced to pay $450 apiece for those puts. Many investors in that position feel cheated. Some are outraged. They believe that some conspiracy was responsible. That's not the case. Those investors ignored settlement risk and have no idea how settlement price is calculated. [6] Please don't let this happen to you. If you choose not to cover, understand that most of the time that's the winning decision, but part of the time it's going be an expensive decision: Paying

---

4. But something very bad may have happened. If this option was OTM at last night's close and you failed to repurchase it, you must now pay $873 apiece for these options.
5. Consider it to be regular expiration in which you were assigned an exercise notice, delivered shares of the underlying and repurchased those shares. Of course, the sale and repurchase of the underlying are imaginary and because no commissions are involved, it costs nothing. Settling options in cash is very convenient for all involved.
6. Because the market was headed lower, many investors, being afraid, sold stocks "at the market." When that happens there are more sellers than buyers and stocks often open at depressed prices. Because the settlement price is determined by those individual opening prices, and because those stocks open at various times, the settlement price is often lower than the actual index price posted. Here's why: While some stocks are already rebounding after the opening, other stocks are not yet open. These stocks may also open at depressed prices. And the settlement price depends only on those opening prices.

that $0.60 for those options doesn't seem like such a bad idea in retrospect. If you prefer to avoid settlement risk, you can roll your front-month options to a different expiration month before those near-term options cease trading.

Assume you have a spread[7] position in which you are short May calls and long June calls. For now, let's ignore why you make this investment, If you prefer to keep the June options, you can cover[8] the May calls and roll the position by selling appropriate June calls to create a new spread consisting of only June options. The point is: If you want to move those short May options to another month, it's better (most of the time) to do so before the May options cease trading.

EXAMPLE

#4

You are long six NDX Jun 2025 calls and short six NDX May 1975 calls. It's expiration week (May) and NDX is currently 1960. You decide it is too risky to hold your short position in May[9] and enter a spread order to:

Buy six May 1975 calls (to close) and sell six Jun 2000 calls (to open). You collect a cash credit of $400 for the spread (that means 4 points for each spread, or $2,400 total).

Your new position is long six NDX Jun 2025 calls and short six NDX Jun 2000 calls.

If you prefer to close, rather than roll, the spread, it's important to understand your choices. One obvious choice is to close by buying in your shorts and selling out your longs. Another choice is to wait for the opening Friday morning. At that time, you sell your Junes and allow your Mays to disappear via settlement. If OTM, the near-term options expire worthless. If ITM, you pay intrinsic value. A reasonable question is: Is that a good idea? The answer is no. If the market gaps higher, you do get a nice price when you sell out your Junes, but as is often the case, the settlement price is even higher than the real world opening price, so you are forced to buy in your Mays (assuming they are ITM) at an elevated price. This is not a profitable situation (most of the time).

There is always another side when talking about risk. If the market opens relatively unchanged—and that does happen—then you are much better off closing Friday morning because you cover your Mays at parity (that's much less than these options cost Thursday afternoon), or they may expire worthless, You sell your Junes approximately where they closed last night. When you make this choice you are taking settlement risk. It's safer and more profitable over the long-term to simply get out of these positions when you can do so—and that means before settlement.

---

7. *A spread (noun) is a position consisting of two or more different options. A spread transaction is a trade in which two or more different options are traded simultaneously. To spread (verb) means to hedge one position by adding a second position to partially offset the risk of owning the first position—as in "I reduced the risk of being short those Dec 50 calls by spreading them against Dec 55 calls."*
8. *Buy to close.*
9. *True, your May position is not naked short and you do own calls to protect against an upside move. If the market rallies, the May calls increase in value much faster than the Jun (they have a higher delta), and if the move is large enough, it results in a loss. Many investors (including this author) feel it's better to eliminate that risk. On the other hand, if the market holds steady and if the May option expires worthless, you can make a very tidy profit by holding this position.*

Cash settlement is a mixed blessing for index traders. Without this feature, index options would not be so popular. Imagine if you owned a portfolio of hundreds of stocks (in an attempt to mimic the performance of the S&P 500, or any other index) and you had to deliver all those stocks when assigned an exercise notice. What a nightmare. Cash settlement simplifies the process for everyone. But the fact that the process is simplified does not eliminate the fact that settlement represents a significant risk for index option traders.

Difference three: exercise rights

The owner of an American-style option has the right to exercise the option *any time* before it expires. European-style options cannot be exercised before expiration. Thus, owners of European-style options who don't want to hold a position have no choice but to sell their options. This represents a small inconvenience for the option buyer and a nice bonus for the option seller who never has to be concerned with being assigned an early exercise notice.

Being assigned early represents a significant risk when dealing with American-style cash-settled index options. Options on the S&P 100 Index (OEX)[10] are popular options to trade, but they present extra difficulties to anyone who sells options.[11] Here's why:

EXAMPLE

#5

Assume you sell two OEX Dec 650 puts and that your timing is unfortunate. The market suddenly drops for several days and falls especially hard one afternoon, and OEX closes at 620 at the low price of the day. Immediately after the close, IBM announces

spectacular earnings and the futures trade much higher,[12] indicating that the market is likely to open significantly higher tomorrow morning. That's good news for someone who sold puts because the anticipated rally presents an opportunity to recover some of your losses. OEX declined all the way to 620, driving your puts 30 points ITM. You hate how much money you are losing on this position, but tomorrow is another day!

The next morning, two things happen:

- *The futures market indicates that the Dow Jones Industrial Average will open about 200 points higher.*
- *You receive an exercise notice on your two OEX Dec 650 puts. Because these options are cash settled, it means you are required to repurchase those options at their intrinsic value, based on last night's closing index price of 620. Thus, you buy your two puts at $30, or $3,000 apiece.*

Sure enough, the markets open strongly higher and the OEX Dec 650 put is trading at 13. Seventeen points better than last night's close! But, it's too late for you. You were assigned an exercise notice and forced to pay $30 for those puts.

This is not a made-up situation to unsettle you. It's a very real phenomenon. (OK, the 200-point rally may be an exaggeration, but when it appears that the market is about to change direction, it's not uncommon for investors who are short deep in-the-money OEX options to be assigned an exercise

---

10. These American-style options expire Friday afternoon, not Friday morning.
11. It doesn't matter if you're naked short the options, or if they are part of a spread. When you are short OEX options, the threat of an early exercise is real.
12. Futures contracts on the indexes trade after the market closes and before it opens.

notice on either calls or puts.) When OEX options become deep in-the-money, there is a significant chance of being assigned an exercise notice. If news occurs just as the markets close, one way for the option owner to sell his or her profitable holding is to exercise.[13] And if you think the loss just described is bad, imagine how much worse it is if you own long puts as a hedge against those short puts and you fail to exercise your long puts. Not only would you repurchase your shorts at the worst possible time (because of the assignment notice), but you now have additional losses because you still own the other part of your spread position.

OEX is a decent product, but if you want to sell options as part of your strategy, I suggest you avoid trading OEX in favor of European-style index options.

Which indexes are European?

Not all indexes are European style. Although we have not yet addressed the specific strategies that allow you to best take advantage of index options, you are usually better off trading European-style, rather than American-style index options. The elimination of early exercise risk is sufficient reason.

The most actively traded options are easier to trade[14] than options with little investor interest. Among the European indexes, consider trading any of these broad-based indexes:

- SPX. S&P 500 Index. This index has more trading volume than any other, which is to your advantage. However, as of this writing, this index trades on a single exchange and there's not as much competitive market making as in other indexes whose options are listed on multiple exchanges. The bid/ask differential in SPX options is so wide that I no longer make any attempt to trade them. My advice is to try SPX options to see if you can accept the conditions.

- NDX. Nasdaq 100 Index. A good portion of this index is comprised of technology stocks.
- RUT. Russell 2000 Index. This index consists of stocks in the small-cap universe and is comprised of the smallest 2000 companies in the Russell 3000 Index.[15] It's significantly more volatile than SPX.
- DJX. Dow Jones Industrial Average (stock of 30 large companies).
- SML. S&P 600 Small Cap Index. Six hundred small stocks comprise this index.

If you prefer to trade the stocks of a specific sector, many sector funds or indexes are available. Those are American-style options.

QQQQ is an ETF with very actively traded options. These are standard American options—if assigned an exercise notice, you deliver QQQQ shares. There's no reason to avoid trading QQQQ options.

BOTTOM LINE: To successfully trade European-style options, you must be aware of how they differ from American options. There's also a tax advantage to trading European-style options (in the U.S.) because trading profits are taxed as part long-term and part short-term capital gains. You can get more information from the IRS.

---

13. Sure, the option owner can simply sell the options, but who's going to buy them? The bids disappear as the news becomes known, and they are under their intrinsic value. Why sell a put or call below parity (its intrinsic value) when you can exercise and receive full intrinsic value?

14. Extra volume provides more opportunity to trade with other individual investors—and that means better prices for everyone.

15. An index composed of the 3,000 largest (by capitalization—the market value of all outstanding shares of a company) stocks. This index can be divided into two other indexes: the Russell 1000 Index, which consists of the largest 1,000 stocks, and the Russell 2000 Index, which consists of the other 2,000 stocks.

1. American-style options trade in the U.S. and European-style options trade overseas.

○ **TRUE** ○ **FALSE**

2. If you are short an American-style option on ABCD stock, the settlement price is determined by its opening price on expiration Friday.

○ **TRUE** ○ **FALSE**

3. Which option owner has more extensive rights regarding exercise: the owner of the American-style option or the owner of the European-style option?

4. What's the major reason for not holding a short position in a European-style option later than Thursday of expiration week?

5. The settlement price of European-style options is almost identical with the opening price for the specific index on expiration Friday.

○ **TRUE** ○ **FALSE**

6. You own six European-style cash-settled SPX options.

A. Are you allowed to exercise them before expiration?

B. Are you allowed to sell them any time before expiration?

C. If the options finish in-the-money, what do you have to do to get your cash?

Chapter 18

Credit Spreads

A credit spread is an option position consisting of two legs—either both calls or both puts. In addition, both options expire in the same month and have the same underlying asset. When initiating (opening) this position, you may trade one of the options first, then the other. But, it's more efficient to enter your order as a spread. The discussion that follows includes specific instructions on how to do that.

If you sell the spread,[1] you collect cash. Hence, it's referred to as a credit spread. If you buy the spread, you pay cash and it's called a debit spread.

Credit Spread	Debit Spread
Buy 10 IBM	Buy 10 MSFT
Oct 90 puts	Dec 32.50 calls
Sell 10 IBM	Sell 10 MSFT
Oct 95 puts	Dec 35 calls

---

1. *Selling a spread means selling the higher priced option and buying the lower priced option.*

Earlier we showed that selling a put spread is equivalent to owning a collar—a conservative investment that allows an investor to protect a position against significant loss. Let's take a closer look at the put credit spread to see why this conservative strategy is appropriate for all investors.

Put credit spreads

If you have a neutral to bullish opinion on a stock (or the entire stock market), you can sell naked puts in an attempt to profit from that opinion. That method is suitable for investors who don't mind accumulating shares of stock when their short-term opinion is wrong and the stock drops below the strike price (as described in Chapter 14).

There's a better (less risky) put-selling strategy you can use. When adopting this strategy, you buy one (less expensive, i.e., lower strike price) put for each put sold. If both options expire in the same month the position is a generic put spread.[2] When selling put spreads, the goal is similar to selling naked puts: to allow the spread to expire worthless, or repurchase the spread at a profit.

Some stocks offer a significant number of spread choices because they have numerous strike prices. Others offer a more limited choice. We'll look at a real-world example, using the Russell 2000 Index (RUT) and consider how to decide which options to trade. As is always true, there is no single "best" answer.

The numbers presented in Table 18.1 were collected during market hours on September 21, 2007. Four weeks remain before the October options stop trading. The final settlement price (see Chapter 17) is calculated from the opening prices on Friday, October 19.

Options are listed for trading with strike prices every 10 points from a low of 550 through 980, but the table only includes Oct 660 through 810 for two reasons:

- This strategy is almost always implemented using out-of-the-money (OTM) options and ITM options need not be considered.
- Options that are too far OTM cannot be used to meet the suggested minimum requirements (described below).

The table shows the bid/ask quotes and delta for 16 different options. When you sell a credit spread, you can theoretically use any two of those options. That means there are 16 x 15, or 240 possible credit spreads. In reality, many fewer choices are practical. When selling credit spreads, there is room for individuality. My personal preference is to sell spreads in which the strike prices are as near each other as possible. For me, that means selling 10-point spreads (spread nomenclature defines a spread by the difference between the strike prices.) when trading RUT options. But it's perfectly reasonable to sell 20- and 30-point RUT put spreads. And some investors sell spreads that are wider.

TABLE 18.1: RUT put options, 28 days before expiration. RUT at $815.55

STRIKE	BID	ASK	DELTA
660	$0.60	$0.75	-2
670	$0.75	$0.85	-2
680	$0.95	$1.05	-3
690	$1.20	$1.30	-4
700	$1.55	$1.75	-5
710	$1.95	$2.05	-6
720	$2.45	$2.60	-7
730	$2.95	$3.20	-8
740	$3.80	$4.00	-11
750	$4.70	$4.90	-13
760	$5.60	$5.90	-16
770	$7.10	$7.50	-20
780	$8.90	$9.10	-24
790	$10.90	$11.20	-29
800	$13.40	$13.80	-35
810	$16.60	$16.90	-42

Choosing your RUT put spread.

Choosing the underlying

If you use this strategy for individual stocks, then it's reasonable to trade options in stocks you have

---

2. If they don't, the position is referred to as a diagonal put spread.

been following. That's much safer than choosing stocks at random. If you don't have a list of stocks, then this strategy is appropriate for indexes. Many indexes have listed options, but if you trade cash-settled options (Chapter 17), be certain to choose an index with European-style options. If you cannot find which indexes qualify, ask the OCC (Options Clearing Corporation).[3]

The most popular indexes with European-style, cash-settled options are SPX, NDX and RUT (Standard & Poor's 500 Index, Nasdaq 100 Index and Russell 2000 Index, respectively). It's also important to be comfortable trading the stock portfolio represented by the index, because selling put spreads is a bullish strategy. If you feel more comfortable trading larger stocks, then SPX or DJX (Dow Jones Industrials) may be your best choice. If you prefer smaller companies, the Russell 2000 (RUT) is appropriate. You can also trade sector indexes. Stay within your comfort zone.

Choosing the strikes

There are several items to consider when choosing the specific strike price to sell. With individual stocks, there are often few choices. But when trading indexes, there are more than enough possibilities.

There are two main schools of thought on which strike price to sell. There's the OTM school and the CTM[4] school. The most popular strategy (and the one I prefer) is to sell options that are reasonably far out-of-the-money (OTM). The idea is to sell option spreads that have a high probability of expiring worthless, but which have enough premium to make them worth selling. The good news for OTM supporters: the probability of earning a profit is excellent. That can be inferred from the low delta (probability of finishing ITM) of these options (Table 18.1). The bad news: the maximum

possible loss is far greater than the potential reward, and the risk/reward ratio is unattractive.

- Maximum gain when selling a credit spread: You never earn more than the credit you receive. Thus, when you sell a spread for $1.00, your maximum gain is $100. You earn that amount if the spread eventually expires worthless.
- Maximum loss when selling a credit spread: If both options in the spread are in-the-money at expiration, then the spread becomes worth the difference between the strike prices. The loss is that maximum amount, minus the premium collected. If you sell a 10-point spread for $1.00, the maximum loss is $9.00. Why is this true? Whenever the put option you own finishes in-the-money, then the option you sold also finishes in-the-money because it has a higher strike price. Whatever your option is worth, the option you sold is always worth 10 points (for a 10-point spread), or $1,000 more.

The other school of thought supports the idea of selling options that are closer-to-the-money (CTM).[5] There are several benefits to adopting this method:

- The premium collected is higher and that translates into higher potential profit per spread.
- The maximum loss per spread is reduced,[6] making the risk/reward ratio more attractive.
- You can earn as much as with CTM spreads, and you generate the same profit potential by selling fewer spreads. That significantly reduces overall risk (defined as the amount you can lose).

Along with the benefits, there are also disadvantages:

---

3. (312) 322-6200 or send an e-mail to options@theocc.com.
4. Close-to-the-money (i.e., not too far OTM).
5. CTM options are also OTM, but they are OTM by less.
6. If you sell an OTM 10-point spread for $1.00, the maximum loss is $9.00. When you sell a CTM spread for $3.00, the maximum loss is $7.00.

- The options sold have a higher delta, and thus, a lower probability of expiring worthless.

BOTTOM LINE: For the CTM school, there is less overall risk, the same overall profit potential and less-frequent profits.

There is a third school (FOTM, or far out-of-the-money), but it's best ignored. These spreads have a high probability of being profitable. But, the premium is small and you cannot collect enough cash to provide a worthwhile return. If you sell index spreads for $0.10 or $0.20, you earn your profit almost all the time. That's not good enough because those premiums are reduced by commissions. More importantly, the market undergoes major moves every so often, and one of these spreads could easily result in a loss that wipes out years of profits. Don't do it. The odds of long-term success are very much against this style of trading. I suggest you never sell a credit spread for less than a certain minimum amount. Each investor can determine a suitable minimum for his or her situation. When trading indexes, don't accept less than $0.40 or $0.50 when selling 10-point spreads.[7] I find those amounts to be too small and avoid selling spreads for less than $1.00. Once again, this is not a rule, just a guide.

If you begin your spread search with an idea of which strike price to sell, there are fewer alternatives to consider. Begin with 10-point spreads if you choose RUT. If you prefer to trade NDX you must choose 25- or 50-point spreads. SPX offers a wide variety of strike prices, but you cannot always find the specific strikes you want.

With so many choices, the obvious question is: How are you supposed to make an intelligent decision? Let's look at one example and discuss the possibilities. But first, some notes about entering orders:

Entering the order

Don't pay the ask price for the option you want to buy and don't sell the bid price for the option you want to sell. Often the bid/ask spreads are wide. Most readers have little experience with option trading, and even less experience with index options. Most index options are notorious for their wide markets, and wide markets make it more difficult for the investor.

Use a spread order—an order which stipulates:

- You must trade both options or neither option.
- You must be filled at your specified (limit) price or better.[8]

Enter a *limit* order, not a *market* order. If you are filled, you sell your spread at your price (or better). If you are not filled, you can change your order to settle for a lower price, or try again the next day. That's an individual choice.

EXAMPLE

Choosing the width of your credit spread

For the moment, let's not choose the "school" and assume the Oct 740 put is a suitable option to sell. The current bid is $3.80 and the delta is -11. Let's consider three different credit spreads in which we buy the Oct 730, 720 or 710 puts.

10-point spread

The RUT Oct 730 put is offered at $3.20 and the delta is -8. Thus, the spread delta is -3 (-11 minus -8). If you pay the offer and sell the bid, you collect $0.60 for the 10-point spread. The "outside market" for

---

7. *Double those amounts for 20-point spreads.*
8. *"Or better" means you receive at least the limit price, but sometimes your order is filled at an even higher price when selling (or a lower price when buying).*

> *this spread is $0.45 wide. That means if you use the individual quotes to determine the market for the RUT Oct 740/730 put spread, the bid is $0.60 and the offer is $1.05. The "outside market" is the price you see on your computer screen[9] when you agree to pay the offer for one option and sell the bid for the other (again, you can get better prices when you trade).*

Here are some important things you should know:

- There is always an "inside market." That means if you have a way to get the information, the specific spread you want to trade has a bid price (using our example) that is higher than $0.60 and an offer price that is less than $1.05. Some brokers provide no help in obtaining that inside market and you are left to your own devices. That's unfortunate, but it's the way the world operates. Some brokers (for an additional fee if the order is filled) send someone into the pit on the trading floor to ask market makers for a quote on your spread. But, this service is usually reserved for customers who trade larger orders.[10] If you are fortunate to have a broker who supplies the inside market, then you have a much better idea at what price to enter your order. In this specific example, it's likely that the inside market is $0.70 to $0.95, or possibly tighter.[11]

- When you don't know the inside market, you must guess the price to enter your orders. After you gain some experience you learn how to enter orders that have a good chance of getting filled. Here's my suggestion: Use the midpoint between the bid and ask prices as your starting point. In this case, that's $0.825 (halfway between the bid of $60 and the offer of $1.05). Shave something off that midpoint and enter your order at that price. Begin by shaving approximately five cents. That means trying to sell the spread at $0.75.

- If you enter your orders online, you must become familiar with your broker's trading software. Don't be afraid to ask customer service for help if you are unable to figure it out for yourself. If uncertain, try entering orders in a play money account (called paper trading) to be certain you don't buy when you intend to sell or make other mistakes due to unfamiliarity with the software.

- If you use a live broker and you want to sell five spreads, tell your broker: "I want to enter an order to sell five lots of the RUT Oct 740/730 put spread at a limit price of seventy-five cents or better." Obviously this statement is for this specific example and you must substitute the appropriate quantity, underlying symbol, premium and strike prices.

- Markets and market conditions change over the years. Sometimes you can receive a quick execution near the midpoint, and at other times it's more difficult to trade. You are probably anxious to get started trading, and if you are willing to sacrifice a little cash to get started, then reduce your offer by $0.05 after a few minutes. If not filled, reduce it again. But (important) you must have some minimum price in mind—you cannot reduce your price until someone buys the spread. Have a little patience, if your personality allows.

- When you enter an order and it's not filled immediately, that order remains visible

---

9. *Assuming you trade online. If not, it's the market your broker supplies when he or she gives you a quote for your spread order.*
10. *It varies by broker. Don't expect this service for orders of fewer than 50 contracts or 50 spreads.*
11. *"Tighter" means the bid and ask prices are closer to each other.*

to market participants and may be filled at any time. If the underlying moves lower, it becomes more attractive for someone to buy your put spread. If the underlying moves higher, it reduces your chances of getting filled. Why? Because the put credit spread increases in value as the underlying moves lower—and the lower it moves the more likely it is that some market participant buys your spread. Conversely, if it moves higher, the spread becomes less attractive.

- Once you determine how much to shave off the midpoint price, you have a better idea where to start the next time you enter an order in the same underlying. If you get filled when shaving $0.20, then you may want to begin by shaving $0.15 next time. If filled quickly, then you probably shaved too much. It's a cat and mouse game and there's no substitute for experience to help you determine at which price to try to sell (or buy) your spreads.

- If happy to sell the spread at $0.70, then you are not obligated to try for a better price. You can offer at $0.70 right away. But extra nickels and dimes add up over the years (it's a way to pay commissions, for example), so don't give them away without at least a minimal effort to get a better price on each trade. A difference of $0.05 on a 10-lot[12] is $50.

When you sell the 10-point spread for $0.75, your maximum gain is $75 per spread (less commission). What are the chances of earning that maximum? The best way to get a good handle on that probability is to look at the delta of the put sold. Remember, the absolute value of the delta is roughly the same as the probability the

option finishes in-the-money. Using the calculator (or referring to Table 18.1), you find the put has a delta of -10.9. Thus, the chance that this option finishes ITM is approximately 11 percent, or 1 in 9. Using the same volatility[13] for the Oct 730 put, the calculator returns a delta of -8.2. This means both options finish ITM more than 8 percent of the time, and if no adjustments are made, you can expect to lose the maximum, or $925 per spread, approximately one time in 12, or once per year, assuming you trade every month.

{ Note: The $925 loss is more than you earn, even if you make the $75 maximum, during the other 11 months. Those numbers suggest two obvious conclusions: Either it's a poor strategy to sell this spread at any price below $1.00[14] or you must prevent losing the maximum by taking some action before that possibility looms.

No one should begin trading options with too little capital. Each broker establishes a minimum requirement, but these requirements are too low in my opinion. If you begin trading with a small number of contracts and have the patience to learn more before trading larger size (more contracts), you can do well. When you use the suggested strategies skillfully, your chances of making money increase, which is why each strategy is covered in detail. The better you understand what you are doing, the better you are going to perform, but the primary factors that determine your long-term success are your risk and money-management skills.

The margin requirement to open a 10-point spread is $1,000, less the premium collected. How is that determined? It's the maximum loss ($925 in this case). Once the margin requirement is met, you cannot receive a margin call.[15] The maximum profit is $75 and the maximum return on investment (ROI) is $75/$925 or 8.1 percent. That's very good for a one-

---

12. Ten option contracts or 10 spreads.

13. When you set the dividend to zero and the put price to 3.80, the calculator sets the volatility to 30.73.

14. If you collect $1.00 every month, you earn $1,100 over 11 months and lose $900 once for a net annual gain of $200. This is not a very good return, but it's not a loss.

15. Some other positions may result in a margin call, but not the sale of credit spreads.

month investment. That's what makes these spreads so attractive, despite potentially large losses.

20-point spread

The RUT Oct 720 put is offered at $2.60. The outside market for the RUT Oct 740/720 put spread is $1.20 to $1.65. The midpoint is $1.425. Enter an order to sell this spread at $1.40, knowing you probably must accept $1.35 (or less).

If you sell this spread at $135, the maximum loss is $1,865 (this is a 20-point spread). The Oct 720 put has a -7 delta, and the maximum loss occurs about one time in 14. The margin requirement is $1,865. The maximum return is $135, and the maximum ROI is $135/$1,865 or 7.2 percent.

30-point spread

The RUT Oct 710 put is offered at $2.05 (Table 18.1). The market for the RUT Oct 740/710 put spread is $1.75 to $2.05. With the midpoint being $1.90, enter an order to sell this spread at $1.80 or $1.85.

Assuming you collect $180, the maximum loss is $2,820 (30-point spread). The delta of the Oct 710 put is -6 and this spread loses the maximum about one time in 16. The margin requirement is $2,820 and the maximum gain is $180 or 6.4 percent.

Deciding how wide the spread should be is an important decision, and it's OK to be flexible. I strongly suggest beginning with the narrowest possible spread for your first trades and deciding if that style works for you. The narrower spreads are easier to handle because maximum losses are smaller, the position has fewer negative delta and rolling (if necessary) is easier for most traders to handle. Your goal is to be comfortable with both the risk and reward parameters of your chosen spread. If you have a strong feeling that 20-, 30- (or wider) point

spreads are best for your comfort zone, go with that feeling and see how it works out for you.

Choosing the strike to sell

This is an important decision. When trading individual stocks, your choices are usually limited.[16] But with high-priced indexes, there are more than enough strike prices for everyone.

When first using this method, try writing options that are further OTM, rather than CTM (closer-to-the-money). It's not that this is the better choice, but it's likely to provide a more comfortable experience. It's easier to learn when you have fewer problems and fewer difficult decisions. Those decisions are easier to handle after you have some real trading experience.

If choosing an OTM option, there are two important requirements. First, the option you sell must have sufficient premium to make the trade worthwhile. Very low priced options are inappropriate, primarily because the second condition cannot be satisfied. Second, when choosing an option to buy (this option is always further OTM than the option you sell), the difference in premium between the two strike prices must provide an acceptable potential profit. Very low-priced options tend to have similar prices, and that makes it difficult to collect more than a few nickels in premium—and that's not something you want to do. Referring to Table 18.1, take a look at the markets for the first two puts listed: the Oct 660 and Oct 670 puts. The bid/ask for this spread is zero to $0.25. How much can you expect to collect for this spread when the market makers are willing to sell it for twenty-five cents? Answer: too little. And it's not much better with the next possible spread, the Oct 670/680. The bottom line is that you cannot go too far OTM because the very low price of the options makes trading a put credit spread undesirable.[17] If

---

16. If you trade high-priced or volatile stocks, such as GOOG (Google) or AAPL (Apple Computer), there are many strikes from which to choose.

17. Don't forget, this is not the entire list of October RUT options. This inability to trade gets even worse as you move further OTM.

you truly want to trade options this far (or further) OTM, you can do so by going out another month to November options (see Table 18.2).

Again, referring to Table 18.1, the Oct 740 put is as far as my comfort zone allows me to go. You may feel comfortable selling the 730 or 720 instead, but the reason I choose not to do that is that the spread premium becomes too small. The outside market for the RUT Oct 720/730 spread is $0.35 to $0.75, and it's unlikely you can collect more than $0.50 for the spread. If $0.50 appeals to you, then go for it. There are no rules, just guidelines. I'd provide a list of conditions that must be met for optimum results, but no such conditions exist. You're on your own in deciding how much profit potential and how much risk to take. In addition, if one person opens the trade with four weeks remaining to expiration and another investor opens the same spread one week later, prices and premium levels are different. With less time, you collect less premium. In return, there's less risk because there are fewer trading days in which something bad can happen.

If you attend the CTM school, there are several acceptable choices. You must decide how far out-of-the-money you are willing to sell put options. For example, if you are very bullish on the underlying, then you may prefer to sell a put spread that is almost at the money. That gives you the chance to earn a higher reward. The Oct 800/810 put spread is $2.80 to $3.50 (Table 18.1) and you should be able to get at least $3.10. If you are that bullish, you can consider selling the 790/810 put spread in an effort to collect even more (with appropriately greater risk).

Other CTM traders would be comfortable selling the 770 or 780 put. There's no best choice. This truly is a question of being comfortable with the risk required to collect the reward. Let's look at one CTM spread and compare the risk and reward with that of the OTM chosen in the previous example.

EXAMPLE

The market in the RUT Oct 770 put is $7.10 to $7.50 and that of the 780 put is $8.90 to $9.10. Notice that the market in the latter put is only twenty cents wide—a rarity for index options priced over $1. The outside market for the Oct 780/770 put spread is $1.40 to $2.00. You can probably collect $1.60, and perhaps $1.65 for the spread (these actively traded index options trade in penny increments).[18] If the price is $1.65, then the maximum loss is $8.35. Notice that risk is five times the profit potential, whereas it was more than 12 times greater ($925/$75) for the 740/730 put spread. That improved risk/reward ratio provides a feeling of security. However, the delta of the Oct 770 put is -20.1[19], reducing the likelihood that this option finishes out-of-the-money to 80 percent compared with 89 percent for the Oct 740 put. By adopting the CTM methodology, you get something, but you give up something else.

The objective in trading these spreads is to find the right combination for your comfort zone. There's no substitute for trading with real money to get a sense of which strike prices appeal to you. Make your best judgment when you begin trading, but have a little patience and don't trade too many of these put spreads until you are comfortable with how they work.

Choosing the expiration month

Front-month options are the most popular choice among those who sell credit spreads. The primary reason is because time decay (theta) is greatest as expiration approaches. Moving out one month (or

---

18. *Thus, you may enter an order to sell at $1.62, for example.*
19. *A put value of $7.30 tells us the IV is 27.7. Using that IV, the calculator produces -20.1 as the put delta.*

two) changes some of the important parameters of the credit spread.

- Because there's more time before expiration, more bad things can happen and there's an increased chance for the underlying to move against you.
- Option prices are higher, which allows you to sell options that are further OTM and still meet your requirements for collecting a minimum premium (see Table 18.2).
- Gamma is reduced. If the underlying moves against you (down when you sell put spreads) the gamma changes more rapidly for near-term options, and that in turn changes the deltas more rapidly. Translation: If the underlying drops significantly, your position delta becomes worse[20] when there is little time before expiration.
- When you collect more cash to open the position, you may be more inclined to close early to lock in your profit. It's easier to pay that last 25 cents to close a spread when you sell it for $1.50 than when you sell it for $0.75. The initial sale price should have nothing to do with the decision to close the spread, but human nature being what it is, most investors consider the size of the profit before deciding whether to close. I don't believe profit is relevant, and the decision to hold or close should be made independent of any other factor.

EXAMPLE

The data in Table 18.2 represent the midpoint prices (the average between the bid and ask prices) for specific NDX put credit spreads. You probably cannot receive these prices when selling the spreads, but the comparisons are still worthwhile. With the index trading near 2092, if you want to sell put spreads that are significantly out-of-the-money, the front-month NDX 1800/1825 spread is unappealing because the credit is $0.35 or less. By moving out one

month, you can collect approximately $1.30 for the 1800/1825 spread. That's a far more appealing price, even though the spread has a lifetime that is four weeks longer. The same alternative (higher premium coupled with longer lifetime) is available with all OTM spreads (Table 18.2).

BOTTOM LINE: If you attend the FOTM school and are considering near-term credit spreads, one way to find a substantially better premium is to trade options that expire in the following month.

It's not always necessary to trade when you actively manage risk. Most of the time all goes well and your credit spreads peacefully expire worthless. At other times, you profitably cover the spread at a low price. "Low" does not refer to a specific price. If your style calls for selling spreads in the $1.50 to $2 range, then paying $0.25 to $0.35 (depending on circumstances) is reasonable. If you sell spreads for $0.50 or less, it's difficult to pay more than five or ten cents to close the position. Time to expiration must also be considered and you should expect to pay a bit extra when there's more, rather than less, time remaining in the lifetime of the options. As you gain experience, you'll determine whether holding or closing early works better for you. But remember, when the spread premium becomes low, there's little to gain (and a great deal to lose) from holding.

TABLE 18.2: Midpoint prices for NDX put credit spreads, NDX at $2091.85

SPREAD	24 DAYS	52 DAYS
1800/1825	$0.35	$1.30
1825/1850	$0.475	$1.60
1850/1875	$0.575	$1.65
1875/1900	$0.825	$2.15
1900/1925	$1.15	$2.60
1925/1950	$1.50	$3.10
1950/1975	$2.10	$3.65
1975/2000	$2.85	$4.45
2000/2025	$3.40	$5.10

How times affects the value of NDX put spreads.
Days = days to expiration

---

20. Unless it's still far out-of-the-money.

This thorough discussion of put credit spreads does not replace hands-on experience. If you have the patience, open a paper trading account and play with a few different credit spreads. If trading an index, consider CTM and OTM spreads that expire in the front month (at least three weeks before expiration). In addition, open one or more spreads in the second month. As time passes, watch the positions. Notice the conditions under which the position makes and loses money. Decide if any adjustments are necessary and which spreads make you feel more comfortable. Keep in mind that the results from your first few trades do not represent a true picture of what lies ahead. Your ultimate goal is to build a portfolio of positions (or one larger position) that allows you to invest in the stock market—but with less risk than that of a buy and hold stock investor.

When selling put credit spreads, the goal is to buy in your short spreads when you have earned a substantial profit (or let them expire worthless). When the underlying moves too far or too quickly in the wrong direction, you lose money. If you find yourself in that unfortunate situation (and you will), it's important to decide when to adjust the position. Closing your eyes and hoping for the best is not a winning strategy.

Risk management

The discussion that follows presents some ideas on managing risk. There is no simple, easy-to-follow formula for deciding when a position should be adjusted. Nor are there specific trades to make. There are always alternatives. Your goal, as risk manager and money manager for your portfolio, is to make those difficult decisions. You must decide whether to "hold 'em or fold 'em."

Not every decision results in the best possible outcome. Part of the time you would be better off not making the adjustment. Another part of the time those adjustments save you a bundle of cash. Don't be harsh on yourself. Remember, when selling credit spreads or iron condors (the subject of Chapter 19) you make money most of the time. Your goal as risk manager is to be certain that losses don't hurt. They are never

pleasant, but if you maintain good discipline, losses are not large enough to threaten your overall profitability.

When to adjust a position

The term, "adjustment," refers to making one or more trades that change your current position. The most common reason to adjust a position is to reduce risk, but locking in a profit also falls under the adjustment umbrella.

Knowing when to adjust a position to reduce or eliminate risk is more of an art than a science. There is no single set of rules to cover all contingencies. The purpose of this discussion is to provide choices and allow you to decide for yourself which style of risk management works best for you and your circumstances. As you gain experience facing these unwelcome decisions, you gain confidence. It's easier to ignore risk and hope all goes well. I've been there, and take my word for it—it doesn't work well over the long term.

When I was a market maker on the CBOE trading floor and held positions with outrageous risk, the results were as expected: I won most of the time, but the occasional losses were horrendous. Why did I allow that to happen? Sometimes I was stubborn and "just knew" the market couldn't possibly go any higher. Or perhaps I decided there was no reason to buy in options I had sold earlier and which were available for 1/16 (options traded in fractions, not decimals a few short years ago). I mention these painful stories with the hope readers take my advice: Don't allow your portfolio to carry more risk than is reasonable for your circumstances. Don't be greedy over that last nickel or dime. Have some patience and discipline and you should be well rewarded.

Keep in mind that the need to adjust credit spreads gone awry comes from two different perspectives. Adherents to the OTM method collect smaller premiums than those who believe in selling CTM spreads, and thus, their maximum losses are larger. While CTM believers don't lose as much per spread when disaster strikes, they begin with a short put option that is closer to the index price and thus, has a higher probability of moving ITM.

One popular method for managing risk is to make an adjustment when the short[21] put option moves into-the-money. The major advantage of this method is that fewer adjustments are necessary. The major disadvantage is that by the time an adjustment is necessary, you are losing a substantial amount. This method does not suit everyone, nor should it. But let's look at it in more detail for those who want to try this method.

As more time passes, the less you lose when the short option *barely*[22] goes ITM. The data in Table 18.3 show the value of the NDX 1925/1900 put spread when NDX is 1925 and expiration approaches. As expected, the spread decreases in value as time passes. There's nothing surprising about that. But, once your short option moves slightly ITM, the effect of additional time is minimal—even when expiration is only a few days away. Conclusion: Holding the position, hoping the ticking clock will save you from a large loss, is not a good idea.[23]

Why is this information important to you? Because it's tempting to convince yourself that no adjustment is necessary (and that's dangerous):

- Holding the position is a gamble. The short option is ATM, and if NDX drops another point or two, it's not too significant. But a larger drop is costly (see Table 18.4).
- If you make an adjustment, you'll lock in a loss and no one likes to do that. By holding, the ticking clock and the positive theta that comes with it can be reassuring. But even a few days doesn't help

enough to take the risk (see Table 18.3).[24]

- And who knows, the market may reverse direction and head higher. This is certainly a possibility and the constant wish of someone whose short options are rapidly becoming ITM options. But, it's also possible that the market decline not only continues, but accelerates.

TABLE 18.3: Value of the NDX 1925/1900 put spread, NDX at 1925

NDX 1925	SPREAD VALUE
52 days	$11.20
38 days	$11.15
24 days	$11.02
17 days	$10.86
10 days	$10.53
3 days	$9.25
2 days	$8.64
1 day	$7.34

How time affects the value of an ATM NDX put spread.
Days = days to expiration

By the time the 1925 put option becomes an ATM option, NDX has already declined from 2092 (that's 167 points!), and unless you have some compelling reason to believe the decline is over, there's no reason why another substantial decline is not imminent. How bad can it be if NDX declines another 10 points? Assuming there are 10 days before the options stop trading,[25] if NDX declines from 1925 to 1915, the spread moves from $10.53 to $13.92.[26] That's a significant loss on top on the previous loss. If you believe that preventing such losses is vital, then taking action is the long-term winning strategy. Again—no one likes taking losses. But selling credit spreads wins most of the time, not all the time. If you expect all your credit spreads to expire worthless, you are likely to be disappointed.

---

21. *The short put option is the one with the higher strike price—the option you sold. The long put option is the one you own and has a lower strike price.*
22. *Later we discuss the situation in which the option moves much further ITM.*
23. *The passage of another day or two helps, but not enough to risk holding.*
24. *This statement is obviously an opinion, not a fact. You must handle your positions to satisfy your personal situation. As you gain experience feel free to override these suggestions.*
25. *Don't forget settlement risk the following morning (discussed in Chapter 17).*
26. *The calculator gives these values for the options with NDX at 1915 (IV 22, time 10 days): $31.70 and $17.78.*

There is one other reason why waiting, hoping the days pass uneventfully, is not the best choice. Please study Table 18.4 because the information is very important. It has already been pointed out (Table 18.3) that the put credit spread (slowly) decreases in value as the days pass. If nothing bad happens, losses are reduced. But as those losses shrink, danger looms. Why? Because negative gamma explodes as expiration approaches. Options quickly move from zero delta to 100 delta, and the value of an option changes dramatically when expiration is very near. The data in Table 18.4 illustrate this important fact.

The data lists the value of the 1925/1900 put spread when NDX declines from 1950 (the short option is 25 points OTM) to 1900 (the short is 25 points ITM) in a single day. Note that the size of the loss increases from about $3 when 52 days remain before the options expire to more than twice that amount with only 10 days remaining. And as fewer and fewer days remain, the potential loss increases dramatically. In fact, sometimes the spread appears to be worthless one day and moves to its maximum value, or $25.00, the next. This is something you must avoid!

TABLE 18.4: Value of the 1925/1900 put spread when NDX declines from 1950 to 1900 in one day

DAYS	NDX 1,950	NDX 1,900	LOSS
52	$9.70	$12.75	$3.05
38	$9.40	$12.97	$3.57
24	$8.83	$13.31	$4.48
17	$8.29	$13.58	$5.29
10	$7.27	$14.07	$6.80
3	$4.17	$15.56	$11.39
2	$3.04	$16.23	$13.19
1	$1.35	$17.58	$16.23
0	$0.00	$25.00	$25.00

How time affects the loss of your short put spread when the underlying declines by 2.5 percent in one day.

NDX 1950 and NDX 1900: Theoretical value of spread when IV=22

This situation catches too many investors by surprise. The uncertainty of where the market opens the next morning when settlement prices are calculated (Chapter 17) makes holding the position through settlement a huge risk. By buying back your short position before expiration, this risk is avoided. When to buy back the spread and how much to pay are individual decisions. It's tempting to wait just one more day again and again, but the bottom line is that you should never go home with this position when the market closes for trading on Thursday, one day before the settlement price is determined.[27] It's just not worth it in the long run. The potential for disaster should not fit within anyone's comfort zone. It's prudent to buy in the position to eliminate all risk.

More on when to adjust

For many investors, waiting until the short option goes in-the-money is not an acceptable strategy because the potential loss is too great. Thus, they adjust sooner. The bottom line is that the sooner you adjust, the more often you make adjustments, and as a result, you may deprive yourself of some profitable situations. On the other hand, by adjusting early, your losses are smaller. It's a compromise. As you gain experience this process becomes easier.

> NOTE: When selling put spreads, it's easy to get spooked the first time the market moves lower. If you sell an option that is 75 points out-of-the-money and it suddenly becomes 65 points out-of-the-money, that's not good, but it's not so terrible. Don't rush to make an adjustment. Instead, when you open the position, try to decide at what point you will seriously consider looking at adjustment alternatives. If that time comes, be prepared to act if you still deem it necessary. It may be disappointing to close a position to avoid serious losses, but it's an essential ingredient for success.

---

27. European-style, cash-settled index options cease trading on Thursday (before the third Friday, see Chapter 17).

Another method for adjusting is to consider your position delta. You may decide to be long[28] a maximum of so many delta, and no more. By following the Greeks (hopefully supplied by your broker), you can determine when you reach that point. One possible adjustment is to close a portion of your position. If the underlying continues to decline, you continue to get longer, and it may become time to close more spreads.

There is only one rule concerning adjustments: Don't ignore them. You can make your own determination as to when it's appropriate to adjust, and that's probably when the position exits your comfort zone. As you gain more experience, that comfort zone widens. That's fine, but don't allow it to widen so far that you never adjust bad positions.

How to adjust a position

If you are considering adjusting a position, you are probably looking at a loss. Don't let that alarm you. Just as they do when trading stocks, too many novices hold losing positions (and quickly take profits on winning trades), hoping (in reality, praying) that everything turns out all right in the end. A happy outcome is possible, but the current loss can easily become a much larger loss. Holding a position, planning to make no adjustment, is gambling, pure and simple. If that suits your investing style, then by all means, gamble to your heart's content. But, if your goal is to invest with limited risk, then gambling is not a good plan. Let's consider some possible methods for adjusting a put credit spread.

Assume you sold 10 NDX 1950/1925 put credit spreads and that expiration arrives in 52 days. NDX was near 2092 when you made this trade, but the market has declined and you are in danger of losing more than you are willing to lose. You sold this spread, collecting $310 for each. The good news

is that 42 days have passed, but the bad news is that NDX has declined to 1970. There are 10 days remaining before the options expire, but the short option is now only 20 points out-of-the-money. Is this a bad situation for you, and if so, what are your choices?

If the implied volatility is unchanged (22), then the spread is worth $7.93.[29] Assuming that that this spread can be bought or sold near its theoretical price (a good assumption for a discussion, but unrealistic in the real world).[30] Your current loss is $483 per spread, or $4,830.

- If this loss is too large for you and your comfort zone, then this discussion still applies to you, except for the fact that you would consider your adjustment choices sooner— perhaps when NDX first declined below 2000. Or perhaps you would sell fewer than 10 spreads. There is nothing wrong with trading 1- or 2-lots if that's appropriate.

- The easiest adjustment is to repurchase some of the spreads sold earlier. Some investors prefer to cover all 10 spreads, getting out of a losing position. Others prefer to repurchase a portion of the position, locking in a loss, but reducing the remaining risk. When this choice is made, further losses are possible, but the opportunity to recover all, or most, of the current loss remains.

- Another option is to "roll" the position. Rolling consists of two separate decisions. First, you must be willing to buy back all the spreads sold earlier, locking in the loss. Second, you must find a new position that meets your needs. Don't open a new position just to reduce risk by rolling. Rolling is an acceptable risk management tool, but it's over-used by investors who, desperate to find

---

28. When a put credit spread goes bad, you become longer and longer as the underlying declines. With other spreads, you may become too short as the market rises.
29. Once again, our trusty calculator is used to determine all values for specific spreads and individual options.
30. The bid/ask spread tends to be wide in these indexes and the bid is likely to be 30 to 40 cents lower and the offer about 30 to 40 cents higher. And that's assuming IV has not increased during the market decline.

some way to salvage a profit, and unwilling to accept a loss, roll the position just to do something. If you cannot find an acceptable new position, then forget about rolling and close or reduce your current spread.

- When you roll a position, you open a new put credit spread with lower strike prices. In addition, the spread is almost always moved out to a more distant expiration month. That new month is usually one month further out, but there's no reason to limit your choices. Choose any spread (and any expiration month) that's acceptable to you. Look for the new spread the same way you choose a spread when you open a brand new position. In other words, the new spread doesn't have to bear any special relationship to the spread you are closing. It's psychologically satisfying to "roll for a credit." That means collecting more cash for the new spread than you pay for the old spread, but that's not always possible, nor is it always wise to open a position that does not fit into your comfort zone. Collecting that cash credit may feel good, but it's not a requirement. Your major goal is to reduce risk.

There's no guarantee that you won't lose more money when you roll the position (if the underlying keeps declining), but your chances of earning a profit increase once you roll the position.

EXAMPLE

You decide to buy back the 10 NDX 1950/1925 spreads and roll the position by selling 10 new NDX spreads that expire in the following month. You choose lower strike prices hoping NDX doesn't decline enough to threaten that new strike price during the remaining 38 days.[31]

If you sell the 38-day NDX 1900/1875 spread, you can expect to receive about $5.50. In this case, you cannot roll to a significantly lower strike for a credit (it costs $2.43[32] to make this roll). There's nothing wrong with paying cash to roll the position. The market moved against you and you are facing a loss. You can hold the current position and hope that loss goes away, or you can act prudently and reduce risk by moving the position to lower strike prices. Your main concern is protecting your assets. You still have a chance to come out ahead. The original spread was sold for $3.10 and you paid "only" $2.43 to roll. Thus, if all goes well and you are able to cover[33] the new spread at a low enough price, you will earn a small profit.

You may prefer to sell the 73-day NDX 1875/1850 spread,[34] which can be sold for approximately $6.60. The good news is that it costs less to roll ($1.33 vs. $2.43) and the strike price is 50 points lower. But the position does not expire for two months.

There is no specific formula to determine which spread to sell. There are usually several reasonable choices. The major requirements for the new spread are:

- The new position must allow you to remain within your comfort zone, and that includes position delta. If you cannot find a suitable spread, consider closing all or part of the current position for a loss and wait before opening a new position.
- The new spread should meet the same requirements as if you were initiating the spread as a stand-alone trade, and not as part of a roll.

---

31. The current position expires in 10 days. The next month's options expire either 28 or 35 days later.
32. You pay approximately $7.93 for the near-term spread and sell the new spread at approximately $5.50.
33. Repurchase, to close the position.
34. Two months is either 56 or 63 days.

- The suggested rolls involve opening a new position in either of the next two expiration months. You may feel more comfortable moving out even further. Look at alternatives and select the spread that leaves you feeling satisfied with the new position.
- It's not necessary to roll. Don't force the trade. If you find a new position that makes you comfortable, then rolling makes sense. If unable to find a suitable position, don't feel obligated to roll, trying to salvage some profit. Choose an alternative method for reducing risk. It's not necessary, nor is it possible, to turn each trade into a winner. Your goal is to grow your assets over time (not profit from each trade), and that means limiting losses.

Another method for adjusting a position involves buying insurance before it's needed. That discussion is postponed until Chapter 20.

When all goes well

You can adjust a position to lock in profits. You may decide a position has earned a suitable profit, and rather than risk holding longer, you close the position to lock in the profits. When the word "adjustment" is used, most investors think about a losing situation in which reducing risk is the primary consideration. Closing a profitable position is also a method for reducing risk.

Conclusion

Selling put credit spreads is equivalent to buying call debit spreads or owning collars. The strategy is bullish in nature and you earn your profit when the underlying doesn't decline below the strike price (or threaten to do so). Because this strategy involves limited risk, the margin requirements are lenient. When you sell a 10-point spread, the most you can lose is $1,000 (less premium collected) and the margin requirement is that maximum loss. When you sell naked put options, the margin requirement is higher. Suggestions: Begin selling credit spreads with the minimum possible distance between the strikes (i.e., 25 points for NDX, 10 points for RUT and SPX). If you prefer a strategy that is more market neutral, then consider selling call spreads in addition to put spreads. This idea is covered in detail in the next chapter.

There is one additional risk involved when selling credit spreads. It's not a risk associated with the strategy per se. It's a risk that results from a poor decision on the part of an inexperienced trader. When you sell a 10-point credit spread for $100, you may notice that the margin requirement is "only" $900 and conclude that such a low margin requirement must mean that the trade is relatively risk free and that you can therefore sell many such spreads. Please do not allow that to happen to you.

Remember that selling one put credit spread is equivalent to owning a collar position on 100 shares of stock. When you decide how many spreads to sell, think about the collar position and decide how many shares you are willing to own. If the answer is 500 shares, then the appropriate number of credit spreads to sell is five. Don't fall into the trap of believing that reduced margin means that you can easily sell 10 or 20 of these spreads and make lots of money. If the stock or index tumbles, the long puts you own limits your losses, but it does not eliminate them. Just as it's up to you not to buy too much stock when investing in the stock market, it's equally as important not to trade too many options when investing your money in the options market.

1. Credit spreads are only for bullish investors.
○ **TRUE** ○ **FALSE**

2. It's a good idea to initiate your credit spread by first buying the option you want to own and then selling the option you want to sell.
○ **TRUE** ○ **FALSE**

3. You decide to sell a 20-point put credit spread. You want to buy the SPX Mar 1520 put. Which put do you sell?

4. You sold the RUT Aug 800/790 put credit spread. It's Thursday afternoon during expiration week and RUT is trading near 810. What, if anything, are you thinking about this position?

5. When the short option in your credit spread becomes an option that is at-the-money, each day that passes makes the position less risky.
○ **TRUE** ○ **FALSE**

6. When entering a spread order, it's reasonable to expect to sell the spread at a price nearer the bid than the offer.
○ **TRUE** ○ **FALSE**

7. Which of the following are credit spreads?
A. Buy Nov 60 put, sell Nov 65 put,
B. Buy Apr 100 call, sell Apr 90 call,
C. Buy Feb 750 call, sell Feb 750 put

Chapter 19

Iron Condors

Buying iron condors is an option strategy for investors who have a neutral opinion on the market, i.e., neither strongly bullish nor strongly bearish. It's also suitable for investors who seldom, if ever, have an opinion on market direction. Iron condors represent an opportunity to earn money when the markets are treading water and are very popular among individual and professional traders. At least one major brokerage firm recommends this strategy to its clients. In addition, there are numerous advisory services who charge high fees to trade this strategy for clients.

An iron condor consists of two credit spreads— one call spread and one put spread—on the same underlying security. All four options expire on the same day. When buying iron condors, the investor's objective is to profit as time passes and each spread decreases in value. Profits are limited to the premium collected. Losses are limited to the maximum value of the call or put spread, reduced by the premium collected.

{ NOTE: *In theory you can lose more than the maximum just described,[1] but a small amount of prudent risk management (discussed below) eliminates that possibility.*

Buying iron condors is essentially the same strategy as selling put spreads, but it includes the sale of call spreads. That introduces the possibility of losing money when the market rallies strongly. In exchange for additional risk, profit potential increases because you collect more premium by selling both calls and puts. There's no need to repeat the same details already covered in Chapter 18. This chapter primarily emphasizes situations that are specific to buying iron condors.

The maximum profit occurs when each spread expires worthless. But investors who understand how to manage risk don't try to collect the last few nickels. Over the longer term it's prudent to buy back individual spreads when they become available at a low price.

Buying iron condors

You can adopt many styles when buying iron condors, making it difficult for newcomers to the world of options to know where to begin. One purpose of this discussion is to minimize the number of choices and help you find positions that keep you within your comfort zone. If you have no option trading experience and are looking for a place to begin, I suggest that you practice trading[2] without using real money. Then you can examine front-month, second-month and third-

month iron condors and determine if one makes more sense to you than another. You can also open positions from the perspective of the OTM, CTM or even the FOTM school.[3]

A note on my personal style:[4] I currently buy 10-point iron condors that expire in two or three months and collect $3 to $4 in premium for each. When feasible, I repurchase the call or the put spread when it's available for $0.30, but only when there are more than four weeks remaining before expiration. It's a time-dependent decision. With less time, I pay less. Holding positions through expiration is too risky, and I want to avoid both settlement risk and expiration risk (Table 18.4). The sooner you bring home (close) the short near-term iron condors, the sooner you can trade new iron condors. That not only reduces portfoloio risk, but also brings in more cash. If you prefer to hold through expiration please remember settlement risk is real and it's usually not worthwhile to try to gain the last few nickels, unless your short options are *very* far out-of-the-money. As you watch expirations come and go, you get a better idea how much the market can move on settlement Friday. Expiration is often uneventful, but don't count on it.

You cannot expect to repurchase your short spreads cheaply every month. The discussion above considers covering when possible by paying 30 cents. The problem arises when your spreads (calls or puts, not the entire iron condor) are not very far out-of-the-money and are priced at $1, $2 or even much higher. It's easy to be stubborn (or confident) and allow the position to remain open. Just recognize that you don't gain as much

---

1. *This unhappy event can occur if the market moves sharply lower and you buy back your put spread for a large loss and the market then reverses direction, causing you to repurchase your call spread for a large loss.*
2. *Most brokers allow you to open a practice, or paper trading account.*
3. *The merits of selling spreads that are out-of-the-money (OTM), closer-to-the-money (CTM), or far out-of-the-money (FOTM) were considered in Chapter 18.*
4. *This is not to suggest this style represents is the best approach. Far from it. It suits my comfort zone and that's no reason to believe it suits yours. The purpose of including this discussion is to illustrate how one trader chose a trading style from among the many, many choices.*

from time decay as you might expect when your short option is very close-to-the-money (Table 18.3), and the risk of holding as expiration nears increases daily (Table 18.4). The frequency of this predicament depends on market volatility. If you prefer to minimize risk, your best choice is to cover the short position and open a new iron condor in an appropriate month. This may result in a loss, but if safety is paramount, this is the proper action to take. If willing to accept more risk, you can hold out on a day by day basis, as long as you understand that risk of loss is increasing as you wait and hope the market makes a favorable move.

Trading iron condors is as much an art as it is a science.

- If you trade only front-month iron condors, you have the most rapid time decay, which is a big advantage. Along with that advantage comes the extra risk of holding positions as expiration nears.
- When you buy iron condors with more time remaining, you have two different ways to remain within your comfort zone. You can receive higher premiums. The obvious advantage of those higher premiums is a better risk/reward ratio (your maximum reward increases and your maximum loss decreases). As an alternative to collecting higher prices for the options you sell, you can slightly reduce the probability of facing an adjustment by selling options that are one strike further out-of-the-money.
- If your style is selling options that are reasonably far OTM, you can go further OTM and still receive good prices because that additional month (or two) significantly raises option prices. Choosing the expiration

month (Chapter 18) is an important decision, one that depends on your style. Choose positions that leave you satisfied with the risk/reward profile. There are two basic and conflicting needs to satisfy: the ability to earn a satisfactory return on your investment and the desire to reduce risk.

A more detailed definition

To be a true iron condor these conditions are necessary (but there is no need to trade a true iron condor):

- All options expire in the same month.
- The difference between the strike prices of the call spread equals the difference between the strike prices of the put spread. For example, sell XYZ Jun 80/90 call spread and XYZ Jun 60/70 put spread. Both spreads are 10 points wide.
- The number of put spreads equals the number of call spreads. If you have a market bias, you may elect to sell fewer put spreads or call spreads, but your position will consist of some iron condors and some call or put spreads.
- The strike prices do not overlap. The strike prices of the call spread are each higher than the strike prices of the put spread. Note that if the middle strike is the same, then the position is an iron butterfly.[5] For example, an iron butterfly is selling XYZ Jun 80/90 call spread and XYZ Jun 70/80 put spread. The 80 strike is common to both spreads.
- When you sell both credit spreads, you buy the iron condor. When you buy both spreads you sell the iron condor.

---

5. "Butterfly" and "condor" are examples of winged spreads. In such spreads, you sell some calls and/or puts and buy an equal number of less expensive calls and/or puts expiring in the same month. The spreads differ because of the strike prices chosen. In the "iron" version, you sell calls and puts. The regular butterfly and condor consist of only calls or only puts. You sell the option that is closer-to-the-money and buy the option that is further-from-the-money. For example, in a condor you would buy the 50/55 call spread and sell the 60/65 call spread. For a butterfly you would buy the 60/80 call spread and sell the 80/100 call spread.

- When you sell credit spreads, you sell the more expensive option. Thus, both your short call and put options are closer to the price of the underlying asset than your long options. That means you lose money when the short option goes ITM or threatens to go into-the-money.[6]

{ NOTE: The term, "threatens," is used throughout this chapter. When your short option is out-of-the-money after the settlement price is determined, it has expired worthless and no longer presents any risk. But whenever the underlying (stock, ETF or index) approaches the strike price of your short option, you are in imminent danger of losing serious money because both delta and gamma have been working against you. In fact, the position is probably already losing money, but that depends on how much time remains before the options expire[7] and the premium you collected. Doing nothing is not a viable strategy. When you find yourself in this situation, it's prudent to take action to reduce risk. See Chapter 18 for more details on adjustment methods. When your broker provides the Greeks, it saves time, but use the calculator if necessary to determine your position delta and gamma. These numbers may help you decide. You may choose to close, or roll, all or part of the iron condor or you may choose to hold (a little longer) without an adjustment. There's never a "best" solution before the fact. Afterward, when the smoke clears, it's easy to see what would have worked out best. Don't fall into the trap of letting that influence you. One action may be best this time, but there's no reason to believe it will be best next time. No one likes to lock in a loss, but it's far worse to allow a losing position to run against you.

Trading iron condors is a topic that can be approached from several different points of view, and volumes can be written on this single investment strategy. Because this book is aimed at option rookies, this chapter will show you how to choose appropriate options to trade.

Buying iron condors is a market neutral strategy that makes money most of the time. As with all methods described in this book, your job is to be certain losses are not excessive.

There are two major psychological shortcomings with this strategy. It's easy to conclude that this method is so profitable that investors may be tempted to take too much risk: 1) It's easy to feel the odds of success are greater than they are in reality; and 2) margin requirements are relatively small and it's easy to sell more spreads than are appropriate for you. If you sell options with a 10 delta, you may (incorrectly) believe the probability that neither option finishes in-the-money is 90 percent, but the likelihood that either finishes in-the-money is 20 percent.[8] If you write a new iron condor every month (selling 10-delta options), you must anticipate that one of your options finishes ITM at least twice per year. There's another problem: Part of the time the option may threaten to go in-the-money, causing you to prudently adjust the position. It doesn't matter if that option eventually finishes OTM, because you already made the adjustment. This is another way of saying this strategy is not a gimmie. You win often, but you must manage risk to stay in the game and be profitable over the long term.

With relatively small margin requirements, you may be tempted to double or triple the number of contracts you trade. Please avoid this trap. It's tempting to load

---

6. At expiration, OTM options are no longer a threat. They expire worthless and you earn the maximum profit. However when time remains, there's still a chance for OTM options to move ITM and cause losses. Remember settlement risk for European-style index options. Just because the options appear to be safely out-of-the-money when the market closes on Thursday, the settlement price is determined at the opening Friday morning, and can convert those OTM options into options are that deep ITM. Options on individual stocks are not subject to settlement risk (because they are American-style).

7. The less time, the less you may have lost to this point. But in this situation, less time remaining doesn't translate into less risk (Table 18.4).

8. The two 10 percent probabilities are additive, and one of the options is expected to finish ITM 20 percent of the time, or one in five.

up on a position that looks like a probable winner, but iron condors are not sure winners. They have a high probability of success, but nowhere near 100 percent.

Entering orders

This topic was thoroughly discussed in Chapter 18, but when trading iron condors there is one further consideration. You must decide whether to:

- Enter the iron condor as a single order.
- Enter the call (or put) spread first, and then enter the other spread when the first spread is filled.

It's far safer—and this is especially true for option rookies—to enter the whole iron condor as a single order. That eliminates the possibility of selling one spread and then discovering that you cannot receive an acceptable price on the other half of the iron condor. If you are uncertain how to enter an order for the iron condor, ask your broker for instructions. These orders consist of four legs (individual options) but should pose no problem for any broker.

If you use a live broker and decide to buy three iron condors consisting of the XYX Jan 100/110 call spread and the Jan 80/90 put spread, and if you want a minimum premium of $405 per iron condor, tell your broker:

"I want to buy 3-lots of an XYZ Jan iron condor for a net credit of $4.05 each. I'm selling both the Jan 80/90 put spread and the Jan 100/110 call spread, both to open."

Choosing the strike prices

We have already covered how to select appropriate options to trade. The same general principles apply when initiating an iron condor position. The only real difference is that you sell two spreads instead of one.

When buying iron condors the ideal situation occurs when the underlying asset trades in a narrow range, the options you sell remain out-

of-the-money and eventually expire worthless. This pleasant scenario does happen. But, it's unreasonable to expect it to happen all the time. You can increase the likelihood that your options expire worthless by selling options that are so far out-of-the-money that there's little chance that they go into-the-money. If you adopt that philosophy, you win almost every time, but you cannot expect to collect much premium—and that premium represents your profit. Thus, if your goal is to earn a decent return on your investment, you cannot sell options for nickels and dimes.

As an extreme example, suppose you sell very far OTM call and put spreads, collecting $0.05 for each. After expiration, your profit is $10, less commissions. The margin requirement for this iron condor is $1,000.[9] Your return on investment is no more than 1 percent. If you earn that amount every month with relative safety, why not adopt this method for at least part of your portfolio? Because the risk/reward parameters for this trade are terrible. If disaster strikes, you may lose up to $990 per spread. Although that's not likely, if it does happen, it wipes out 99 months of profits (and that ignores commissions). If you lose only half that amount, and if it happens once every four years, your trading is still not profitable. There's an additional problem. If it becomes necessary to adjust this position, human nature being what it is, almost every trader would refuse to adjust because he or she collected so little cash when opening the position. That's foolish thinking (adjustments should be made when risk management so dictates, and the decision is not related to the premium originally collected). It's simply a bad idea to sell spreads for such small amounts.

In Chapter 18, we discussed choosing the strike prices for a put credit spread. The thought process is the same when trading iron condors, except that you must also consider your choices

---

9. *That means that these are 10-point spreads.*

TABLE 19.1: Russell 2000 Index (RUT) Options, 42 days before expiration, RUT at $790.42

STRIKE	CALLS B/A	DELTA	STRIKE	PUTS B/A	DELTA
800	$28.45	49	620	$2.45	-5
810	$23.15	44	630	$3.05	-6
820	$18.45	38	640	$3.65	-7
830	$14.35	33	650	$4.35	-8
840	$10.80	27	660	$5.20	-9
850	$7.90	22	670	$6.15	-11
860	$5.50	17	680	$7.20	-12
870	$3.70	13	690	$8.45	-14
880	$2.45	9	700	$9.85	-16
890	$1.50	6	710	$11.35	-18
900	$1.00	4	720	$13.05	-21
			730	$14.90	-23
			740	$17.10	-27
			750	$19.45	-30
			760	$22.05	-33
			770	$25.05	-37
			780	$28.30	-41

Choosing RUT call and put spreads for your RUT iron condor. BA = midpoint between bid and ask.

when selling a call spread. Many brokers offer lenient margin requirements when trading iron condors—there is no additional margin requirement when you sell the call spread. In other words, the margin requirement for the put spread covers the iron condor position. But only if the position is a true iron condor.

Let's consider opening one iron condor position. Table 19.1 contains data for RUT, the Russell 2000 Index. RUT is priced at 790.42 and it's 42 days before the October options expire.

Sell OTM options

Most investors who adopt this strategy, including this author, prefer to write options that are not near the current market price of the underlying—with the proviso that the premium must be sufficient. It's not possible to define sufficient because that number depends on the nature of the underlying and the comfort zone of the individual trader. But remember, when the premium is too low, there's little money to be made.

By choosing options with strike prices that are far out-of-the-money, an investor may feel safe and believe the options will expire worthless.[10] Don't get overconfident.

Puts

Let's consider which put spread to sell You probably cannot sell these spreads at the prices in Table 19.1 because these are the midpoints between the bid and the ask prices, but for this discussion, assume you can.

EXAMPLE

The 620/630 spread[11] is 160 points out-of-the-money, has a delta of +1 and finishes OTM 94 percent of the time. That's about a 20 percent move when the index is priced near 800 (RUT is 790.42). The premium is $60 and if this position expires worthless you earn 6 percent on the $1,000 margin requirement. That's a nice return for six weeks. But, if you plan to repurchase this spread before it expires, the return becomes less attractive. Because this is part of an iron condor position, there is a special consideration. The sale of the call spread generates additional cash and requires no additional margin,[12] increasing the return on investment. This spread is a possibility.

The 630/640 spread can be sold for $60. This is a no-brainer. If you can collect $60 for the 630/620 spread, there's no reason to accept only $60 for this spread. It is, after all, 10 points closer-to-the-money.

---

10. The strikes may appear to be far OTM right now, but tomorrow they may be ITM!
11. Lower strike prices are available.
12. Assuming you sell a 10-point spread that expires in the same month.

NOTE: When dealing with indexes that have many different strike prices, you may occasionally encounter a situation in which one or two of the individual options appear to be priced out of line. That happens when an individual investor enters an order to buy or sell a few contracts at a limit price—a price that differs from the market maker's price. That may be why the 620/630 spread appears to be priced so attractively, compared with the 630/640 spread. A customer may be offering to sell the 620 puts at a relatively low price.

To find an appropriate put spread, consider each possibility,[13] looking for one that feels right. The higher the strike, the more you collect in premium, but (obviously) the more likely the spread is to require an adjustment before expiration. Once again, there is no "best" spread to sell. You can sell options that are further OTM and settle for less premium, or you can accept a greater risk that your short options threatens to move ITM and collect a higher premium. Keep in mind that you can afford to settle for less cash from this put spread because you collect additional cash from the call spread.

When short an option that threatens to move in-the-money, sometimes it's prudent to cover that short and accept the loss and roll the position. If that happens, don't forget to cover the other part of the iron condor at a low price. It must be FOTM if you are considering adjusting the other part. You cannot expect smooth sailing all the time. But the less often you are short options that threaten to move ITM, the better. The primary reason for trading spreads from the previous example (selling options that are far out-of-the-money) is to avoid being forced to make adjustments. In this scenario, my choice

is to sell the 670/680 put spread and collect a premium near $1.05.

It takes trading experience, but after you sell these spreads for a few months, you'll have a much better idea of how to stay within your comfort zone. If you are someone who can treat fictional trades with respect, then paper trade without using real money. But for that to prove beneficial, you must know how you would react if using real money. It takes time, so have a bit of patience. Leave your ego behind[14] and concentrate on earning money.

Calls

It's time to choose a call spread to go along with the put spread to complete the iron condor. The suggested put spread is reasonably far OTM. It's customary to select a similar call spread. But for educational purposes, let's look at call spreads from a different perspective— one that is CTM.

{ *NOTE: Don't assume that the recommendation is to have one OTM spread and one CTM spread. It's better to choose both spreads using similar criteria, unless you prefer to open a position with a market bias. If somewhat bullish, you may decide to sell CTM puts and OTM calls. Unless you have a proven track record for predicting market direction, it's best to avoid this and remain market neutral.*

EXAMPLE *Sell CTM options*
With RUT near 790 (Table 19.1), there are several different strikes that fulfill the close-to-the-money criteria. The 800/810 call spread is priced near $5.30. That's a very attractive premium, but the call is merely 10 points

13. In Chapter 18 we discussed how to choose between selling a 10-, 20- or 30-point spread. That discussion is valid for iron condors as well.
14. No one likes to admit to trading 1- or 2-lot spreads. But the truth is, it's a very intelligent thing to do. If you discuss your trading with friends, there's no need to disclose how many options you are trading.

OTM. Too close for my comfort, even for investors who prefer CTM spreads. The 810/820 spread is priced near $4.70. When selling spreads at these prices, your losses are limited. If, for example, you sell a put spread that is also CTM, you can collect $3.25 for the 770/780 put spread. That's $7.95 for the iron condor. When you collect that much, the maximum loss is only $2.05, and there's less to fear when one of the options goes ITM. CTM spreads have two advantages: you collect a high premium, and your maximum loss is reasonable. Unfortunately, there is one disadvantage: there's only a 15 percent chance that your short options expire worthless. (From Table 19.1: The 780 put finishes ITM 41 percent of the time and the 810 call finishes ITM 44 percent of the time; 41 + 44 = 85 percent ITM.) Nevertheless, this style fits some investors because the risk/reward ratio is attractive.

The 820/830 call spread at $4.10 is also a consideration—a slightly smaller premium ($0.60) in return for being an additional 10 points OTM. Deciding which spread suits you best becomes easier after you make the decision a few times. Always, you must consider risk, reward, your market bias and most importantly whether the position allows you to be comfortable with your investments and allows you to sleep at night, without being concerned about your portfolio.

As a non-trader of CTM spreads, it's difficult to know which I would choose. But, the 820/830 spread had a lot going for it.

Margin requirements

Once you understand iron condors, including the risk and reward potential and how to manage risk, there's no need to trade a true iron condor. If it suits you, you can modify iron condors by adopting any of the following:

- Sell more call spreads than put spreads.
- Sell more put spreads than call spreads.
- Vary the width between the strike prices.

For example, sell the SPX 1650/1675 call spread and sell the SPX 1350/1400 put spread.

Basically any variation that comes to mind can be used, but there are advantages to using true iron condors. The primary advantage is that most brokers (sadly, not all) have lenient margin requirements for true iron condors. If you modify the spread in any way, those advantages disappear.

Risk management

Managing iron condor risk differs from put credit spreads in an important way: Don't ignore positions that appear to be very safe. Assume the market takes an unfavorable move to the upside and you decide to roll your call spread to higher strike prices in another expiration month. Your position now consists of the new call spread and the old put spread. This is not a good situation because you have a very inexpensive put spread (the options must be pretty far OTM for the call spread to have required an adjustment), and that provides little offset to your call position. In other words, this position is far from market neutral.

If you accept the premise that you don't know whether the market's next big move is higher or lower, then why own this position when it performs poorly if the market continues higher? You want a position that's more market neutral. (Isn't that why you're trading iron condors?) To achieve that market neutrality, it's best to roll the put position. The easiest way to do that is to simply place a bid (that has a reasonable chance of being filled) to buy back that put spread (locking in the profit on this part of the iron condor and eliminating the risk of holding it). Also enter a new order to sell a put spread that completes the iron condor that you prefer to have at this time.

Assuming you rolled to a suitable call spread, do the same with the put spread. You may have a profit or loss on the closed iron condor, but that's not your main concern. You rolled the position primarily to reduce risk, but it is also important to open a new position that you want to own—one that you expect will be profitable.

The point is that there's little to gain by owning an inexpensive spread. It's best to "get it off your sheets"[15] and sell a put spread that has a chance to contribute to your future earnings.

Another method for reducing risk has been discussed before, but bears repeating because it works very well: Don't hold positions near expiration. The problem is that it's not always easy for traders/investors to adopt this technique because it requires a willingness to close a short position at prices that may appear to be unattractive. Part of adopting this risk management method involves opening credit spreads and/or iron condors when two or three months remain before expiration. The plan is to close those positions three or four weeks[16] before the options expire.

The major benefit of using this method is that it eliminates the ever-increasing risk of a significant market move. As shown in Table 18.4, that risk increases very rapidly as expiration approaches. This technique also eliminates settlement risk.

As an offset, time decay accelerates as expiration nears (except when your short option is nearly ATM, see Table 18.3), and the rate at which profits accumulate increases. By holding the position, you gain both increasing profits and increasing risk. The recommendation here is to eliminate both by closing positions and opening others[17] (with a more distant expiration date).

When adopting this risk-management method, you sacrifice the ability to maximize profits in return for owning safer positions. For some traders, that's not a satisfactory tradeoff. But, if you meet your investment objectives by taking less risk, why take more risk? I use this technique as often as possible when trading my personal account.

---

15. Market-maker terminology for closing the position. It simply means removing the position from your daily statement.
16. If you prefer to hold a week longer, that's reasonable. But risk increases every day. The basis of this risk-reducing method is to hold no positions as expiration nears.
17. The new positions have less negative gamma, and thus, are less risky.

Quiz

Answers on page 220

1. Iron condors are the ideal strategy when you are very bullish.

○ **TRUE** ○ **FALSE**

2. It's almost impossible to lose money over the long term when you sell iron condors in which both spreads are very far out-of-the-money.

○ **TRUE** ○ **FALSE**

3. No matter what happens, if you sell a 10-point iron condor on a European-style index, and if you collect $300 and hold the position through expiration, you can never lose more than $700.

○ **TRUE** ○ **FALSE**

4. When you sell a 20-point iron condor, the margin requirement is:

A. $4,000 ($2,000 each for the call spread and put spread)
B. $2,000
C. It depends on the strike prices

5. Do these four trades comprise a true iron condor?

A. Sell 10 IBM Nov 90 puts
B. Buy 10 IBM Nov 80 puts
C. Sell 15 IBM Nov 110 calls
D. Buy 15 IBM Nov 120 calls

6. When you initiate an iron condor position, it's possible to estimate the probability that all options expire worthless. How do you do that?

7. If you sell an OTM put spread and a CTM call spread, it's not a true iron condor.

○ **TRUE** ○ **FALSE**

Chapter 20

Advanced Risk Management

Although this book is primarily for option rookies, you won't always be a rookie, and when you return to these pages to further your options education, you will be in a better position to use more advanced trading and risk management methods. You may not be ready to adopt the methods described in this chapter now, but it's included to make your trading more successful down the road. This sophisticated method for protecting your investment portfolio works like an insurance policy. When you buy insurance, most of the time, the insurance is "wasted," and that's good news.[1] But if the insurance is needed, you'll be glad you have it.

---

1. When you buy homeowner's insurance, aren't you pleased that your house doesn't burn and you don't collect on that insurance policy? But if a disaster strikes, that insurance is badly needed.

Pre-insurance means buying *extra* insurance to protect a specific position or an entire portfolio. When you sell credit spreads or iron condors, you already own insurance because you own one option for each option sold. That's your protection against unlimited losses. In this chapter the discussion concerns owning extra insurance to reduce the risk of large, but limited losses, such as those resulting from a stock market surprise. This method of adjusting option positions before that adjustment is necessary (let's call it "pre-insurance") is rarely used, primarily because investors seldom consider fixing a problem that does not yet exist. Sometimes this insurance provides limited protection (a loss is still possible) and sometimes you earn a profit from a situation that otherwise would have resulted in a substantial loss.

If you are first starting to trade, or if your bankroll dictates that you own small positions (single contract spreads or positions consisting of a few contracts), then this type of adjustment is probably unsuitable for you. But, you won't always have a small bankroll, so consider this idea as food for thought.

Chapters 18 and 19 discussed selling credit spreads, a strategy suitable for an investor with any outlook for the market, including:

- Put spreads, when neutral to bullish.
- Iron condors, when neutral (or without an opinion).
- Call spreads when neutral to bearish. Although call spreads were not discussed specifically, think of this strategy as the mirror image of selling put spreads.

Option rookies have the best opportunity to really *understand* how options work by starting their trading careers with one of the three basic conservative strategies. Covered call writing allows investors who already trade stocks to make a smooth transition into the options world. Naked put selling is equivalent to covered call writing and thus, it should be easy to move from writing covered calls to writing naked puts. Owning collars is the most conservative of the three basic conservative strategies because it entails owning one put option for each covered call. When we discuss pre-insuring a position, the concept should already be familiar because it's similar to the insurance that converts a covered call position into the less risky collar.[2]

Moving beyond the three basic strategies

The underlying premise for recommending the sale of credit spreads:

- Owning collars is a conservative stock market strategy.
- Selling put spreads is equivalent to owning collars (Chapter 15).
- Selling put spreads is appropriate for all types of investors, from those who are wildly speculative to those who are extremely conservative.
- The three basic strategies are all bullish in nature, and credit spreads can be used by investors who prefer to be market neutral, bullish or bearish.

The main purpose of this book is to teach you to use options to earn money with reduced risk and remain within your comfort zone. If you are not yet ready to sell credit spreads or buy iron condors, that's OK. It's more important to get some hands-on experience with methods you understand that fit nicely into your investment philosophy. Too many investors trade first and hope to understand later.

---

2. *When you own a collar position, you own stock, sell calls, and buy puts. Those puts represent an insurance policy. If you need a refresher, collars are covered in Chapter 13.*

When you feel comfortable with any of the basic strategies, it's not difficult to switch to the sale of put spreads—and you may even decide to consider that as your primary option strategy. It is, after all, the way most investors approach the stock market—with a bullish bias. The difference is that when you sell put spreads, you own a hedged portfolio, and thus, have much less risk than the traditional investor who owns stocks and mutual funds. Although those bullish investors have unlimited upside potential, you have enough upside potential to earn a very good return on your investment. And if you compound those earnings (perhaps in a retirement account), the chances are excellent that your option trading can provide for your future financial security. Isn't sacrificing some of that upside potential for extra downside security an intelligent tradeoff?[3]

The added advantage of selling credit spreads is that it allows you to be market neutral rather than bullish, if that idea appeals to you. Don't forget the bottom line—if trading the three basic conservative strategies feels better, then you may prefer to use those methods—even though selling put spreads is equivalent to owning collars (Chapter 15).

If you decide to adopt these methods as your primary money-making option strategies, then this chapter contains information that's important for you. The repetitive mention of the importance of risk and money management shouldn't make you believe these methods are extra risky. They aren't. Selling put credit spreads is a traditional investment method. The reason it's not better known as an investment method is because brokers shy away from recommending it to their customers, and it's not easy for investors to learn how to successfully adopt these methods. This information is important to you because it offers a clear explanation of how to initiate and manage credit spreads and iron condors.

But no strategy is guaranteed to bring profits. Sometimes you have many consecutive months with nary a problem, and the profits just roll in. At others times, the markets are turbulent and you may be forced to adjust positions month after month. Allowing you to survive during those turbulent times is the reason that risk management is essential.

This book was not written to teach you how to choose a strategy and then leave you stranded. The goal is to help you earn money over the long term—and that involves explaining how to open positions, close positions and, most importantly, manage risk.

Pre-insurance

By combining a bit of option buying with the sale of credit spreads, you build a position that retains a high probability of being profitable, but with an extra insurance policy. And when not profitable, the insurance aspect of the position goes a long way toward protecting you against large losses—and under the appropriate (but rare) circumstances, produces extra profits.

 NOTE: Many investors consider pre-insurance to be too expensive because a portion of potential profits must be sacrificed to buy the insurance. They prefer to buy insurance only when needed. Either method of risk management is acceptable. What is not acceptable is ignoring risk.

Choosing which options to buy

When buying options as insurance, there are important considerations. You can buy options that expire in any month, and you can buy options with any strike price. To keep this discussion to a reasonable length, let's only consider a few of the possibilities.[4] When you become a more experienced options trader you are in position to generate your own ideas and modify any suggestions made in this book.

---

3. To this author, the answer is yes. But not everyone agrees.
4. In theory any options can be used as insurance, but as time goes by, options with strike prices that are far out-of-the-money lose much of their effectiveness. Thus, if you own a position in which you sell a put option with a 1,000 strike price, don't consider buying puts with an 800 strike price as insurance. Use options much closer to the 1,000 strike price.

To get a clear picture of pre-insurance and what it can (and cannot) do for you, let's examine three scenarios varying the method of insuring a portfolio composed of iron condors. In each example, we follow the position as time passes.

Setup for figures used in this chapter

Let's say today is Wednesday, two days prior to September expiration. Thus:

1. When October positions are opened, the time to October expiration is 30 days.
2. When November positions are opened, the time to November expiration is 65 days.
3. When December positions are opened, the time to December expiration is 93 days.

Scenario 1: Buy an iron condor that expires in approximately two months (Nov). Buy insurance that expires one month later (Dec).

Scenario 2: Buy the same iron condor and buy insurance expiring in the same month (Nov).

Scenario 3: Buy the same iron condor and buy insurance that expires one month earlier than the iron condor (Oct).

Whenever you sell an iron condor, you are subject to the risk of market movement. If for example, the market rallies, the call spread portion of the iron condor loses money, and the put spread portion makes money. At first, these nearly balance each other. That's why the downward slope of the curve (Figure 20.1), showing the rate at which money is lost when the underlying moves, is gentle when the underlying is near the center of the graph. As the underlying moves more and more away from that center, the downward slope of the graph accelerates, until it flattens as the maximum loss is approached. The slope also steepens as time passes because risk increases as expiration nears.

For each day that passes, the position makes money. When enough time passes, you may want to close the position and take your profit (assuming the underlying has not moved so far that there is no profit). Maximum profit occurs when expiration arrives and all options expire worthless. It's important to understand the extra risk (and reward potential) that comes with holding these positions as expiration nears because you must make the decision: hold longer for extra profits and extra risk, or close early to eliminate that risk (and the possible rewards).

But other factors are at play. Implied volatility constantly changes for these index options and the effect of IV on daily profits and losses is significant. Why? Because iron condor positions are short vega (volatility). As IV changes, the value of the position changes—usually by more than a single day's time decay. There are many variables that affect the value of your portfolio on any given day.

The best way to manage these positions is to be aware of your maximum profit and decide when to close the position. This is especially true as expiration nears. For example, if you sell an iron condor that expires in 35 days, collecting $250, and for some strange reason you can close the position one week later for a $200 profit (you are extremely unlike to see this happen), it's wise to do so. With only $50 of potential remaining, risk vs. reward becomes unfavorable.

If your broker provides graphs similar to these, take advantage and use them.

> **How to read the profit/loss graphs in this chapter: The price of the underlying asset (The Russell 2000 Index, or RUT, in this example) is plotted along the horizontal axis and the change in the value of the position is plotted along the vertical axis.**

{ *NOTE: When you look at the graphs, it appears that all positions result in losses and that there are no potential profits. That's because profits come as time passes, and these graphs don't reflect the passage of time. Each graph is based on the assumption that the position is opened the same day the graph is created. Thus, none of the graphs shown in Figures 20.1 through 20.9 reflect profit potential. In each case, the profit potential is the premium collected when selling the iron condor, reduced by premium paid for insurance. You can calculate theta for the position, giving you the theoretical daily time decay.*

Scenario 1

Figure 20.1 shows the profit/loss profile when selling 40-lots of the RUT Nov 740/750 put, 900/910 call iron condor. You collect $3.00 for each, or $12,000, making your maximum loss $28,000.[5]

As seen in Figure 20.1, the position is slightly bearish (because you earn a profit if RUT declines from 823 to about 805). Typical of iron condors, losses increase as RUT moves away from its current price.

In Figure 20.2, the effect of buying two calls and two puts can be seen. The calls cost $640 each and the puts cost $860, or $3,000 total. Twenty-five

percent of the proceeds from the sale of the iron condors was reinvested to buy insurance.

Has the insurance helped? Is the value of the portfolio protected? Yes and no. If RUT undergoes a major, unexpected decline (approximately 20 percent to 660) losses decrease from $17,000 to about $9,000. Similarly, the resulting loss if RUT soars 17 percent to 960 is reduced from $20,000 to near $9,000. The question a trader must ask is whether it's worthwhile to invest a quarter of the cash collected to acquire this protection.

This protection is helpful, but not worth the cost.

You may ask whether it's reasonable to be concerned with such large changes (20 percent) in the price of the underlying. Isn't it more practical to consider what happens when RUT moves 5, or even 10 percent? Yes it is. If you look at the graphs closely, you can see that when RUT moves about 5 percent to 780 or 860, insurance provides a small benefit. Again, this insurance is not worth the cost.

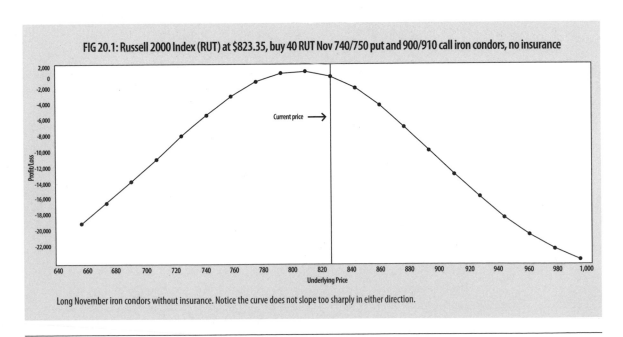

FIG 20.1: Russell 2000 Index (RUT) at $823.35, buy 40 RUT Nov 740/750 put and 900/910 call iron condors, no insurance

Long November iron condors without insurance. Notice the curve does not slope too sharply in either direction.

5. *The maximum value of 40 10-point iron condors is $40,000. Subtracting the $12,000 premium, the maximum loss is $28,000.*

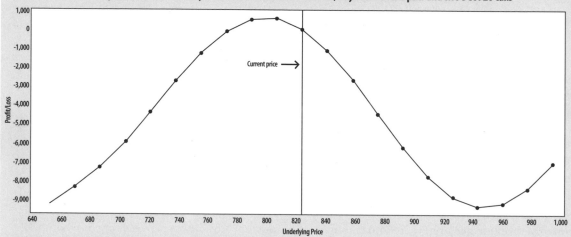

FIG 20.2: Russell 2000 Index (RUT) at $823.35,
buy 40 RUT Nov 740/750 put and 900/910 call iron condors, buy two Dec 690 puts and two Dec 920 calls

Long the same November iron condors, but with insurance that expires in December. Notice that larger moves produce smaller losses, compared to the position in Figure 20.1, which has no insurance.

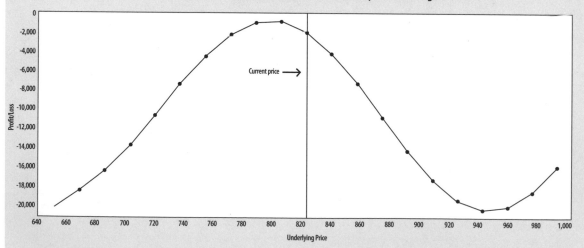

FIG 20.3: Russell 2000 Index (RUT) at $823.35, buy 40 RUT Nov 740/750 put and 900/910 call iron condors, buy two Dec 690 puts and two Dec 920 calls 35 days later than Figure 20.2

Long November iron condors, with December insurance. Notice that the passage of time has made the insurance less useful and substantial losses are possible.

Let's take another look at this position as time passes. As you know, options are a wasting asset and the options you buy lose considerable value as time passes. In addition, as expiration nears, the iron condor position becomes more risky (Table 18.4). That combination suggests that insurance may be even less effective as time passes. Figure 20.3 illustrates this position 35 days later.

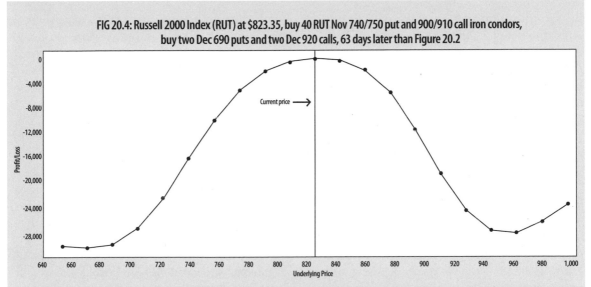

FIG 20.4: Russell 2000 Index (RUT) at $823.35, buy 40 RUT Nov 740/750 put and 900/910 call iron condors, buy two Dec 690 puts and two Dec 920 calls, 63 days later than Figure 20.2

Long November iron condors, with December insurance. Two months later than Figure 20.2. Notice that the trend continues—the passage of additional time makes the insurance even less useful.

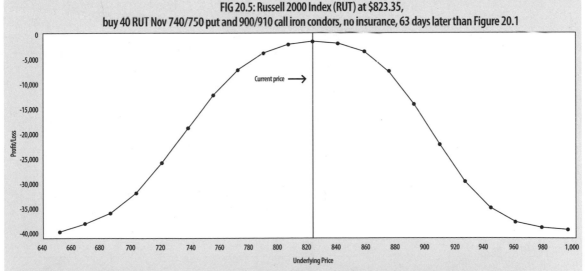

FIG 20.5: Russell 2000 Index (RUT) at $823.35, buy 40 RUT Nov 740/750 put and 900/910 call iron condors, no insurance, 63 days later than Figure 20.1

Long November iron condors with no insurance. Nine weeks passed since the position was opened (Figure 20.1), and there are two days remaining before expiration. The passage of time produces profits for the iron condor seller when all goes well, but the risk of incurring large losses increases. Compare P/L when RUT trades near 680 or 940 in Figure 20.1.

Notice that the general shape of the curve remains the same—if the underlying move is large enough, the rate of loss deceases, or even reverses. As expected, insurance is less effective and the potential loss is significantly greater than it was 35 days ago, increasing from roughly $9,000 to between $18,000 and $20,000. To show that this effect continues, Figure 20.4 represents the same position after an additional 28 days. For comparison, Figure 20.5 shows the original iron condor without insurance, at the same point in time.

Figure 20.5 makes it clear that holding the position into expiration increases the danger of a huge loss. The portfolio value approaches its worst possible result (worth of -$40,000). Owning insurance that expires 28 days later is insufficient to provide more than $10,000 worth of protection (Figure 20.4).

This is not a very attractive method for pre-insuring an iron condor portfolio.

Scenario 2

In this scenario, the options bought as insurance expire at the same time as the iron condor, or one month earlier than in scenario 1. Because the options expire sooner, they are less expensive and you can buy options that are closer-to-the-money. By spending $2,980 you buy three extra 910 calls and two 720 puts.[6] The risk profile is shown in Figure 20.6, and it's apparent that same-month insurance provides better protection (compare Figure 20.2).

This is an interesting result. It turns out that owning three calls instead of two and owning options with strike prices that are closer-to-the-money is more important in providing insurance than owning more expensive options with longer lifetimes. You were able to buy better options this time because these options cost less.

Let's see if this holds true when times passes. Figure 20.7 shows the risk profile for same-month insurance 35 days later.

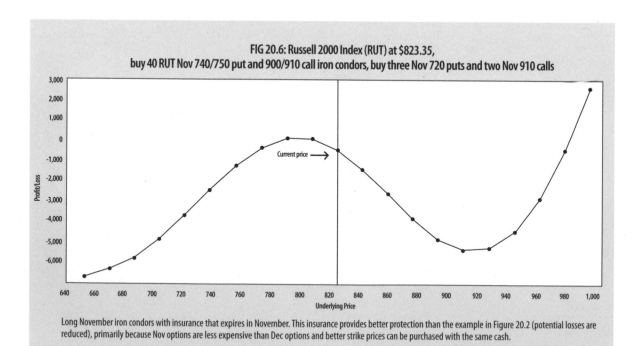

FIG 20.6: Russell 2000 Index (RUT) at $823.35, buy 40 RUT Nov 740/750 put and 900/910 call iron condors, buy three Nov 720 puts and two Nov 910 calls

Long November iron condors with insurance that expires in November. This insurance provides better protection than the example in Figure 20.2 (potential losses are reduced), primarily because Nov options are less expensive than Dec options and better strike prices can be purchased with the same cash.

6. It's not necessary to buy an equal number of puts and calls. Puts trade at a higher implied volatility and are more expensive than calls (equally far OTM). In this example, each call is $420 and puts are $860. This strike prices are illustrative, and you may elect to buy slightly different strikes.

When you compare Figures 20.3 and 20.7 you see that same-month options continue to provide better insurance than next-month options. The disappointing feature seen in Figure 20.7 is that a significant market move still results in a substantial loss.

Because scenario 2 provides better insurance than scenario 1, let's take this idea one step further and consider the purchase of insurance that expires one month before the iron condor expires. As a rookie, you don't have the perspective of a more experienced trader, but this is an uncomfortable idea for many investors who don't like the idea of owning insurance that expires while that insurance is still needed.[7]

Scenario 3

In this scenario, you sell the same 40-lot of Nov iron condors and buy insurance that expires in 30 days. Because these options are so much less expensive than longer-term options, you can afford to buy options with more desirable strike prices. To protect against the 900/910 call spread, you buy 880 calls. Do these calls provide better insurance than the 910 and 920 calls bought in scenarios 1 and 2?[8] Similarly, you buy 770 puts as protection against the 740/750 put spreads. Does this provide better insurance the 690s and 720 purchased in the other scenarios?

The answers can be seen in Figure 20.8, the risk profile for the iron condors insured with near-term options. The two Oct 770 puts cost $6.90 each and three Oct 880 calls are $3.40 each. Net insurance cost: $2,400.

This profile shows very limited risk: $3,000 upside risk and no downside risk. That's protection! The

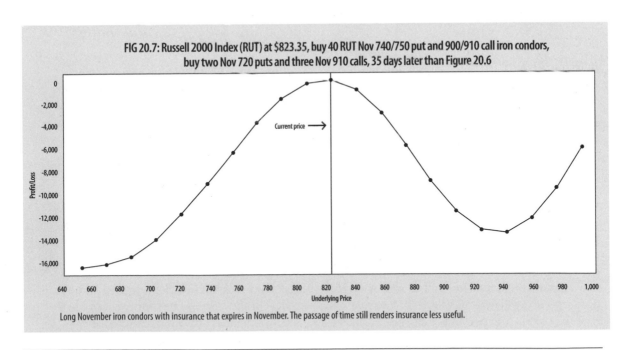

FIG 20.7: Russell 2000 Index (RUT) at $823.35, buy 40 RUT Nov 740/750 put and 900/910 call iron condors, buy two Nov 720 puts and three Nov 910 calls, 35 days later than Figure 20.6

Long November iron condors with insurance that expires in November. The passage of time still renders insurance less useful.

7. When the options you buy as insurance expire, the iron condor's expiration remains one month in the future, and you don't want to own this position without insurance. That gives you two choices: close the position now or buy more insurance. If you agree with the earlier idea (Chapter 18) that it's worthwhile to open positions in the second and third months and close them when they become front-month options (to avoid expiration risk and settlement risk), then these methods are consistent. When you own front-month options as insurance, then you close the iron condor position when insurance lapses (expires).

8. In those scenarios, the 880 calls were far too costly to buy.

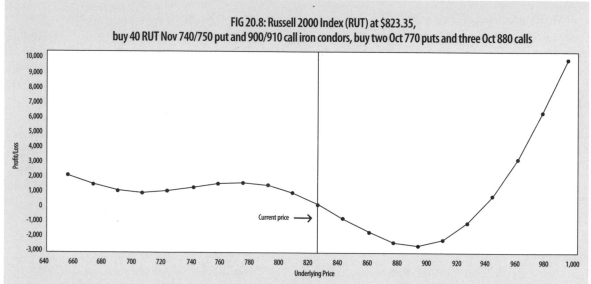

FIG 20.8: Russell 2000 Index (RUT) at $823.35,
buy 40 RUT Nov 740/750 put and 900/910 call iron condors, buy two Oct 770 puts and three Oct 880 calls

Long November iron condors with insurance that expires in October. Compare Figures 20.2 and 20.6. These near-term options provide much better protection at the same (or lower) cost. Note the strike prices of the Oct options are much higher for puts and lower for calls and are more effective as insurance. On the negative side, they expire before the iron condors.

question is how does the passage of time (28 days) affect the profile? Figure 20.9 supplies the answer.

In Figure 20.9 you see that insurance does its job. These near-term options not only cost less ($2,400 vs. $3,000) but only two days before the insurance expires, the position is still well protected against a catastrophe. The maximum loss is between $7,000 and $8,000 compared with twice that amount when using same-month options as protection.

The conclusion is clear. Buying near-term options provides the best insurance for an iron condor position that expires one month later. However, despite this conclusion, this type of insurance does not work for everyone. When you adopt this style of pre-insurance, you must be willing to close your iron condor position when insurance lapses.[9]

If you are considering the idea of buying insurance that expires before the iron condor (or other) position it's protecting, there is one additional concern: The possibility that rapid time decay for the few near-term options may be greater than time decay for the iron condors. The reason trading iron condors works is because of theta, or the time decay that you collect daily. The position represented by Figure 20.8 has positive theta ($95 per day), almost zero delta (short 26 delta), and as with all iron condors, the position is short vega (821). These Greeks are specific to this snapshot in time for this specific position, yet if you adopt this methodology, you can anticipate that your position will be short vega and have positive theta. Positive theta is the key.

---

9. *When your short options (in the iron condor) are both pretty far OTM, it's very tempting to hold longer. You can do so, but it's riskier without insurance. In today's world, the possibility of a serious terrorist attack, a political assassination or a sudden announcement of huge importance from the U.S. Federal Reserve can move markets. Do you want to take that chance? I recommend closing the near-term iron condor and re-establishing a second-month iron condor with near-term insurance.*

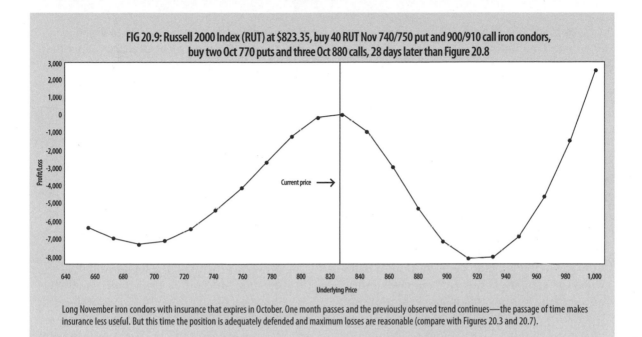

FIG 20.9: Russell 2000 Index (RUT) at $823.35, buy 40 RUT Nov 740/750 put and 900/910 call iron condors, buy two Oct 770 puts and three Oct 880 calls, 28 days later than Figure 20.8

Long November iron condors with insurance that expires in October. One month passes and the previously observed trend continues—the passage of time makes insurance less useful. But this time the position is adequately defended and maximum losses are reasonable (compare with Figures 20.3 and 20.7).

BOTTOM LINE:

1) Near-term options provide the best insurance for an iron condor position that expires in the second month. These options are significantly less expensive than options with longer lifetimes, and you can afford to buy options that provide better protection (strike prices that are CTM).

2) Second-month options are appropriate as insurance against an iron condor position that expires in the third month, but these options are expensive and you cannot expect this insurance to provide the same protection as near-term vs. second month iron condors (because you cannot afford to buy options with more attractive strike prices).

3) Near-term options are less expensive than longer-term options, allowing you to choose between buying more options that are further OTM or fewer options with better strike prices. It's preferable to buy options with better strike prices.[10]

4) Near-term options provide significant protection, but at a price. Is it enough protection for you and your comfort zone? Is it too costly? Would you prefer to pay for insurance only when needed? That's for you to decide, but the recommendation is to consider using this method to gain excellent portfolio protection.

5) If you decide not to adopt this method now, paper trade and gain insight into how it works—especially when the markets move. Dull markets may make you believe that insurance is a waste of money, but volatile markets may convince you otherwise.

6) The fact that you are using pre-insurance does not mean you can ignore the possibility of adjusting a position. Pre-insurance goes a long way toward making your positions

---

10. *Owning more options, each further OTM, only pays off in the event of a big disaster (or huge rally).*

less risky, but be alert if risk increases to an unacceptable level.

Is insurance for you?

There is one significant problem that may present itself every once in a while when you own pre-insurance that expires before the iron condor. Part of the plan when owning this type of insurance is to shut down (close) the iron condor position when your insurance lapses.

The latest time to close the iron condors is either Thursday afternoon, or very early Friday morning (third Friday of the month). Why? Your insurance options offer protection, but only until the market opens Friday morning—that's when the settlement price of your near-term options (the options that insure your portfolio) is determined.[11] After the market opens, those near-term options have expired and can neither increase in value nor offer protection. Those options may have expired worthless, or they may be ITM. If they are ITM, you receive the cash value of those options before the market opens for trading next Monday.

The main point to understand is that you are now without insurance. If you still own the iron condors, you have a decision to make. You can close (the original plan), or you may decide to stay short the iron condors without insurance or to buy more insurance that expires in the same month.

The plan was to close those iron condors, but sometimes you won't like the prices at which you can shut down the positions. Thus, you can close the positions at those unfavorable prices, planning on opening new iron condor positions (with insurance) in a new month, or accept greater risk by holding your current positions. You don't have to do anything. Holding without insurance

is acceptable, but it's not how you planned to manage risk. Buying new insurance is better than owning no insurance, but same month insurance is not as effective as owning insurance that expires before the iron condor position. Why would you consider violating your original plan and continue to hold?

- The underlying may be priced right so that each spread is far enough out-of-the-money that you are comfortable holding. The plan should not be to hold through expiration. Instead it should be to gain a few more days of time decay before taking your profits. Remember, the longer you hold, the more dangerous a substantial market move becomes (Table 18.4). And if there's a big, overnight surprise, you may not have a chance to adjust or close the position before it's too late to prevent a large loss. Don't be greedy.
- You may feel that the options are priced too high, forcing you to pay far more than you prefer to buy back the iron condor. When this happens it's important to understand that a) You cannot earn a profit every month; and b) if you pay a high price to buy back your front-month iron condor, you should be compensated for doing so because you can collect a better price for the iron condor you plan to sell in one of the other expiration months (due to high implied volatility).

Minimizing the importance of large losses is critical to long-term success, Insurance serves that purpose but most of the time it is not needed and reduces your profits.

---

11. Assuming you are trading European-style index options. If trading stock options, you have until late Friday afternoon to close.

1. If you sell a put spread and collect a cash credit, should you buy puts or calls as insurance (assuming you elect to own insurance)?

2. When you buy pre-insurance, you will probably earn a quick profit when:

A. the Federal Reserve cuts interest rates by 0.25 percent.
B. the President of the United States undergoes minor surgery.
C. terrorists blow up the Eiffel Tower and Washington Monument simultaneously.
D. the price of oil reaches $120 per gallon.

3. Is this good advice: If you buy a 1-lot iron condor, buy insurance.

4. Investors who believe pre-insurance is too expensive and elect not to own it are making a big mistake.

○ **TRUE**   ○ **FALSE**

5. Which of the following are true? Near-term options provide better insurance for iron condor positions because:

A. The options are less expensive.
B. You can afford to buy more options.
C. Options with better strike prices are available at the same cost per option.
D. They have a much slower rate of daily time decay.

Chapter 21

Double Diagonals

Under certain market conditions there are advantages to owning positions with options that expire in different months. Those spreads are referred to as diagonal spreads. In theory you can own the option that expires first or the option that expires later. For practical reasons, we'll only discuss diagonal spreads when you own the option that expires later.[1] As with credit spreads, either calls or puts are used to create diagonal spreads. For the purposes of our discussion, we sell the diagonal spread. Thus, we sell the call with the lower strike price or the put with the higher strike price.[2]

---

1. For individual investors who don't qualify for "portfolio margin" (more lenient requirements for customers with larger accounts), margin rules stipulate that the option you own must expire at the same time, or later than, the option sold, or else the option sold is considered to be "naked short." Those naked short options not only have much larger margin requirements, but many brokers don't allow naked (we know they are not really naked, but you cannot argue with margin rules) call options in your portfolio.
2. In contrast with same-month credit spreads, when you sell the diagonal you do not always sell the higher priced option.

For example:

Buy SPX Dec 1550 call   Buy MSFT Apr 35 puts
Sell SPX Nov 1525 call   Sell MSFT Feb 40 puts

The rest of the nomenclature remains the same. The above spreads are a 25-point SPX diagonal call spread and a 5-point Microsoft diagonal put spread.

When you sell both a diagonal call spread and a diagonal put spread at the same time, the position is called a double diagonal. Any months may be chosen, but the most common strategy is to buy and sell options that expire in adjacent months. These double diagonals are very similar to iron condors. The only difference is that the options you buy expire in a later month.

Why consider diagonals?

When you sell a typical put spread (or iron condor), sometimes the underlying approaches the strike price of your short option as expiration nears. As previously discussed, that's a risky proposition, and the prudent course of action is to close or roll the risky position. Wouldn't it be better if, in addition to those spreads which have become dangerous to hold, you owned positions that made money under those conditions? Diagonal spreads can do just that. But, diagonals have their own risk/reward parameters and you must be careful not to increase risk.

Let's begin with profit potential. After all, that's the main reason for adopting an investment strategy.

Trading style

In the example that follows, we are selling the S&P 500 Index (SPX) March 1350 puts. If you choose to buy the Apr 1300 put, you are opening an SPX 50-point diagonal put spread. If you decide to buy the Apr 1275 put, you would have a 75-point diagonal

put spread. Based on what you already know about selling credit spreads, the maximum value for the spread is the difference between the strikes (x 100), which is $7,500 for the 75-point spread and $5,000 for the 50-point spread. Thus, there is less overall risk when you sell the 50-point diagonal spread.

On the other hand, when you buy the April 1300 put, you must pay more for the position (the higher strike put is more expensive than the lower strike put). Sometimes you cannot collect a cash credit when opening a diagonal spread, making it a debit spread. There's nothing wrong with paying cash for these positions, but some investors have a style that demands they collect cash (it's then a credit spread) to remain within their comfort zones. It's a choice between collecting more cash when you initiate the position vs. having less risk. Deciding which is more important allows you to trade intelligently. Because diagonals are different from same-month credit spreads, it's probably a good idea to paper trade diagonal (and double diagonal) spreads for a few months before investing real cash.

When selling call spreads, the choice is made in a similar manner. Choose the March call you feel comfortable selling and determine if there is an appropriate April call option to buy as a hedge.[3] When you sell an iron condor, it's commonplace to sell an equal number of put and call spreads and for each spread to be the same width (difference between strikes). Many brokers do *not* give their customers a break with margin requirements for double diagonals, as they do with iron condors,[4] so the incentive to have put and call spreads that resemble each other is eliminated.

Style also comes into play when deciding how far out-of-the-money you want your options to be. Those of you who prefer CTM options when trading iron condors or put credit spreads will probably feel comfortable selling CTM options for double diagonal spreads. Once again, I caution

---

3. *Although it is seldom specifically stated in the sample trades, any time you buy one option as part of a spread position, it's a hedge against the option sold.*
4. *Thus, the margin requirement for the double diagonal is the margin for the call spread plus the margin for the put spread.*

you against using options that are very far OTM and which trade at relatively low prices.

EXAMPLE

Let's assume SPX is trading at 1501, March expiration is seven weeks from today and April expiration is four weeks later. You choose the strike prices to buy and sell as usual, creating positions that satisfy your profit and loss requirements and allow you to remain within your comfort zone.

Assume you decide to sell four Mar 1350 puts at $12.10 each.[5] Let's consider the possibility of buying one of two April puts:

- *Apr 1300 put at $13.60[6]*
- *Apr 1275 put at 11.70[7]*

Let's assume you elect to buy the Apr 1300 puts. The debit for the put spread is $1.50. If you buy the Apr 1275 put instead, you generate a credit of $0.40.

When you look at the calls, you notice that calls trade with a much lower implied volatility, because calls that are equally far OTM are much less expensive than puts. You decide to sell four Mar 1600 calls at $9.00[8] and buy four Apr 1625 calls, paying $11.80[9] each. Paying cash may not please you, but the fact that the maximum value this spread can reach is only $2,500 (compared with $5,000 for the put spread) probably more than compensates for any disappointment.

You pay a $2.80 debit to sell the call spread and a $4.30 total debit for the double diagonal.

If your comfort zone requires collecting a credit for these positions, that need is covered later in this chapter.

In the following tables, the value of the double diagonal spread is listed under various conditions. Because we are beginning with reasons for opening such a position, let's consider the most favorable outcome first. In Table 21.1, you see the potential profit when expiration is only one day away (i.e., it's Thursday and time to decide if you should close the position or take settlement risk) and the SPX put option you sold is ATM.

This spread is long vega and the profit or loss is *very* dependent on the implied volatility. You paid a debit of $4.30 for this double diagonal. If you get a miracle finish, but if IV drops to 20, you barely

TABLE 21.1: Value of double diagonal SPX spread as IV varies, SPX at $1,350 one day before Mar expiration, 29 days before Apr expiration

PUT IV	MAR 1350 P	APR 1300 P	CREDIT	APR 1625 C	CALL IV
20	$5.70	$10.33	$4.63	$0.00	10
25	$7.11	$16.29	$9.18	$0.00	15
30	$8.52	$22.85	$14.33	$0.01	20
35	$9.93	$29.58	$19.65	$0.14	25
40	$11.34	$36.47	$25.13	$0.60	30
45	$12.75	$43.45	$30.70		

When you have a double diagonal spread, if the underlying index is very near the strike price of the near-term puts when expiration day is nigh, the practical[10] maximum profit is earned. Note that profits increase dramatically as IV increases.

Credit = price of Apr 1300 put less price of Mar 1350 put, or the value of the double diagonal spread. Value of call is ignored.

---

5. IV = 29, delta = -14, vega = $125/point, theta = $38/day.
6. IV = 30, delta = -12, vega = $177/point, theta = $25/day.
7. IV = 31.5, delta = -11, vega = $168/point, theta = $19/day.
8. IV = 17, delta = 18, vega = $150/point, theta = $27/day.
9. IV = 17, delta = 19, vega = $192/point, theta = $23/day.
10. The theoretical maximum profit is earned when the settlement price equals the strike price of the short option, but it's very poor strategy to hold overnight, waiting for settlement to be determined Friday morning (Chapter 17). If you held the position this long, don't be greedy.

earn a profit because the position is worth only $4.63 (Table 21.1). This should not concern you. If the market drops this far, IV will almost certainly be much higher.

As IV is near 40, each spread earns a profit of more than $2,000. If this happens to you, would you be willing to pay more than $1,100 to cover your short-term option that's going to expire tomorrow? Isn't that a lot of money to pay when there's only one day remaining?

Yes, it *is* a high price to pay. But, look at your long Apr 1300 put. It's worth nearly $3,650. To safely sell this high-priced option, you must buy back your Mar 1350 put[11] to lock in your profit.

In Table 21.2, we consider a similar situation. This time SPX is trading at $1,600, the strike price of the March calls. Note that profits are even higher with the call spread than they were with

TABLE 21.2: Value of double diagonal SPX spread as IV varies, SPX at $1,600 one day before Mar expiration, 29 days before Apr expiration

CALL IV	MAR 1600 C	APR 1625 C	CREDIT	APR 1300 P	PUT IV
10	$3.42	$9.62	$6.20	$0.00	20
15	$5.09	$18.06	$12.97	$0.03	25
20	$6.76	$26.79	$20.03	$0.24	30
25	$8.43	$56.25	$47.82	$0.82	35
				$1.86	40

When you have a double diagonal spread, if the underlying index is very near the strike price of the near-term calls when expiration day nears, the practical maximum profit is earned. Notice that profits increase substantially as implied volatility increases.

Credit = price of Apr 1625 call less price of Mar 1600 call, or the value of the double diagonal spread. Value of put is ignored.

the put spread under these ideal conditions. That may be surprising because IV is going to

be significantly lower if SPX is $1,600, compared with IV when SPX trading at $1,350. The reason the calls are even better than the puts is because the call option is only 25 points OTM, whereas the put option is 50 points OTM.

This scenario (SPX at strike price day before expiration) was presented as an example of an ideal finish for your position. If you own a double diagonal, it's very difficult to hold as expiration nears because the position has become profitable and the risk of turning a good-sized profit into a large loss is real—and that possibility becomes more and more likely with each passing day.[12] Thus, each day, you must decide whether to accept the gain, or hold longer and accept a higher risk and a higher potential reward.

If the market rallies and IV drops, you can easily lose more in your April put than you gain as the March put declines in value. And if there's a large decline when the market opens on settlement Friday, you can lose more on the March put than you gain on the April. Of course, there are scenarios in which you earn even more money by holding through settlement, but your potential losses exceed the potential gains. These miracle finishes are pleasant, but it's often wrong to hold through settlement.

If you hold the position, despite this advice, be absolutely certain you understand that once the market opens on expiration Friday, your March option has expired and you are naked long your (expensive) April options. Is that a risk you want to take? Sell, or hedge those April options immediately.

What should you do with the other end of your double diagonal—the end that is now FOTM? You can sell and collect a few nickels. Or you can hold and keep those options as an inexpensive insurance policy against other positions. It's not a clear decision, but I keep my FOTM options because they are

---

11. *If you get more sophisticated, you can sell your April put and buy a much less expensive put option to hedge the Mar put overnight (March 1340 put?). Don't gamble by selling your April put and remain naked short the March put. Settlement risk is real. The safest thing to do is to close the position and be pleased with the result.*
12. *In Table 18.4 we showed how the high gamma of the front-month option increases risk as time passes. The diagonal spread is less risky than the put credit spread in this situation, but the risk of holding into expiration still exists.*

too inexpensive to sell, and insurance is always worthwhile. These FOTM options are likely to expire worthless, but they are worth very little right now and may become valuable later, when you can sell and add to your profits. However, if selling these options brings in significant cash,[13] then it's worth selling and increasing your profits.

It's unlikely that your position performs as described above. If the underlying moves too rapidly in one direction, then these positions perform similarly to iron condors. Thus, the positions lose money. But, the good news is that the passage of time is much more beneficial to these positions, compared

TABLE 21.3: Value of double diagonal SPX spread as time passes, SPX at $1,350, IV 29 (March puts) and 30 (April puts)

TIME	MAR 1350 P	APR 1300 P	CREDIT
49 days	$53.94	$46.54	($7.40)
35 days	$46.04	$40.72	($5.32)
28 days	$41.41	$37.54	($3.87)
21 days	$36.09	$34.15	($1.94)
10 days	$25.21	$28.29	$3.08
3 days	$13.97	$24.12	$10.15
2 days	$11.44	$23.49	$12.05
1 day	$8.11	$22.85	$14.74

As time passes, the diagonal spread increases in value. If the short put is threatened, it's possible to close the position and collect net cash, depending on how much time has passed. Compare with data in Table 18.3. In that situation (put credit spreads and iron condors), you always pay cash and lose money when closing. With double diagonals, profits are possible.

Time = days before March options expire. April is 28 days later. Calls are ignored.

with iron condors. In Table 18.3 we noticed that the passage of time was beneficial, but when the short strike price was threatened, you already lost money and continuing to hold the position was risky.

The situation is much better with double diagonals. In Table 21.3 we see the effect of the passage of time on the double diagonal, when the put is ATM. In this table, the assumption is made that IV remains constant as time passes.

The passage of time is beneficial to this position. This spread was initiated seven weeks before March expiration, and in this example, you paid $4.30 per double diagonal. If the market drops suddenly, you have a loss and must pay more cash to close. But that loss is reduced as time passes (Table 21.3), and the position even becomes profitable if enough days go by. When you sell iron condors (or put credit spreads), the passage of time is helpful, but a similar decline in the price of the underlying always results in a loss when the short strike is threatened.

That's the main difference between these spreads. In return for owning long vega and the risk that IV declines, you are compensated by much better time decay and the possibility of making money if the short strike is threatened.[14]

The data in Table 21.4 shows the same situation when the call strike price is threatened. But this time, the whole double diagonal becomes profitable sooner.[15]

Implied volatility

Double diagonal spreads are not always a good idea. The time decay makes these positions look good, but the fact that you must be long vega to own them is important. When implied volatility is high, you must pay a relatively high price for the options

---

13. Significant does not necessarily mean a great deal of money. If one side of the double diagonal spread has produced a profit of $3.00 and if you can sell the other side for another $1.00, that increases profits from $300 to $400 per spread, and that's a significant difference.
14. "Short strike is threatened" means that the underlying is poised to drive through the strike price of your short option.
15. With 21 days remaining, the call spread is worth $4.15 and you paid only $4.30 for the double diagonal. In another day or two this position can be closed for more than it cost to open. If the market threatens the put spread instead (Table 21.3), the break-even point occurs fewer than 10 days before March expiration.

TABLE 21.4: Value of double diagonal SPX spread as time passes, SPX at $1,600, IV 17

TIME	MAR 1600 C	APR 1625 C	CREDIT
49 days	$43.31	$43.46	$0.15
35 days	$36.15	$37.85	$1.70
28 days	$32.10	$34.86	$2.76
21 days	$27.56	$31.71	$4.15
10 days	$18.70	$26.37	$7.67
3 days	$10.06	$22.65	$12.59
2 days	$8.18	$22.10	$13.92
1 day	$5.75	$21.53	$15.78

As time passes, the diagonal spread increases in value. If the short call is threatened, it's possible to close the position and collect net cash. Depending on how much time has passed, with double diagonals, profits are possible.

Time = days before March options expire. April is 28 days later. Puts are ignored

you purchase. When IV is relatively low, you buy your long options at a much more favorable price. One benefit of that is the ability to open diagonal spreads and collect a cash credit. If that cash credit is essential for your comfort zone, then you must wait for times when IV is low to open double diagonal spreads.

In Chapter 7 we showed how increasing the implied volatility of an option plays a vital role in determining the market price of that option. That idea is reinforced in Tables 21.1 and 21.2, where you see how the price of an individual option changes as IV changes. For example, when IV moves from 35 to 40, the value of the Apr 1300 put moves higher by almost $700. Because you are buying vega when you open a double diagonal position, it's to your advantage to own diagonal spreads when IV is relatively low, rather

than relatively high. As rookies, you may not have a good idea how to determine whether IV is high or low, based on its historical levels. By looking at the VIX (CBOE volatility index graph), you can get a good idea of how current levels compare with the past.[16]

Risk

When selling iron condors, you can limit potential losses by choosing strike prices that are near each other. When you choose diagonal spreads, unless you pay a significant cash debit for the position, the strike prices chosen must be further apart—and the further apart, the greater the potential loss. Thus, choosing strike prices that are near each other produces a less risky position, but you must often pay a large debit to acquire that diagonal. A large debit introduces a new risk.

EXAMPLE

Assume you choose a diagonal NDX Mar-Feb put spread and pay $1,000 debit. For this discussion, strike prices are not important. The usual risk when owning a put diagonal spread is a quick market decline, forcing an adjustment.

When you pay a significant debit for the put spread,[17] you face an additional risk. If the market rallies, your diagonal call spread is threatened when you own a double diagonal. But that rally can also turn your put spread into a loser. If the rally is large and if IV shrinks enough, then the price of your March put options shrink. Sure, it's great that your Feb put option heads to zero, but if the March option declines to $4.00, then your spread can be closed for only $400 when you paid $1,000. Refusing to pay large debits eliminates this possibility.

When implied volatilities are elevated, options cost more and it becomes difficult to establish double

---

16. VIX graphs are available on the Internet at sites such as cboe.com.
17. The discussion is also applicable when you pay a large debit for the call spread.

diagonal spreads at a favorable price. Thus, this strategy is best reserved for times when IV is low, rather than high, even though double diagonal spreads have obvious advantages over iron condors (primarily they are more profitable as time passes).

If you prefer to trade as simply as possible, you don't have to pay attention to actual implied volatility. All you have to do is try to find a good double diagonal that suits your comfort zone. That includes opening the position for a credit or small debit *and* keeping the strike prices relatively near each other.[18] If IV is low enough, you will find such spreads. If IV is too high you won't find suitable spreads. Thus, there's no need to pay attention to actual IV.

When IV is high, it's better to sell iron condors because you receive higher credits for your spreads. When IV is low, it's better to sell double diagonal spreads[19] because you collect cash credits with positions that are not too risky (strikes not too far apart).

Additional thoughts

1. When trading double diagonals it's always tempting to allow more time to pass, because that's beneficial to the position. However, you must recognize that profits can disappear in two ways:

   - If the market moves to threaten one of your short options, a further move will be costly. It's prudent to close or roll to prevent large losses (and doing that remains the name of the game for long-term success).
   - If you have a good profit due to time decay and favorable movement in the underlying, that profit can be reduced significantly if the

underlying reverses direction. Sometimes it's a good idea to close diagonal positions and take your profits. Then you can open a new position with more distant expirations.

2. Double diagonals can be opened by selling front-month options and buying second month options.

   If you prefer to sell options that are further OTM, or if you prefer safer positions with less negative gamma, then you may want to open a position by selling options that expire in the second month and buying options that expire in the third month. As with iron condors, this method allows you to close positions earlier.

3. If your portfolio is short enough vega from current positions to make you uncomfortable, the addition of a few diagonal spreads reduces your vega exposure. If that short vega comes from iron condors, don't sell more of the same front-month option when you choose your double diagonal. That strike price is already a danger point for you, and if the market drives through that strike, you don't want additional jeopardy. Instead, consider selling further OTM options and buying appropriate long options as a hedge. For example, in Chapter 20 you sold the RUT Nov 740/750 put, 900/910 call iron condor. A suitable diagonal that adds protection[20] where you need it involves selling the Nov 730 put and buying an appropriate Dec put. There is no specific put to suggest, because implied volatility affects which puts you can afford and the size of the debit that must be paid to construct a suitable position. Just remember that the nearer the strike

---

18. It's difficult for investors to agree upon how far apart to choose strike prices for double diagonals. Different traders have different preferences, and no one is wrong. For me, RUT calls should be 20 to 30 points apart and puts, no more than 40. For SPX, 40 to 50 points is my maximum. For NDX, I prefer 50 points but have used 75-point differences. This is my comfort zone. Choose your own.
19. Sell means to sell the lower strike call in the earlier month, to own the higher strike call in the outer month, sell the higher strike put in the early month and buy the lower strike put in the outer month.
20. If time passes, this spread affords protection, but not if the decline comes quickly.

prices are to each other, the more the spread costs, but the less you can lose if things go badly. If you can find a suitable spread,[21] consider selling the November 920 calls and buying an appropriate December call.

4. As with iron condors, you can purchase a few additional calls and/or puts to provide pre-insurance.

5. Margin requirements are much larger for double diagonals than for iron condors. The typical iron condor may be 10 points wide, requiring margin of $1,000. The double diagonal spread is going to be wider, and even if it's 20-points wide, the call spread and the put spread often have a margin requirement of $2,000 (difference between the strikes) *each*.

Double diagonals represent an additional strategy for your investment arsenal. They work best when IV is low, but they can be used to reduce the risk of holding positions with short vega at any time.

---

21. *The Nov 920 call may be priced too low to allow you to construct a good diagonal call spread. Don't force the trade just to get protection. It may be preferable to move out one month and choose an appropriate iron condor that expires in December, rather than November, and add a Jan-Dec double diagonal to that position. An alternative may be to sell the put diagonal and ignore the calls in this special situation.*

1. Double diagonal spreads are not subject to settlement risk.
○ TRUE ○ FALSE

2. You own a double diagonal position, the market trades in a small range over the next four weeks and the short-term options expire worthless. Is this a good result?

3. With one week remaining before expiration, if the market makes an unfavorable move and is heading toward the strike price of your short call option, would you rather own an iron condor or a double diagonal?

4. Margin requirements are essentially the same for iron condors and double diagonals.
○ TRUE ○ FALSE

5. The implied volatility for an actively traded stock has ranged between 40 and 70 over the past three years. IV is currently 75. Are you better off with iron condors or double diagonals?

6. When you collect a cash credit for a double diagonal, a profit is guaranteed.
○ TRUE ○ FALSE

Afterword

I hope that you have felt welcome entering the options universe and that you've learned a fair amount about options along the way. The ideas presented here have been developed over the course of 30-plus years of trading options. If you understand the principles behind options and know how they work, you are in a good position to make money adopting the strategies outlined in this book.

Every method covered in this book has been selected because of its compatibility with a generally conservative investing philosophy. In my experience, the major downfall of many new option investors is the tendency to trade more than their financial capacity (and trading experience) allows. Don't be in a hurry—you have the rest of your life to make money with options. Get familiar with options by paper trading, and then start to trade with real money. You have the tools here to become a successful, long-term options trader.

Options are investment tools. Use them wisely. Options are versatile. Use them to reduce risk.

If you have questions (no investment advice, please), I'll try to respond: rookies@mdwoptions.com

Mark D. Wolfinger
Evanston, Illinois

Quiz Answers

Chapter 1

1) False. Only the seller (writer) of an option can be assigned an exercise notice.

2) In-the-money: Nov 30 call, Feb 30 call, Dec 30 call, Dec 25 call, Jan 35 put. Out-of-the-money: Oct 35 call, Feb 30 put.

3) Yes. $400. Stock price ($104) minus strike price ($100) is intrinsic value per share. An option represents 100 shares.

4) $4,500.

5) $30,000.

6) The option writer (seller) has NO rights.

7) There is no such procedure. The call seller may not request that an option be exercised.

8) This purchase is called a closing transaction because you are buying options to close a position. You have a capital gain of $95 per contract, or $190 less commission. Your obligation to deliver 200 shares of QUIZ at $40 per share is cancelled and you no longer have a position in these options.

9) $400. The stock price is immaterial. Note: The question does not ask for the option's intrinsic value, just the premium (the selling price).

10) Yes. The answer to this question is not covered in the chapter, but I hope you know enough about buying and selling stocks to understand that if you own an asset, you are always allowed to sell. Sometimes you sell at a higher price and earn a profit. Sometimes you sell at a lower price and take a loss.

11) No. When you sell an option you already own, your position is cancelled and you have neither rights nor obligations.

12) $80 profit, less commission.

Chapter 2

1) Four.

2) Not possible. If the puts are listed, then the calls must be listed.

3) Nov and Dec. The next two calendar months are always available for trading.

4) Three possibilities

    a. The stock price is rising and traded at 60 or higher yesterday.

    b. The stock price is falling and traded at 70 or lower yesterday.

    c. A customer requested that the exchanges list Oct 65s.

5) Before the recent rule change, you would own six ZZZ Aug 20 calls. Today you still own two ZZZ Aug 60 calls, but the deliverable (items delivered to the option owners account, upon exercising the option and paying the strike price) is now 300 shares per contract.

6) It's a great result. The put options you sold are going to be worthless if the deal is completed. It's a good idea to repurchase those puts at $5 per contract, if possible. This is insurance against the possibility that the deal falls apart.

7) Only c and d make sense.

    a. The options do not expire worthless. They finished 5 cents in-the-money and will be exercised automatically if you do nothing.

    b. You cannot be assigned an exercise notice because you own the options.

8) They expire (the options no longer exist) and are worthless.

Chapter 4

1) False. You should expect to buy at the ask price.

2) True.

3) Two basic reasons:

    a. You can get a better price using limit orders (most of the time).

    b. You avoid getting the order filled at a horrendous price.

4) Barron's.

5) No. Someone made an error. You established $3.00 as the maximum price you are willing to pay, and your broker cannot force you to accept the fill at a higher price. You have the right to reject the trade, or ask your broker to pay the $20-per-contract difference.

6) You shouldn't be. Your broker is obligated to fill your order at the best available price. By sending the order to the AMEX, that obligation was not satisfied. In addition, it's wrong for anyone to sell options at a price above the NBBO (National Best Bid and Offer).

7) d. Sell to close. First, it's an order to sell. Second, you are eliminating a position you own and that's the definition of a closing transaction.

8) False. It's only advantageous to your broker and is harmful to you.

Chapter 6

1) a. True.

    b. False. Interest rates are usually unimportant.

    c. False. All inputs are known, except for volatility.

2) The value of a call option increases as the stock price increases. The value of a put option decreases as the stock price increases.

3) You should not agree. Sometimes the option premium is so unfavorable for your chosen strategy that it's better to avoid trading the options than accepting the current market price. In other words, if you are an option seller and the premium is far below its fair value, over the long term you will be a more successful trader if you avoid selling those undervalued options. Similarly, if you are a buyer and prices are much higher than fair value, it's usually best not to play. NOTE: Any single play, whether it's a buy or sell, can be a winner. But, on average, you don't want to trade options when the probability of success is diminished. This is covered in greater detail in Chapter 7.

4) Put owners. The higher the dividend, the more the stock price decreases when the stock pays that dividend. As an aside, you might argue that a dividend increase is good for the longer term, and thus, call owners benefit. But for the purposes of evaluating an option, higher dividends make calls worth less and puts worth more.

5) False. Knowing the fair value of an option is beneficial, but it's not mandatory.

6) False. The calculated value of an option depends on the numbers plugged into the Black-Scholes equation. And different people use different values for the estimated future volatility of the stock. That volatility difference can make a significant difference in the calculated option value.

Chapter 7

1) False. Beta has nothing to do with the value of an option. Options trade above fair value when the implied volatility of the options is higher than the forecast volatility for the stock.

2) True.

3) False. That's when options tend to become overpriced.

4) If the volatility is 20, then a one-standard-deviation move is up or down by 20 percent

    a. 32 percent of the time. A stock moves less than one standard deviation about 68 percent of the time.

    b. 5 percent. That's a two-standard deviation move, which occurs approximately one year in 20.

5) False. You may want to avoid the details, and any mathematics, but you should understand at least this much: Options are not always priced fairly. Sometimes you get a bargain and sometimes you get a bad deal. And that's true for both option buyers and option sellers.

Chapters 10 through 12

1) False. When you sell calls, your returns are limited.

2) True. You have more frequent profits and fewer losses.

3) False. CCW is ideal for investors who want steady returns, year after year.

4) a. Selling to open.

5) a. No control. The option owner makes that decision.

6) b. ATM.

7) a. ITM.

8) c. Six months. The more time remaining, the higher the premium.

9) When rolling, you collect additional cash, and that cash provides a cushion in the event the stock continues to decline.

10) True.

Chapter 13

1) A collar is a covered call with the addition of a long put option.

2) False. Collars are very conservative positions.

3) False. Losses are limited to a pre-determined level. Collars require less maintenance than the vast majority of option positions.

4) True.

5) No. It does mean that you can make slightly more money by not buying the put option. But it also means you can lose substantially more. The put option was not bought to make money. Instead, it was bought as an insurance policy, and insurance costs something. In this case it reduces potential profits.

6) False. The call limits your profits.

Chapter 14

1) False. The loss may be large, but it's limited. The stock can fall no lower than zero, and if forced to buy stock at the strike price, the most you can lose is the strike price x 100, less premium collected.

2) Having enough cash in your account to buy the shares, if and when assigned an exercise notice.

3) True. To close, you merely purchase the put. To close the covered call position, you must buy the call and sell the stock, and that involves twice as many transactions.

4) False. By selling 10 puts, it's possible that you find yourself owning 1,000 shares (instead of 400)—and that entails much more risk.

5) False. Some stocks are much riskier than others. Some stocks have news pending and that news may result in the stock gapping much lower. Pay close attention to the underlying. It's important and you must choose carefully.

Chapter 15

1) Short 300 HHH shares. This requires some thinking on your part, but if long calls and short puts equals long stock, then long puts and short calls equals short stock.

2) No. You must pay less than $600 for the trade to be worthwhile. Sell the put spread instead.

3) $6,000. The difference between the strike prices, multiplied by 100: (100 x $60).

4) False. It's a futile endeavor for the individual investor.

5) a. No. You own the ATM (at-the-money) option and control the exercise decision.

   b. No.

   c. Yes. The owner of the 120 call may not exercise. The safest course of action is to sell the call spread to close your position.

6) No. The September position is not what you want to trade. You want to sell the June put spread or buy the June call spread.

Chapter 16

1) 70. You are long 200 shares of stock and that's always 200 deltas. You are short two options, each with a 65 delta, and that's -130 deltas (minus because you are short calls). Total +70.

2) Make money. You are long and the stock moved higher. You will make approximately $70 because you are long 70 deltas and the stock moved one point. Delta measures the change in the option (or entire position) price as the stock price changes by one point.

3) You own options. Thus, you are long gamma and vega. You are also short theta. Because you own puts, you are short delta.

4) $3.20. When the option's vega is 4.0, it means the option's value increases by approximately $4 for each one point increase in implied volatility. The five-point increase corresponds to $20 per contract.

5) More than $200. Because of gamma, the put delta has increased as the stock declined. A further decrease in the price of the underlying results in ever-increasing losses. Another way to look at this is to say the delta was approximately -20 when you sold the puts (because you lost $20 per put when the stock declined one point), and because of gamma, the delta is larger (more negative) now.

Chapter 17

1) False.

2) False. The settlement price is the closing price Friday afternoon.

3) American. Can exercise any time, whereas European option own can only exercise at expiration.

4) The danger of a large adverse market move at the opening on Friday. Such a move may turn a worthless option into a big loser.

5) False. It's often substantially different.

6) a. No.

   b. Yes.

   c. Nothing. Your broker automatically transfers the cash into your account.

Chapter 18

1) False. Put credit spreads are for bullish investors. Call credit spreads are for bearish investors.

2) False. It's far better to enter both orders simultaneously via a spread order.

3) The SPX Mar 1540 put. The puts are 20 points apart and expire in the same month. You sell the higher strike price.

4) The spread appears to be expiring worthless. But, anything can happen tomorrow morning, when the settlement price is determined. I intend to buy back this spread later today. Note that you may not be able to sell the 790 put because there are no bids. Don't let that bother you. The key part of eliminating risk is buying back the 800 put. It's OK to forget about selling the put you own.

5) False. This difficult concept may not be suitable for rookies. But the intention of this book is to help you really understand how options work. It's true that the passage of time reduces the value of the spread, and in general, the passage of time is your ally. This situation is the one exception. Once the index has moved such that your short option is at-the-money, if the index suddenly drops by a significant amount, the fewer days remaining before the options expire, the larger the loss (see Table 18.4). That's one reason why holding a spread when the index has moved near the strike price is not a long-term winning strategy.

6) True.

7) a and b are credit spreads. c is long 100 shares of synthetic stock.

Chapter 19

1) False. If you anticipate a major move in either direction, iron condors are not suitable. They work best for traders who have a neutral outlook or who have no opinion on market direction.

2) False. The premiums you earn are so small that significant loss that occurs only once every several years is more than enough to make this a losing strategy.

Chapter 19 cont.

3) True. When expiration arrives, the worst case scenario occurs when one of the spreads is completely ITM and worth 10 points. You can lose more than this amount only when you adjust one of the credit spreads and the market then reverses direction and you close the other credit spread—both with large losses.

4) b. $2,000. But some brokers insist on imposing a $4,000 requirement.

5) No. A true iron condor contains an equal number of put spreads and call spreads. (You have 10 true iron condors plus five put spreads.)

6) Find the delta for each option sold. Subtract each delta from 100, giving you the probability that each option finishes OTM. Multiply those two probabilities to determine the overall probability that both finish OTM.

7) False. The distance each spread is from the underlying price is not relevant in determining whether a position is a true iron condor.

Chapter 20

1) Puts. This spread cannot lose money if the underlying rallies. The only time you need insurance is when the underlying declines.

2) c. These events would result in panic, at least temporarily.

3) No. When you sell an iron condor, those puts and calls you own as part of the spread act as your insurance policy. For very small positions, there are no appropriate options to buy as extra insurance.

4) False. Pre-insurance is not for everyone.

5) a, b, and c. Only d is false.

Chapter 21

1) False when options are cash-settled and European style. True for options on individual stocks.

2) Probably. If you collected a credit when opening the position, you can collect another credit now to close the position. If you paid a debit, it's almost a certain that you can sell your options for more than the original debit. However, if you paid a relatively high debit, and if IV has dropped significantly, the value of your long options has been hurt by the IV decrease and by the passage of time. Thus, it's possible that you have a loss because the value of your options is less than the original debit.

3) Double diagonal. This position is probably profitable and you can collect that profit and remove all risk by closing. The iron condor position is losing money and becoming more and more risky to hold This is far from an ideal situation for an iron condor.

4) False. Iron condors require much less margin.

5) Iron condors are better when IV is high.

6) False. There are no guaranteed profits when trading double diagonals.

Bullish vs. Bearish Options Strategies

Here are six profit/loss graphs that provide a quick snapshot of how specific strategies perform when the market moves higher or lower. This is intended to help you compare and contrast strategies and assess their usefulness. The horizontal axes represent the price of the underlying asset. The vertical axes represent profit and loss. (These graphs are laid out in the same manner as the figures used in Chapter 20.)

These strategies are mentioned or described in this book and are not the only bullish, bearish, or neutral strategies that exist. Keep in mind that on occasion, a given strategy may not produce the expected result. That can happen when there's a significant change in the implied volatilities. For example, owning a call option may not provide a profit when the stock moves higher, if implied volatility drops by too much.

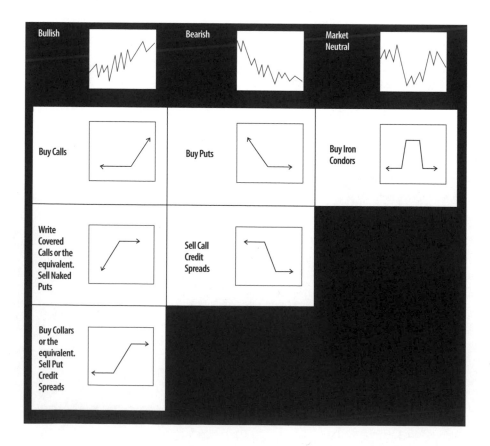

Glossary

1256 contracts: IRS code Section 1256 states that any gains or losses from the sale of options on broad based indexes (for example, SPX, NDX, RUT) are subject to the 60/40 rule (60 percent of gains and losses are long term and 40 percent are short term, regardless of how long securities are held).

1-lot: The trade of a single option or option spread. Thus, 20 lots refers to a trade of 20 contracts or spreads.

A

American-style: An option that may be exercised any time after it is purchased, providing the exercise occurs before the option expires.

Ask: The price at which an option (or stock) is offered for sale.

Assignment notice: The method used to inform an investor that an option sold has been exercised by its owner. The more formal terminology to describe this process is "you have been assigned an exercise notice." Once the notice has been received, it cannot be reversed and the assignee is obligated to fulfill the conditions of the option contract.

At-the-money (ATM): An option whose strike price equals (or very nearly equals) the price of the underlying asset.

B

Bear spread: A spread designed to profit when the underlying declines. A put debit spread or a call credit spread.

Beta: The relative volatility of one stock compared with the volatility of a large group of stocks (such as the S&P 500 Index). Not used when discussing options.

Bid: The price buyers are willing to pay for an option or stock.

Bid/Ask spread: The difference between the bid and ask prices. When this spread is narrow, the markets are said to be tight, which is beneficial to the investor. When the markets are wide it's more difficult for the investor to get a satisfactory fill when entering an order.

Box spread: A riskless position with a known payout. It's composed of one bullish call spread and one bearish put spread with the same strike prices and expiration date.

Bull spread: A spread designed to profit when the underlying rallies. A call debit spread or a put credit spread.

Butterfly spread: A three-legged winged spread built by combining one bull spread and one bear spread (equal distance between the strikes).

C

Call: An option that gives its owner the right, but not the obligation, to buy 100 shares of the underlying asset at the strike price any time before the option expires.

Carry, cost of: The cost of owning a long position. It's the interest paid by using cash to purchase an asset or the interest not earned because cash is tied up in the asset.

Cash-settled: An option that doesn't require the delivery of a physical asset (such as shares of stock) when exercised. Instead, the intrinsic value (in cash) of the option is transferred from the account of the investor who received an assignment notice and delivered to the account of the exerciser.

Chicago Board Options Exchange (CBOE): The second-largest securities exchange in the U.S. and the first to list options for trading, the CBOE today offers a wide array of investment products, including options on equities, indexes, interest rates, and exchange-traded funds.

Class: The term used to describe all the puts or all the calls of a specific underlying asset. For example, "IBM calls" represents an option class.

Closing transaction: The purchase or sale of an option that offsets all or part of an existing position. For example, when you sell options you previously bought, it's a closing transaction.

Collar: A conservative investment strategy consisting of three parts: long stock, long put, short call. This position has limited profit potential and limited loss potential. The collar is composed of a covered call position with a long put option.

Condor: A four-legged winged spread, built by combining one bull call spread and one bear put spread, with the condition that each put option has a lower strike price than each call option. In addition, each spread must be of equal width (distance between the strike prices).

Credit: The cash collected from an option transaction.

Credit Spread: A spread whose seller collects cash.

D

Debit: The cash paid to complete an option transaction.

Debit spread: A spread whose buyer pays cash.

Delta: 1. The expected change in an option's price when the underlying asset moves one point. 2. The probability than an option finishes in-the-money.

Derivative: An asset whose value is based on the value of another asset.

Diagonal spread: Similar to a credit spread, with the exception that the long option expires in a different month than the short option.

Deliverable: 1. The items received when a call owner exercises the call and pays the strike price. 2. The items sold when a put owner exercises the put and collects the strike price. Usually 100 shares of the underlying stock, but when there's corporate action, such as a merger or spinoff, the deliverable may involve stock, cash, bonds, etc.

Dividend: A taxable distribution of the earnings of a corporation to its shareholders.

Dividend, exercise for: The process of exercising a call option one (or more) day before a stock goes ex-dividend for the purpose of collecting the dividend. (Shareholders, but not option owners, collect the dividend.)

Dividend, risk of losing: The possibility that a covered call writer is assigned an exercise notice before the stock goes ex-dividend. When that occurs, the covered call writer no longer owns the stock and does not collect the dividend.

Dollar delta: The delta of a position, multiplied by its share price.

Double diagonal: A position composed of one diagonal call spread and one diagonal put spread.

E

Equivalent position: A position with the same risk/reward profile as another. The positions appear to differ, but are essentially identical. For example, a covered call and naked put.

European-style: An option that cannot be exercised, except for a brief period shortly before the option expires.

Exercise: The process by which an option owner implements the rights granted by the option contract. The call exerciser buys (or the put owner sells) 100 shares of the underlying asset at the strike price.

Expiration: The time, after which, an option is no longer a valid contract.

Expire worthless: To be out-of-the-money when expiration arrives. When an option expires without being exercised, it becomes worthless.

Extrinsic value: An option's time value or the portion of an option's price that is not intrinsic.

F

Fill: The completion of an order to buy or sell options (or stock).

Fungible: Interchangeable.

G

Gamma: The expected change in an option's delta when the underlying asset moves one point.

Gap opening: The first trade of the day that occurs at a price that differs significantly from the previous trade.

H

Hedge: A position that offsets (or partially offsets) the risk holding another position.

I

In-the-money (ITM): An option with an intrinsic value. A call is ITM when the strike price is below the asset price. A put is ITM when the strike price is above the asset price.

Inside market: The tightest market. Often an individual investor only sees the outside market for spreads and is unaware of the true highest bid or lowest offer.

Intrinsic value: The amount by which an option is in-the-money. When added to the time value, the sum represents the option premium.

Iron butterfly: A three-legged combination built by selling one call credit spread and one put credit spread with the same expiration, with the additional requirements that the call options are equally far apart from each other as the two put options and each spread has one strike price in common. For example, sell GE Jun 40/45 call spread and 35/40 put spread.

Iron condor: A combination built by selling one call credit spread and one put credit spread with the same expiration and four different strike prices, with the additional requirement that the call options are equally far apart from each other as the two put options. For example, sell GE Jun 40/45 call spread and 30/35 put spread.

L

Leg: 1. (noun) One part of a spread or one part of a position. 2. (verb) To open one part of a spread at a time, as in "He legged into the trade." Thus, not entering the order as a spread.

Limit order: An order to buy or sell with restrictions. The order establishes a minimum price (when selling) or a maximum price (when buying) at which the order may be filled.

Locked market: A situation that occurs when the bid price equals the ask price because customer orders are sent to a designated exchange and the broker refuses to send it to an exchange where it can be filled. When the market is locked, the option can only trade at that locked price until either the bid or offer disappears.

Long: 1. A situation in which the investor owns an asset, as in: "She is long 300 shares of IBM." 2. A bullish bias, a position that profits when the asset increases in value.

M

Margin: When investing, the amount of collateral that must be put up in a purchase of stock, options, futures, etc.

Margin call: A call from a brokerage firm or clearing house to a customer to bring margin deposits back up to minimum levels required by exchange regulations.

Market maker: A professional trader who stands in a trading pit on the floor of an options exchange and continuously displays bids and offers for all options trading in that pit. In today's electronic environment, the market maker may be represented by a computer that displays bids and offers.

Market order: An order to buy or sell that is to be executed as quickly as possible at the best price available when the order reaches the trading pit. Electronic market orders are filled instantly.

N

NBBO: Acronym for National Best Bid or Offer. That quote takes the highest published bid (displayed for all to see), and the lowest published offer on any options exchange and combines them into one bid/ask quote.

O

Obligations (of an option seller): If (and only if) assigned an exercise notice, the option seller must honor the conditions of the option contract. Thus, the call seller must deliver 100 shares of stock in exchange for being paid the strike price. The put seller must buy 100 shares at the strike price.

Options Clearing Corporation (OCC): The organization that handles the clearing of all option trades and regulates the listing of new options.

Open Interest: The number of outstanding option contracts. It's the number of options that have been sold to open that have not yet expired or been repurchased in a closing transaction. The OI is recalculated daily, after the market closes for the day.

Opening transaction: The purchase or sale of an option that initiates a new position or adds to an existing position.

Option: A contract that grants to the buyer the right to buy or sell a specific asset at a specific price for a specified period of time. This potentially (if assigned an exercise notice) obligates the seller to buy or sell a specific asset at a specified price for a specified period of time

Out-of-the-money (OTM): An option with zero intrinsic value. A call option whose strike price is higher than the price of the underlying or a put option whose strike price is below that of the underlying.

Outside market: The widest possible market, i.e., the published bid and offer. Most of the time there is a tighter, or inside, market.

P

Parity: 1. The price of an option equal to its intrinsic value. 2. An option with no time premium. When an option trades at its intrinsic value, it's trading at parity.

Pin Risk: The risk associated with being short options when the underlying stock closes at the strike price on expiration Friday. The investor never knows whether the options will expire worthless of if an assignment notice is on its way.

Portfolio margin: The margin requirement for a portfolio based on the risk of the portfolio as a whole, and not on the requirements for each component of the portfolio. This type of margin is beneficial to option investors who hedge positions.

Preinsurance: Buying puts and calls as insurance before an adverse market move increases risk to an unacceptable level. Usually used when an investor sells credit spreads and/or iron condors.

Premium: The price of an option in the marketplace.

Put: An option that gives its owner the right, but not the obligation, to sell 100 shares of the underlying asset at the strike price any time before the option expires.

R

Resistance: A price level at which a stock's rising trend was previously halted.

Rho: The change in the value of an option when the interest rate changes by one percent.

Rights (of an option owner): The ability to exercise the option and demand that the seller fulfill the conditions of the contract.

Roll (a position): A transaction in which an existing position is closed and an appropriate new position is opened. Rolling is often used as a risk reducing strategy, but can be used to lock in profits.

S

Scalp: The repeated buying and selling of securities in an attempt to earn small profits.

Series: All options of the same class having the same strike price and expiration date.

Settlement price: The price of a security on which the value of all expiring options is based. The settlement price for European-style, cash-settled index options is calculated from opening prices on the third Friday of the month. The settlement price for all stock options is the underlying's last trade at the close of business on the third Friday of the month.

Settlement risk: The risk associated with holding positions (long or short) in European-style index options after those options cease trading on Thursday afternoon, one day before the settlement price is calculated. The risk is that a substantial market move can significantly change the value of those options.

Short: 1. The condition of having sold an asset the investor doesn't own. 2. A bearish bias, a position that profits when the asset decreases in value.

Slide: Escape, as in not being assigned an exercise notice at expiration, despite the fact that the option you are short is ITM by a few pennies. The term is also used when you are not assigned an exercise notice on an ITM option and thereby collect a significant dividend.

Spread: A simultaneous transaction involving two or more options. Also an order submitted in an attempt to execute such a transaction.

Standard deviation: A measure of the dispersion of (distance between) a set of data.

Standardized: Options became standardized when they were first listed for trading on an exchange. That means strike prices and expiration dates were placed at regular and predictable intervals.

Straddle: One call plus one put with the same strike price, expiration date and underlying security. An investor can buy or sell straddles.

Strangle: One call and put with different strike prices, but the same expiration date and underlying security. An investor can buy or sell strangles.

Strike price: The price at which the owner of an option has the right to buy or sell the underlying.

Support: A price level at which a stock's declining tread was previously halted.

Synthetic equivalent: An option position that behaves exactly the same as a different option position. For example, a covered call and a naked put are equivalent positions when the strike price and expiration date are identical.

T

Theta: The daily rate at which the value of an option decays.

Threat: The increasing likelihood that the underlying moves beyond the strike price of a short option position.

Time premium: The portion of an option price devoted to the possibility that the underlying moves in the right direction. In other words, the premium investors pay for hope. The portion of an option's price that's due to volatility, time remaining and, to a lesser extent, interest rates. The option price minus its intrinsic value.

Time value: See time premium.

U

Underlying: The asset from which the value of an option is derived. Also the asset received when a call owner exercises the option or the asset that must be delivered when a put owner exercises the option.

V

Vega: The change in the value of an option when the implied volatility changes by one point.

Volatility: A measure of the tendency of an asset to undergo price changes.

Volatility, estimated: Also called forecast volatility. An educated guess as to how volatile the underlying will be between the current time and the option's expiration.

Volatility, historical: An exact measurement of how volatile the underlying has been over a specified period of time.

Volatility, implied: The future volatility (from the current time until the option expires) of the underlying as predicted by the option premium. Also, the volatility, plugged into an option calculator, that makes the actual option price equal to its theoretical (fair) value.

W

Wasting asset: A security whose value erodes as time passes.

Index